DIE FOR ME ARGENTINA

A Novel

95,673 Words

By Johan Wassenaar

For Maria Diaz

CONTENTS

Johan Wassenaar

Johan Wassenaar

CHAPTER ONE

Freshly liberated from the strict discipline of a Catholic Convent in fashionable Barcelona, Angélica was sent to live with her father in a remote, Argentinean farming community when her mother died. She entered puberty in the care of a businessman woefully unprepared to deal with his attractive, fledgling daughter.

San Miguel de Tucumán lay wedged between tall Andean mountains and a steamy-hot, endless plain of sugar cane and tropical produce fields, leaving it isolated in far northern Argentina. In this provincial ambience Angélica was anxious to make friends amongst the privileged school children of the otherwise poor city and soon fell in with the more daring fringe of her teenage peers. She bonded with another motherless girl and to be cool, they began descending into promiscuity. When her friend moved away, she became more discerning in her social choices and began dating an older architecture student at the National University. Long on sincerity with a serious mind, Angélica opened like a sunflower to the rays of Fernando's profound affection.

Despite his mother's matriarchal misgivings, they kept seeing each other and to win her approval, Angélica entered university to major in psychology. Their romance flourished into a deep commitment, leading to marriage.

Life with Fernando was idyllic. For the first time, she had stability in her life and was full of hope and energy. Once he had joined an architectural firm and felt professionally established, they had a son.

Mounting political unrest and lawlessness in the province, concerned them, but they remained optimistic and ambitious until, suddenly, Marxist rebels emerged from the mountains to take control of most of the two northern provinces of Argentina. Rabid ideologues began commandeering their lecture halls to recruit converts, disrupting proceedings so badly that it effectively closed the university.

By confiscating farms and businesses, the rebels brought the Tucumán economy to its knees. Suddenly, life in San Miguel was harshly confrontational with unqualified rebels taking control of the province's civil services.

Angélica clung to Fernando until life without him seemed impossible. He sought ways to work with everyone—even persuading political fanatics to adhere to sensible planning concepts. There were few opportunities to prosper and he had to invent planning services to make ends meet and to hide his growing desperation from his wife. Gripped in unspoken fear, they frantically made love and she became pregnant again.

Finally, the Army came to quell the rebellion and for a time fighting in the streets disrupted life. Once the rebels were expelled from the urban areas, the economy rebounded as seized property was brought back into production. Fernando continued to go to work even when, at times, there was nothing to do. It took most of a year before all vestiges of the rebel invasion had been removed.

Optimism was running high when the discredited government of Isabel Peron was deposed in a bloodless military coup. The new ruling Junta's first order of business was to root out the considerable residual following of sympathizers they left behind. Military security details began appearing everywhere to search for "subversives". A night-time curfew was proclaimed and intimidating arrests began being made in raids on homes, in the streets and at places of work. The raids turned increasingly brutal, driving fear into the hearts of everyone. People locked themselves in their homes or hid away wherever they could. Young adults were being arrested in growing numbers on suspicion of collaborating with the rebels and were indefinitely held for interrogation.

To celebrate their son's second birthday, Angélica pleaded with Fernando to stay home, especially since the occasion coincided with the end of the steamy-hot rainy season and for once there were cool breezes flowing down from the mountains. He declined, fearing that it would make him seem suspicious.

Angélica's anxiety was running high as she waited for Fernando to join her for the little birthday party she had prepared. The premonition, that something bad was about to happen, had been with her all day and she became increasingly emotional as nightfall approached. Finally, she phoned his parents.

"Forgive me; Suegro...is Fernando still there?"

"Angélica! I'm so glad you called! He didn't come to see us today. Did he say anything about being late?

"No, Suegro, he always calls if he's late. Something *dreadful* must have happened. *What* are we to do?"

"Calm down...we'll give it half an hour more. If we haven't heard from him then, I'll come and get you in the car. It's no longer safe for you to stay there on your own."

"Please come <u>soon</u>! I'd like to call on your neighbors...perhaps someone saw him."

"We've already tried...they won't answer their doors...every one's afraid."

* * *

It was morning before Angélica could start her frantic search, combing the neighborhood, questioning everyone she encountered. By sheer luck she found a frightened boy who had hidden in a bush when he saw someone being attacked and dragged away.

"Please tell me exactly what you saw? What did he look like?"

"Señora, there were three or four men in a green car...it had no license plates. They drove up to a man walking in this direction...some of them jumped out and tried to grab him. He was tall like an athlete and broke loose to run. The car went after him...another man jumped out and caught him. The others came running and began hitting him with their sticks and fists until he fell to the ground. They opened the trunk, tied his hands behind his back and threw him in with his bleeding face to the floor."

"Did you see his face? What did he look like?"

"I saw Señor Diaz' son...the one with the small moustache."

"Oh my <u>God</u>! Why would they arrest *him*? He's my *husband*!"

"I'm so sorry, Señora. Please don't say that I told you...my *padre* will beat me."

She dashed home to her father-in-law, "Suegro, I found a boy...he saw Fernando being dragged away last night! Before they do dreadful things to him, you *must* use your influence to get him released....You *have* to convince them that he's not involved...that he's responsible!"

"Yes, I'll go...just don't expect miracles...everyone's terrified. They're keeping their heads down. Some officials say I'm too outspoken...that I've had to do legal battle with them...some are afraid to even talk to me!"

"Suegro, we don't have time! They're arresting everyone who just looks suspicious to them. Some of my friends have been tortured to give them information!"

"Yes, it's terrible. We shouldn't have let the unions join the terrorists and should've stopped all the corruption. Then we wouldn't be in this mess!"

"Suegro, <u>please</u>! What happened...happened. We must find Fernando *immediately*! The soldiers who drove out the rebels...now mishandle ordinary people the same way," Angélica pleaded. "We must persuade them to release him. *Please* Suegro!" she urged, close to tears.

"Be calm my child. We'll find a way to get him freed. His arrest could have been a mistake. That's what comes from having a name as common as 'Diaz'," he tried to make light of the moment.

Out of concern for her feelings, she sensed that he wouldn't tell her everything he knew. She could feel his anguish about the crackdown on young adults and adolescents. Having grown up in Spain under Franco, she already knew that Tucumán, the only province to have succumbed to Communist rule, would be treated most harshly.

She tried easing information out of him.

"Suegro, you fought long and hard to uphold justice. There's *no way* for them to legally process so many arrests every day!"

"You've no idea how many people are begging me to find their missing children. No one will say why they were taken or where they are. They don't keep records. I can't even get information from my closest colleagues...they're so afraid. They simply say...anyone taken must have been 'subversive'."

"Suegro, you *can't* give up! We *must* keep trying!"

"I <u>am</u> trying. Just don't be upset when people say that Fernando <u>must</u> have done something wrong to be arrested. I have <u>all</u> my friends and important connections searching for him."

"Suegro, you say that to make me feel better. You know that Fernando has disappeared!"

"My child, I don't know what to say."

* * *

Angélica couldn't give up. Without Fernando, life would be unthinkable. She kept calling her friends as well as officials, wanting to know where they had taken him. Finally, a friend secretly called her. She had seen Fernando in bad shape being held in a special detention center set up in a converted, old school building in Famaillá, a small town down the river.

"Suegro, I've found him!" She shouted with joy as she barged into his office.

"Where is he?"

"Suegro, this woman in my class was engaged to our sociology professor. They were after him and tortured her to tell them where he was. They did the most dreadful things to make her talk, but she didn't know where he was. They kept beating, starving and forcefully raping her. Whey they decided to kill her so she couldn't tell what they had done to her, an officer who found her attractive stopped them and forced her to become his mistress." Gasping for breath she cried out, "She saw Fernando there!"

"How did he look?"

"He was filthy. His clothes were torn and full of dried blood. She told me how hideously they torture everyone to make their victims feel worthless and cause so much pain that they say almost anything to stop the suffering. Once they've gone that far, they can't trust their victims not to tell about their horrible ordeal and simply make them 'disappear'. But Fernando is still *alive*! Suegro, let's get him released *immediately*!"

* * *

They quickly went to see the head the Federal Police in Tucumán.

"Commandant, we've always been honest with each other. You must tell me if you've seen my son."

"My friend, I regret to admit it. He was here for about three days. I recognized him and had them untie, clean and treat him so that he could help fuel the vehicles we use to transport detainees."

"Where is he now, Commandant?"

"I wish I knew. He left, driving one of the vehicles. I never saw him again."

Dispirited and exhausted, they dragged themselves home. Dr. Diaz kept contacting everyone in authority with whom he still had influence; even the General governing the Province. Their answers were always the same—no one knew where his son was.

As a last resort, he filed formal petitions in every known jurisdiction with a writ of habeas corpus to produce the body of his son. None of his petitions were answered.

* * *

Having all but given up hope, Angélica received a call from a Colonel Lopez in Buenos Aires, saying that he knew where Fernando was being held.

Elated, she ran to her father-in-law to persuade him to follow the Colonel's instructions. Skeptical as he was, they flew to Buenos Aires to meet him at an inn near the city's center.

"Dr. Diaz," the Colonel began "I've heard good things about you from my colleagues in Tucumán and since I was approached by your son during a regular inspection of one of my barracks, I thought I'd let you know."

"Colonel, have you any idea why he's being held? He was never charged with an offense."

"No, sadly, I can't say that I know. But, this much I can do. Since the facility is under my control, I could, with some difficulty, arrange for you and his lovely wife to visit him."

"That's thoughtful of you, Colonel. How do we go about arranging such a visit?"

"First of all" the Colonel replied, taking Dr. Diaz aside and lowering his voice "I have to take care of a few of my junior officers. As you know, they're poorly paid and to be sure that they won't talk about me bending the rules for you, I need to compensate them."

"I'm not sure that I understand, but how much money do you need?"

"To be on the safe side—which would be to your benefit too—I need five thousand American dollars."

Dr. Diaz cringed, but agreed to return with the money that afternoon. They rushed to a bank and after much difficulty, returned

Johan Wassenaar

to the inn with the cash for the Colonel. He appeared ill at ease counting the money, but smiled when it was all there. "Meet me at the Army barracks at La Tablada tomorrow morning at eight o'clock. I'll arrange for you to visit your son there."

"Thank you Colonel. Is there any way to get him discharged?"

"I'm sorry...I don't know of any."

Dr. Diaz and Angélica were too excited to sleep and were at the barracks well before the doors opened. They asked the officer on duty to see Fernando Diaz, as Colonel Lopez had arranged.

With a surprised look the officer answered.

"I'm terribly sorry, Sir, but there's no one by that name or title in charge of these barracks!"

Dr. Díaz had to sit down.

"God Almighty, show me the way to survive this destruction of human dignity." he pleaded out loud. He arose to comfort Angélica and held her in his arms.

"Oh, Suegro, how will I ever explain this moment to my son and my unborn child?" she asked, weeping softly.

He held her until she was calm and had turned up to look into his eyes.

"Suegro, after this, how can you go on pretending that there's virtue left in this tortured land?"

"Angélica, God will wreak vengeance on the perpetrators of these unspeakable deeds; only then can anyone restore that virtue. We should dedicate our lives to making that happen."

"Suegro, I swear, I'll be there with you."

CHAPTER TWO

They returned to the inn to phone home.

"Papa, I have terrible news. I don't know what to do. I even think they're after me too!"

"Darling, I hate to say this, but you're right...you can't come home. You have to go where you can hide...perhaps in a crowd where no one knows you...in Buenos Aires, or even better, do you have your Spanish passport with you?"

"Yes, what will that do for me?"

"You'd be safer across the river in Montevideo. The way things are...our Spanish Embassy in Uruguay may still be able to help you."

"What will I do for money?"

"Borrow some from old Diaz. I'll pay him back. But listen, I've more bad news. The soldiers ransacked your home. They left with the place turned upside down. They also took Fernando's car. Remember how you told me about Marxist fanatics commandeering your classes to recruit students to join the revolution. Well, the General up here is rounding up all the students who attended those classes—Sociology and psychology majors top his list."

"Those revolutionaries didn't just recruit, Papa. They forced our professors to sit down and shut up while they threatened us with violence if we didn't sign up."

"It's clear that they want to arrest you, because they barged into your mother-in-law's home, demanding to know where you were."

"I hope they didn't harm my suegra or my baby?"

"No, but they were so crude, I'm ashamed of bringing you here—especially after Barcelona. I lived through the Spanish civil war and should have known better."

"Papa, don't say that. After all those years, it brought us together when mother died. I love you very much and will do all I can to survive. Look after yourself, Papa."

She compared notes with her father-in-law.

"I'm ashamed of what we've become. I feel so small and powerless...having to admit that you have to leave my country. My problem is...we used up most of our cash paying that awful Colonel."

"Never mind, I have some in my purse, and once I get to Montevideo I'll arrange for my father to send me money."

"That may take a while, so take what I have and try not to spend more than you absolutely have to."

"Suegro, you've been my pillar of strength. I'm terribly frightened, but with God's will, I'll manage."

* * *

Angélica used to love Buenos Aires for its metropolitan character and worldly ways. It was acknowledged as one of the world's leading cities, representing a polyglot of cultures and ethnic backgrounds. Parts of the city looked like London; others resembled Paris, Milan and Rome. The predominant ethnic components were reflected in its *Porteños* dialect, which reflected the lilting tone of its Italian immigrants. In stark contrast, San Miguel de Tucumán was a depressing mixture of wealth and abject poverty with not much in between—a fertile breeding ground for revolutionaries infiltrating across the massive mountain ranges at its back door.

None of that mattered now. She had to flee the country in the least conspicuous way with her meager bag of earthly belongings. With knots of fear in her stomach she took a crowded streetcar to the ferry docks. It wasn't until she was in line at the ticket counter that she realized what "across the river" meant. The Rio de la Plata mouths into a vast tidal estuary with Montevideo and Buenos Aires far apart on opposite ends. The ferry ride took all of three hours and cost nearly all her money.

Not knowing what to expect at the other end, she was too depressed and scared to stay in the confines of the passenger cabin and left for the fresh air on the stern deck as the city began to disappear into the distance. She couldn't rationalize the shock of what had happened to her. How would she survive without the love and support of Fernando? How would she survive as a wanted person with no money in a strange city? Out of sight and alone, she vented her pent up angst and wept softly.

* * *

Kevin Bartholomew stood back in the shadows of the ferry dock keeping track of the secret Argentinean and Uruguayan agents among those boarding. All except one of the faces were familiar to him. He waited until they were casting off to board unnoticed and spotted the suspicious agent shadowing a young woman with conspicuously little baggage and a bewildered expression on her beautiful face. He positioned himself in the rear passenger cabin and observed the suspicious man taking a seat two rows back from the frightened woman. As they cleared the port, she left the passenger cabin for the stern deck. The snoop behind her remained seated. From the way she moved, Kevin got the impression that she was probably pregnant. He waited a while before slipping out onto the stern deck and found her leaning over the rail, sobbing. Resting his hands nonchalantly on the rail and purposely staring out over the river, he surreptitiously offered her a clean handkerchief while addressing her in a low, calm voice.

"Señora, Please don't look at me...I don't wish to intrude...there must be something I can do to help you."

She wiped away her tears with his handkerchief.

"It's kind of you to ask...you sound like a Gringo...what would you know about Argentina?"

"You're from Catalonia...what does *anyone* know about Argentina? Things happen, but no one talks about them. What do you *need*?" he asked.

"Innocent people are being tortured and killed...I don't want to be one of them."

"Why would they to kill you?"

"They think I know too much," she explained.

"Do you?"

"Yes, they abducted my husband. I had to find him...now I may know too much."

"What will you do if you survive?" He asked.

"Pay them back for their evil brutality."

"How far are you willing to go?"

"*Toda la manera*...All the way...*al fin*...to the end." She answered with determination.

"There are hundreds like you trying to stay alive, but so far you are the first seeking vengeance. Like you, I want revenge...so I will try to keep you alive.

"When you get off the boat, take a taxi to this address," he said, as he slipped her a card with a street address wrapped in an American twenty-dollar bill.

"There's a man following you. He's sitting two rows behind where you sat. When you get to the ferry dock, hang back until most people have gone ashore. Then go quickly to the first taxi and ask to be taken to the address on that card. Stay in the taxi until an old woman with gray hair and spectacles opens the front door of the house. If she reaches down to pick up the doormat and shake it, go to her. If she just turns around and goes back inside, have the taxi take you to the Sheraton Hotel and go directly to room five-forty. Memorize the number—don't write it down and don't talk to anyone."

"Is it *that* dangerous in Montevideo?"

"For someone being followed, it could be very dangerous. Stay out here for ten more minutes. When you come in, be careful not to make eye contact with me. *Adios Señora.*"

Kevin returned to his post at the rear of the passenger cabin and waited patiently until the suspicious man got up to use the toilet. Assuming the fake identity of a supervising Argentinean agent, he paused until the man was washing his hands before addressing him.

"I know that you're neither Argentinean nor Uruguayan Intelligence. It's my job to know who you represent. If you don't cooperate, I'll turn you over to our agents," Kevin lied.

"Who do you think you are...telling me what to do?"

"I work for the special branch of the Junta's intelligence service. I supervise our foreign agents. You would be well advised to do as I say. I need to know who pays you and why you are spying on that woman," Kevin lied again.

"I am a private investigator. Alfredo Villalobos sent me to see where she's going."

"What will you do with that information?—whatever you do, don't try to lie to me."

"I think he wants to hand her to the Argentineans to claim the reward for her arrest."

"How much is the reward?"

"I have no idea. I just do as I'm told."

"Now listen carefully! When we get to Montevideo, stays on this boat...go back with it to Buenos Aires. We'll be watching you, so don't try to get off."

"How will I get paid for my work?"

"Ask Señor Villalobos. That's his business. *Adios, Amigo*"

* * *

Dumbfounded, Angélica returned to the passenger lounge. It was as if this stranger could read her thoughts? Were her emotions as obvious to everyone else? If so, she'd be in trouble. She tried to imagine what Fernando would have done and concluded that he would have trusted the Gringo.

Like Buenos Aires taxis, her cab was an older model Mercedes diesel which had seen better days. But, by the driver's choice of music, he seemed well educated. Montevideo wasn't as glamorous as Buenos Aires and all she saw were long rows of almost identical buildings.

They arrived at the address in a suburb north of the city. After several minutes, an old woman emerged, looked at the taxi and went back into the house. Both she and the driver turned their heads looking for any tell-tale sign of what the old woman may have seen. There was no one around and they left for the Sheraton hotel. Instead of driving up to the front entrance, she asked the driver to let her off at the street corner.

Her heart pounding with fear, she crossed the street and walked the length of the block, surveying the front façade of the hotel. There was a basement parking garage entrance to the right of the main entrance. She crossed back over, entered the hotel through the parking garage and scrambled into the first elevator to the fifth floor. She was still shaking as she tried softly to knock on the door of room 540.

Kevin looked through the peephole and quickly let her in.

"Why did you send me to that house?" She asked still shivering.

"I first had to find out why that man followed you. He's a bounty hunter being paid to deliver you to the Argentineans for a reward. For God's sake, what did you do to justify a price on your head? But that can wait until we can disguise you to look and behave like a different person. Think hard and choose that person carefully...you may have to live in her skin for the rest of your life."

"God, you're devious! I suppose in the world of espionage that's OK. So who do you suggest I change into?"

"Perhaps you could start wearing flashier clothes and makeup...show more cleavage and leg, walk in a sexier way, as if you were my high-class mistress. That way, they won't see you as a threat."

"You're not just trying to seduce me, are you?"

"Why would I want to sleep with a pregnant woman in deep mourning?"

"Who's going to pay for all this? I have no money!"

"Someday you'll repay me. Before anyone sees you, let's slide down to the clothes stores below to dress you up. It would be best if we pretended to be lovers, OK?"

"If you say so, but, first, who are you and what do I call you?"

"While we are on their list of suspects, we don't want to know too much about each other. They torture people more cruelly than you could imagine and I won't risk having my cover blown. You can call me 'Bartholomew' after the famous Portuguese explorer, Bartholomew Dias. What would you like to be called?"

"I'll tell you when I see what the new 'me' looks like."

Alone in the elevator on the way down she remarked.

"I have strong tastes in fashion, so let me pick out things for you to critique. Once I know what I'll be wearing, I'll have my hair done appropriately."

"Sounds good to me."

* * *

Hours later she looked like a high-flier from Barcelona with an auburn tinge to her hair, ready to paint the town red.

"I don't think they'd recognize you even in your home town! Now we have to work on your outward behavior. You mustn't look too intelligent. Your interests should appear superficial, but shrewd, if you know what I mean."

"Sure, you want me to be the vamp that plays like an airhead, but bets like a pro."

"You've got it. Can you keep it up consistently?"

"I think so. It'll keep my mind off my real problems."

"Well then, let's test drive the new you over dinner in the fancy dining room upstairs. Don't talk about your personal life. I'll do the same. Before we go, what's your new name?"

"I fancy 'Alicia de la Rosa.' It goes with the new me."

CHAPTER THREE

The dinner crowd in the swanky penthouse dining room, overlooking the Rio de la Plata, was fashionably cosmopolitan. With style Alicia made her flirtatious entrance on the arm of Bartholomew, much to the satisfaction of the dinner patrons. She looked radiant and they kept their conversation lively with interludes on the dance floor. Bartholomew liked Alicia's slick dancing style to Latin rhythms and they fell into putting on a show, dancing the tango.

"I've been thinking of the best strategy for you," he began.

"You should study for a degree in psychology and when things cool off in Argentina, you can set up a psychotherapy practice where the locals suffered severe trauma at the hands of the Junta and the Marxist rebels. Then you'll be able to accumulate a treasure trove of information about the horrendous torture of patients, some of whom may agree to testify when you can finally take the bastards to trial."

"That's deception...but fits in well with the new me," she mused aloud.

"Going down that path, you may have to remain Alicia for the rest of your life. That could be tough on your emotions...I hope you have a strong enough mind. For now, enjoy dancing with me."

Looking over her shoulder, Bartholomew saw the familiar face of the Spanish Ambassador seated at one of the best tables.

"Look over there...the big table next to the window. The tall handsome man...you need to meet him," he said as he steered her in that direction.

"I'll introduce you and do the talking."

They left the dance floor and approached the table.

"Good evening, Ambassador."

"Oh, hello, Kevin, I meant to call you. Could you stop by my office tomorrow morning?"

"I'd be happy to. Allow me to introduce my Spanish friend, Señorita Alicia de la Rosa," he said as he presented her.

"Charmed to meet you, Señorita. Where are you from?"

"Barcelona, Your Honor."

"Ambassador, the Señorita has a problem with the Argentine government which she'd like to discuss with someone at your Embassy."

"Call me tomorrow morning. I'll make an appointment for her."

"Thank you, I'll come by around eleven o'clock."

Kevin took Alicia by the arm and moved away.

"So you're really 'Kevin', and important enough to be the Spanish Ambassador's friend?"

"I've done business with him," he answered. "We've been bridge partners for years. A nice guy when you can trust him."

"Why? Is he dishonest?"

"Until last year, he represented Generalissimo Franco. That requires clever duplicity."

"That doesn't make him dishonest!"

"No, but don't expect him to sympathize with socialists. Fortunately, he also despises the Argentinean Junta."

"What should I say to him or his people?"

"Tell them that they 'disappeared' someone close to you and also treated you badly. See what they may be willing to do to be of help."

"How did you know that they took someone from me? You're not supposed to know anything about me."

"You forget you told me that they took your husband."

As she listened she stiffened and went pale.

"Don't look now, but over your left shoulder sitting at the table nearest the piano there's an extortionist. He called himself 'Colonel Lopez'...he could recognize me."

"Turn your back on him so that I can take a look...That bastard's a rip-off artist in Buenos Aires. He hired the bounty hunter to follow you! It's just as well we changed you to Alicia. Where do you know him from?" Kevin asked.

"He called me..." and she described what had happened.

"He comes here regularly to hide his money. Let's get out of here. Walk on my side away from him."

They rode the elevator down to the fifth floor in silence and didn't talk until they were safely in his room.

"Now I already know too much about you for my own good and for your safety. We'll have to be extra careful. I have an apartment here which we'll move to tomorrow. You can stay there while I'm away on business. We also need to get you more clothes. As you've seen, there are many eyes watching, and you need to stand out as Alicia de la Rosa," he advised.

There were two double beds in the room and after the upheavals of her tumultuous day, the new Alicia fell into a deep sleep. As dawn approached, she surfaced to go to the bathroom and seeing her changed appearance in the mirror, the reality of it all hit her with force. She didn't know whether to laugh or cry. It had to have been God's will that brought her together with this incredible person who went so far out of his way to identify with her. What did he expect in return?

He was still fast asleep and she struggled between, going back to her isolation or, joining his warm body in bed. Against her natural desire she went back to her own bed.

When she awoke, he was already dressed, had packed his bag and had ordered coffee for both of them.

"I hope I didn't offend you by not crawling in with you," Alicia began. "I wanted to, but thought you'd think of me as a dependent sissy."

"I'm glad you didn't. Affection shows and is easily exploited by one's enemies," he responded.

"Can you really sense what I'm thinking?"

"If you'd seen yourself dancing up there last night, you wouldn't say that. You became Alicia de la Rosa and I will know everything about you. You'll flourish in the limelight and play hard ball when you have to."

"Does she have to be that heartless?"

"Your enemies have no hearts. Given half a chance they'll mutilate you. Your experience with 'Colonel Lopez' is typical. He knew you'd be motivated to seek revenge and that he could wring more money out of your situation.

"But enough. Have some coffee, get dressed in your new street outfit and while I do my business, go downstairs and get two more outfits to wear in public. Charge it to the room. I'll be back to get you around noon. Be packed and ready to leave. OK?"

He left to keep his appointment with the Spanish Ambassador.

* * *

Still very nervous, Alicia shopped thoughtfully while keeping a sharp eye out for any peculiar behavior around her. She sat down in the coffee shop to read the paper and eat a light breakfast.

To her astonishment "Colonel Lopez" came in and sat down. She stayed behind her newspaper to observe him. He exhibited the same charm to the waitress as he had used on her Suegro. This was obviously his way of operating—supreme deception, never to be believed. She waited until he was being served, with the waitress obscuring his view, and left unnoticed.

She was rehearsing her lines for her meeting at the Spanish Embassy when Kevin returned.

"As far as the staff at the Embassy knows, you are Alicia de la Rosa from Barcelona who has lived briefly in Buenos Aires where the intelligence police did great harm to you. You need help to be safe in Montevideo. And, by the way we need to get your Spanish passport changed. Can you give it to me?"

She rummaged in her purse and pulled out her passport. It was in the name of Angélica Beron and gave an address in San Miguel de Tucumán.

"This is not your married name, I take it."

"No, what time is my meeting?"

"Your meeting's at two o'clock. You can walk there from the apartment. May I see the clothes you bought?"

"I just bought two street outfits. I've packed them, ready to leave. But first, I have to tell you. That *bandito*, Lopez, came into the coffee shop while I was there."

"He didn't recognize you. So keep up the charade."

"Why me?"

"By now he's found out that you're a Spanish citizen and was told by his informants that you are wanted for not showing up in San Miguel. His real name is Alfredo Villalobos, a common crook. Other than his bribes for information, the Junta officers don't like him and wouldn't mind if he 'disappeared.'"

"What if he had recognized me?"

"He would have taken you back to Buenos Aires."

"Bartholomew, I'm scared!"

"So am I...we had better get used to it and try not to spend our energies on fear. Save it to think smart."

"Let's go to your apartment, please" she suggested in panic. "I'll feel more secure there."

"You must have been very dependent on your husband and now lack the capacity to be on your own."

"I'm scared out of my wits...you have to help me get over that dependency."

"By changing into Alicia de la Rosa, you'll overcome it"

* * *

His apartment was on the fourth floor of a building near the city center. It had two bedrooms, a living room and a small kitchen with a dining alcove. The furniture was somewhat Spartan, but functional and clean.

"OK, hang up your things and model the outfits you bought this morning."

"Are you afraid I may have spent too much money?"

"Alicia doesn't say things like that. Obviously, I want to see how you look in them."

She modeled the first dress which was chic enough for Alicia.

"I think you should wear a bright silk scarf with it...to add some color. Remember, Alicia wants to be noticed. Straighten your back and show off your elegant breasts. Let's see the other outfit."

She reappeared in a stylish blue pant suit with a white ornate blouse.

"Now that one <u>flies</u>! No one would imagine that you're pregnant. Wear it to the Embassy."

"Yes, Lord and Master!' she said, "Alicia shouldn't have to put up with male chauvinism like yours."

"You're right. I'll tone it down. I'm becoming too familiar with Alicia."

"Can you be familiar with her without also being so with me?"

"Yes, you're taken, she's free. The Embassy's three blocks to the left. Ask at the reception desk to see Gloria Gomez. Remember, you're Alicia. I have business to attend to. This is your key. Make sure no one follows you. Hasta la Vista."

"Bartholomew thank you for everything," she said as she reached up to touch him.

The door closed behind him, leaving her to wonder alone who he was and what his purpose with her could be. He poses as an American businessman, but his knowledge and connections are more involved in local politics and clandestine activities. Against her conscience, she rummaged through the papers on his desk. His formal title was "Business Development Manager, Latin America" for an industrial machinery manufacturer in California. All the notes and messages she found dealt with contacts in the governments of Uruguay and Argentina and key figures at various Embassies. In his phone directory she also found the names of an assortment of women and the phone numbers of several Bridge Clubs.

She wondered if the name of the person he had lost was one of them and felt a slight tingling of jealousy at the thought.

Clearly, through the more glamorous Alicia, he was opening new vistas for her. She was excited about her new role, even if it was no more real than a flight of fantasy.

She examined herself in the mirror and after a few final touches of makeup, left for the Embassy.

* * *

Gloria Gomez cordially received her and asked two male staffers to join them in a small conference room.

"How may we be of assistance? I understand you escaped pursuit by members of the Argentinean Intelligence and came here for your own safety?"

"That's correct."

"How did you learn that your life was in danger?"

"I was shadowed on my way to Montevideo...they're still watching me."

"We don't have the means to guard people at this Embassy and have to refer you to the Uruguayan police."

"What do you know about Argentinean agents in Montevideo?"

"There are many...they come and go as they please."

"Isn't there a Uruguayan force to protect your staff and visitors?"

"Yes, Colonel Raúl Vildoza is responsible for protecting visiting dignitaries to Uruguay. Where can he reach you?"

"My friend, Bartholomew, has kindly allowed me to use his apartment," and she gave them Kevin's phone number.

* * *

Alicia was disappointed. There wasn't much *they* could do for her.

On her way back to the apartment she stopped to buy a newspaper and sat down on a park bench to read it. Strangely, there was absolutely no mention of all the abductions taking place in Argentina, or for that matter, in Uruguay. It made her feel even more lonely and afraid. As she put down her paper she caught the eye of a strange man who had obviously been staring at her. She quickly departed in a direction away from Kevin's apartment. To her chagrin the stranger immediately stood up and followed her. She caught site of a streetcar approaching and was narrowly missed as she sprang across the tracks and disappeared into the crowd on the opposite sidewalk. There were several shopping arcades which she used to circle back to Kevin's apartment.

Her heart was pounding as she unlocked and flung herself through the front door. It felt incredibly lonely to be there alone and she compulsively called her father in Tucumán.

"Papa I'm scared out of my wits here. What's happening there?"

"They're still busy arresting your classmates and are angry that they lost you. So far they haven't dared bother Dr. Diaz, but they have questioned Fernando's mother several times. We still don't know what happened to him."

"Give me your office Telex number...I can't use this phone...they'll be on to me!"

The sound of her father's voice brought her back to reality. She knew that she could never revert to being Angélica. She had to have the extraverted, driven character of Alicia to withstand the entrenched power of the arrogant regime that was out to get her. Instinctively she knew that in her fight to expose the perpetrators she would not be alone. However, at that moment the burden seemed overwhelming and she gave vent to her grief and frustration.

Kevin returned to find her sobbing and praying for deliverance. He felt great empathy with her and took her into his arms.

"You have the gift of endurance to go forward where most demur and silently succumb to gross inequities. I value that quality in you. Keep trying and you will always be my hero, Alicia."

"It is hard to be Alicia. If you didn't believe in me, I couldn't do it. A man followed me when I left the Embassy...I talked to my father. It's a most unhappy scene up there. They're rounding up my classmates...many of them will die after being tortured. The Spanish Embassy can't help me. They say I should talk to Colonel Raúl Vildoza...what does he have?"

"He's the only truly professional law enforcement officer in Uruguay. He looks after the most important visitors here."

"I'll introduce you to him, but what can we ask him to do?"

"Just someone I can call when all else fails."

"Is that all?"

"I wish you could be here, but I must learn to stand on my own. Now I live in your pocket...you own me. That's not fair to Fernando, but I can't do without you."

She turned her head and almost kissed him.

* * *

They went shopping locally for food and returned for her to show her epicurean skill while he immersed himself in bookwork for his monthly business report.

"What exactly do you do? I saw something about an industrial manufacturer in California."

"Snoop! That's in the best tradition of Alicia not to believe what people say without checking their veracity. We make all kinds of machinery. I'm responsible for Latin American sales, which principally means Argentina, Chile, Venezuela and Brazil."

"How come you know so many Government people? Are you someone's secret agent?"

"No, our business involves governments and to do business safely, a company needs to understand the political risks."

"Why did you go so far out of your way for me?"

"I'm not sure. On the ferryboat it was clear...I had to help you survive. I didn't know that you had the flamboyant Alicia within you."

"And now?"

"You've got me hooked on your ambitious program. Others will follow, but you are the first one to commit yourself unconditionally to bringing justice to that cabal in Buenos Aires."

"Is that all?"

"No, but I don't want to talk about it. Tomorrow, we're having lunch with the Ambassador and then I'll introduce you to Colonel Vildoza, because I'll be leaving for São Paulo and on to Buenos Aires. I'll be gone all week."

"Life will be lonely without you. Before you go, my father uses Teletype to communicate with Barcelona. How can I talk to him from here?"

"Since I move around, I use my customers' Telex machines. In Montevideo my best customer is a big printing company. I'll set it up so you can send and receive from their plant"

"What are you going to say to your father? Don't make it anything personal."

"I want him to convince Fernando's father to sue the *bandido* for fraud."

"You don't give up easily, do you, Alicia?"

"No, I have a good instructor, but now I'm ready to serve you dinner, Your Honor!"

"Did you know that sarcasm is the lowest form of wit?"

"Yes...and that it takes a small mind to recognize it?"

"Beating Alicia will require sharp intellect."

"...and discerning taste," she added.

They were both tired and turned in early. Halfway through the night Alicia awoke from a nightmare. Someone was chasing her and the faster she ran, the closer her pursuer came. As he pounced, she woke up yelling. Startled, Kevin jumped out of bed and found her shaking with fright. He held her until she had calmed down and then tucked her into his bed. Embarrassed, she apologized for waking him.

He looking at her bump and he asked, "Does it kick yet?"

"Not yet, but you should be able to hear its heart beat."

He put his ear to her stomach and could hear the rapid fetal heartbeat of her baby.

"Is it a boy or a girl?"

"Since I already have a son, it would be nice if this one's a girl."

"What will you call her?"

"Angélica would call her 'Maria.'"

"When is she due?"

"Early next year."

"Does it matter in which country she's born? You won't be back in Tucumán that soon."

"I don't care where she's born, but how long before I'll be safe there again?"

"You will never be completely safe there, but with care Alicia could live there in about two year's time...say late seventy-eight. The Junta will feel secure enough then to slow down their inquisition."

"Wow, that's a long time. Do I have to stay here?"

"No, you could go back to Barcelona, but the activity you're after will start here. I think it will come in the form of lawsuits by injured foreign nationals in their own courts. For instance you could seek compensation for the loss of your husband—assuming that he's dead—in a Spanish court and that action could be initiated through this Embassy. However, as far as I know, there's no precedent as yet in international law to sue in a jurisdiction other than the one in which the loss occurred."

"I can't stay away from my son that long. His grandmother loves him, but a son should feel his mother's influence."

"Which mother, Angélica or Alicia?"

"I'm not ready to contend with a dual personality."

"It may not be so bad. Tucumán was the only province that submitted to Marxist rebel rule. It will be singled out for more aggressive treatment. So the 'ant subversive' phase will be over sooner there. Your cue to return will be when they reopen the National University in San Miguel."

"That's a very indefinite program for a little boy missing his mother. Suppose my situation here safe enough, could we arrange to have him live with me?"

"I wouldn't count on it if I were you. It all depends on how busy Alicia is, organizing her resistance to the Junta's madness."

"I'll have to work consistently to bring fleeing Spaniards and other nationalities together. I could manage that as well as my children. Don't forget, I'll be giving birth five months from now...in January."

"OK, we can think about that tomorrow. Let's get some sleep," he suggested.

"Aren't you at least going to give me a hug?" she asked.

"You are obviously hurting, which makes me want to comfort you. But I don't want to send the wrong message. Above all, I respect your grief over losing Fernando. I know how dependent on him you became. You can't transfer that trust to me...I may not be able to help you."

"Why not?"

He turned to embrace her.

"You must learn to understand that we live in constant jeopardy...hunted by hateful, vicious people. Either of us could be gone in seconds and for me, having to do business in Buenos Aires—even with top officials in the Junta's regime—the risks are very high. It would be easier to learn to be more independent."

She responded, spilling her grief and fear by clinging to him and weeping tears of pain mixed with a sense of exhilaration.

CHAPTER FOUR

She woke up to his stirrings in the kitchen. He brought her a cup of coffee and sat down on the side of the bed.

"We've a lot to do today. I'd like to start, as I always do, with a brisk walk. There's a nice pathway along the shoreline just a block away. Are you up to joining me?"

"I'd love to come."

It was a beautiful sunny morning with the white beach stretching out along the peninsula jutting out between the main estuary and Montevideo Bay, where the port was located. Starting at the Spanish Plaza, they walked eastward along the beach where many of the tourist hotels were located along a park-lined boulevard. They'd been walking briskly for about a mile when Kevin realized that they were being followed.

"Slow down the pace, turn left in behind that hedge upfront and be prepared to embrace me and be kissed passionately. There's a man tailing us and I want to confuse him."

"Is that your only reason?"

"I really don't know...just do it...now!" he said as they moved behind the hedge and embraced. She lifted her face as their lips met and he began kissing her with overt verve and obvious passion. He could feel her heart pounding and had to wonder how much of it was out of fear. For the moment it didn't matter, it had left the man with nowhere to go, but continue on the trail.

They turned back when he was out of sight and on the way back sat down at a park table adjacent to a wide area of the beach.

"You have to do what suits you best, but I would caution you not to think you'll get vengeance for the isolated case of your husband's disappearance," Kevin began self-consciously. "In my opinion, you need to combine a number of atrocities into a case against a single important officer. You need to show that it was a deliberate, far-flung program to terrorize people by committing grossly inhuman deeds."

"I had to laugh, when you suggested using a therapy practice to document such cases," she responded "that's exactly what I was doing when the university closed."

"How far along were you?"

"I've one semester to go to finish my bachelor's degree and two more to complete my master's."

"That's good news," Kevin complemented her. "To get back to your strategic options, being local, you could point your finger at the officer in charge of Tucumán, General Bussi. You need to find specific atrocities to charge him with."

"That would be very dangerous," she cautioned. "Bussi has strong local support from the conservative leadership. Don't forget, he rescued them from the harsh Marxist rebel regime! After that experience, I can understand their anger at radicals. They summarily confiscated their lands and put them in the hands of their cronies, who wrecked them. I'm sure they won't care if a few innocent people are caught up in Bussi's 'anti-subversive' net.

"By the way, as a Gringo, how do you know so much about that obscure corner of Argentina?"

"My company supplied most of the drive gears for the sugar mills. For a time, I visited Tucumán quite often."

"I wonder if you met my father, Sergio Beron."

"Yes, when you showed me your passport I recognized the name. We were competitors."

"What a small world!" She exclaimed

"Hey, we have to move along. We're meeting the Spanish Ambassador for lunch," he reminded her.

As they walked, he tried to prepare her for the meeting.

"I told the Ambassador that you'd be living here and that you wished to meet as many victimized Spanish citizens as possible. I told him you wanted to document their experiences for the record in the event that, someday, justice could be served."

"Is that what you want me to do?"

"It's not what I want. It's a matter of positioning Alicia as a magnet for victims that have grounds for cases against the officers of the Junta. Given that mantra, you'd better forget Angélica if you want to live. In Montevideo and perhaps later in Madrid, you'll have to be the elegant, smart, Alicia with high level connections, actively working to bring justice to Argentina. What you did in San Miguel has little to do with Alicia's political agenda."

"What about you? That kiss wasn't just to throw off our follower...was it?"

"No, but regardless of me, you have to remain Alicia one hundred percent of the time."

"Does that mean I'm free to do as I please?"

"That's up to you. Just don't sell your body for important favors."

"Is that what you think I was trying to do with you?"

"No. With me you've been honest."

"What about you?"

"I feel too vulnerable to say."

* * *

Wearing her new dress, now with the addition of a bright silk scarf, Alicia entered the restaurant on Bartholomew's arm to join the Ambassador's party in a private room. There were several guests and a few staff members to whom the Ambassador introduced them as his friends, Alicia de la Rosa and Kevin Bartholomew.

"Since I know that some of you are thinking along similar lines, I invited all to tell you what Alicia has her heart set on doing," the Ambassador explained.

"You are most kind, Ambassador," Alicia began. "I suffered the loss of someone very dear to me at the hands of Argentinean military under most inhumane circumstances and, while I know that it may take many years—perhaps even decades—I, along with others— would like to begin preparing for the time when we can bring our transgressors to justice. That could best be done as a tightly organized group with strength in numbers and political influence."

A professional-looking man responded.

"My name is Carlos Vargas. I share your sentiments and am willing to work with you, but how do we ensure our group's security?"

"In my opinion, you have to do it from foreign soil. They'll kill you in Argentina. This is as good a base as any," Kevin answered.

Vargas responded.

"I agree, but isn't it too close to the enemy to be secure?"

Alicia stepped in to resolve the issue.

"The alternative venue would be Spain and it's already crawling with Argentinean agents. Besides, this is where our best candidates for the group will pass through first. Once they reach Spain, they scatter."

An intense discussion ensued ending in a consensus that Alicia and Vargas would act as coordinators and that the group would meet weekly at different safe houses.

Kevin and Alicia accompanied the Ambassador on the short walk to the Embassy.

"Ambassador, how can we be sure that all those in attendance were trustworthy?" Alicia asked.

"My staff checked them out carefully. I would suggest that your committee do the checking from now on—with our help, of course. You should divide the movement into cells of just a few people each, to make infiltration more difficult."

They carried on to the offices of Colonel Vildoza and waited in the lobby for an usher guided them to his office.

"Colonel, it's kind of you to see us at such short notice!"

"Oh, Kevin cut the theatrics. I'm Raúl Vildoza, Señora"

"Colonel, Alicia de la Rosa," she said as she gave him her hand. He bowed and kissed it.

"My friend, Kevin, explained the purpose of your stay and I'll do as much as I can to make your stay a safe one. Señora, do you know how to handle a pistol?"

"It's Señorita, Colonel. I've used one, but I wouldn't call myself a good shot."

"Call me tomorrow. I'll send you to our firing range where you can practice. I'll loan you a small automatic pistol which will slip easily into your purse."

"Is it that dangerous here?"

"It helps to be prepared. We keep a sharp eye out for new agents from Argentina and know the ones already here. I'll warn you if we spot something unusual in your area."

Then he dropped what he thought would be a bombshell, "Kevin you probably didn't notice. You were being shadowed on your walk this morning. No harm was done, the two of you looked so lovey-dovey, he probably thought Alicia was just your latest mistress, and lost interest."

"I told you I was a good actor!" Kevin quipped.

"Acting my foot! Go well, you two."

"Are you really that famous for womanizing?" Alicia asked after they'd left.

"He's a big tease when he likes someone. We've done each other lots of favors."

"Bartholomew, why do you live here? Surely it would be more efficient to use Buenos Aries, Santiago, São Paulo or Rio."

"I like it here. It's not too congested, nice people, no taxes, easy currency controls, good climate, inexpensive living, great airline service and communications. That reminds me, we have to go over to Max's printing place to get you set up for Telex use," He reminded her. "That's how I'll keep in touch with you when I'm on the road."

"Do you really have to leave tomorrow? Without my 'lovey-dovey' the agents won't be thrown off track so easily...besides I could become addicted to your style of doing so."

* * *

At home over dinner they reviewed the details of her plans with Vargas to lead the "Spanish Committee", as they began calling it.

"Life would be so much simpler if only I could just be Alicia."

"With Angélica's child in your womb, another in San Miguel and an obligation to Fernando's family?"

"Do you have to be so realistic?"

"Yes. I have to face reality even if it may cast me in a redundant role."

"That sounds resentful."

"No, I want to see our sacrifices bear fruit. Both of us may not make it...even worse, they could hold one of us hostage to control the other."

"Please don't scare me even more than I am. I was thinking ahead to my problems when I'm back in Tucumán. I'll be with my children, the family, my father and friends, all expecting me to behave like Angélica."

"That's a difficult problem you'll have to master. The characters of your two identities are too different to reside together. You have to become Alicia *exclusively*."

* * *

When she awoke he was gone. There was a note wishing her well, saying that his flight was too early to wake her.

Suddenly, she was without his support and focused her thoughts on flying solo in an unfamiliar, hostile, environment. She was relieved that her first appointment was at the shooting range. At least, she'll have the comfort of a weapon.

The instructor handed her a small handgun and showed her how to maintain and operate it. Then he took her to the shooting range, gave her earmuffs to put on and stood behind to show her how to stand, hold the pistol and aim it to fire.

After an hour's training she felt comfortable using the weapon and was allowed to fire at targets in various ways.

After another hour of target practice, including dynamic targets, Alicia received a passing grade, a small box of ammunition, a handgun with a cleaning kit and was dismissed.

Emboldened, but still fearful, she made her way home using different streets she than the ones she was familiar with. She had gone but two blocks before she noticed the man following her. He looked vaguely familiar and she began dodging him by weaving through shopping arcades as she had done before. He must have anticipated her tactic, because he closed in and refused to be shaken. Finally, a block away from Kevin's apartment, she passed narrowly in front of a car emerging from an alley, turned into it and hid in the rear doorway of a store. The car barred the agent's way for long enough to lose sight of her and he continued along the street. Alicia entered the store and waited to one side near the front entrance until she was sure that he had lost her and continued home without incident to sit down for a well-deserved rest. She felt scared and lonely without Bartholomew, but it helped her assess her situation more realistically.

She didn't know if she could stomach staying in Montevideo and the rest depended on conditions in Tucumán. Her baby was due in January. Essentially, she had to plan her activities around a five to six month stay somewhere away from Argentina.

She went to the printing plant to Telex her father and seek his advice. If at all possible, she wanted him to bring her two-year old son to her and to convince her mother-in-law to come and help her look after the new baby. But where?

* * *

Alicia called Carlos Vargas to come to Kevin's apartment. They took the roster of twelve names and assigned four of them to each of three separate cells as the Ambassador suggested.

"We have to be careful not to wind up supporting fanatics with their own violent agenda. That would defeat our cause," she cautioned.

"Yes, but *what* is our cause?"

"I can't speak for the group. My objective is to expose the most evil transgressions of the Argentinean Intelligence to the world, to force Argentina to think seriously about its lack of moral fortitude. I don't want to risk sounding shrill in the company of fanatic leftist, pointing fingers at the excesses of a hardline regime."

"That distinction will drive some of our militant members away," he indicated.

"I'd be happy to see them go," she exclaimed.

"Do you really mean that?" he asked.

"Does that surprise you? To err on the left is just as bad as doing so on the right. I dare say, without the extremists on our left in

Argentina, there wouldn't be the need for a military correction," Alicia defended her stance.

"I suppose the foreigners in our group are more egocentric in their motivations," he observed.

"Then we don't need them. Are you willing to counsel the group on this issue and let me know who stays in and what other grievances they may have?"

"Yes I'd be delighted to do so...I happen to agree with your philosophy."

"Tell me," Alicia asked "aren't you afraid of being pursued here in Montevideo?"

"Not as acutely as I was in Córdoba, but I still keep a sharp eye out for their agents. There are many of them, but fortunately, they're poorly organized and trained," he answered.

"What do they look like? How does one recognize them?" Alicia prodded.

"They look awkward, insecure and just don't blend in with the locals," he explained. "Such a person followed me this morning, but had to turn away when I went through the Spanish Embassy on my way here.

"What if he's still waiting for you when you leave?"

"I'll stay in crowded places until I can lose him and then go home. Sometimes, if I can't lose my tail, I'll go into a public library and start reading reference material in the stacks until he tires and leaves."

"You make it all seem so trivial and common-place...I look forward to hearing from you again."

She was satisfied that Alicia was coming into her own. The more assertive role gave her a good feeling about herself. She wondered how much further she'd have to go to meet Bartholomew's standards. It was uncanny that this stranger could just walk into her life and bring about such a profound change in her outlook."

CHAPTER FIVE

Carlos Vargas impressed Alicia and she asked the Ambassador's secretary about his background. He came from Segovia, just north of Madrid, to start a medical practice in Córdoba and wound up marrying his nurse. She was abducted while she was pregnant and disappeared. He lost his temper while trying to find her and threatened the authorities. A warrant was issued for his arrest and he fled across the border at Conception de Uruguay.

Given this information, she knew that she could trust his resolve to expose the terrors of the Argentinean authorities and invited him to meet her at the picnic table on the beach.

This time she kept her eyes wide open, had the loaded pistol in her purse and stopped unexpectedly to make random changes in direction, to assured herself that she wasn't being followed. Vargas sat reading the morning paper.

"*Buenos Dias, Señor* Vargas. It was good of you to come."

"It is my pleasure, *Señorita* de la Rosa. What's on your agenda?"

"I'd like to hear your ideas for putting officers of the Junta on trial in Spain. I hear some judges in Madrid want to try Chile's President, General Pinochet, in Spain."

"There are frustrated Federal Judges in Spain who would have loved to try Generalissimo Franco, but he died and they lost their chance. A Spanish judge can't deliver a subpoena to Pinochet in Chile. While he's in power he's immune to prosecution. Further, it's questionable under international law, whether someone can be tried in a foreign jurisdiction for a crime committed in another country."

"So, that avenue isn't our solution."

"Not for a long while. There would have to be major shifts in international law before something like that could happen."

"What kind of shifts?"

"Hypothetically, it seems to me that the standoff between east and west must end first. Until then the Soviets and the Allies each will continue to pour resources into unstable countries to cause extreme political rifts—Without Khrushchev, there wouldn't be a Fidel Castro or a Ché Guevara. They are part of fanatical Marxist group who threaten chaos in countries like this one and Argentina. Then the militaries in those countries get paid and armed by the Allies to shoot the rebels down...and we wind up with a slow-burning civil war where one can't tell who the rebels are...as always, innocent people get hurt."

"So what's the solution?"

"Education."

"If that's your cure, why are you talking about publicizing the rotten deeds of the Junta?"

"Before education can work, there has to be universal representation. That means the current totalitarian Argentinean regime has to go. They have to be made to embarrass their foreign supporters into dropping them. If we could shame the Americans into withholding credit and weapons, the Junta would fall."

"And then we'd be back in Perónist chaos."

"Not if the public learns to change its values and refuses to condone any form of state violence. That's why we *must* reveal as much of their vulgar misdeeds as possible. The national media is under tight Government control, so we have to find ways to appeal to strong international media."

"That makes our program impossibly ambitious."

"Not really. As I think Shakespeare put it: 'There's a tide in the affairs of men, which, taken at the flood, leads on to fortune'. When the Junta runs out of people to terrorize, there'll be thousands, if not tens of thousands of seriously aggrieved persons with grotesque stories to tell. If we can help start a trickle, it may well become a flood. We have to be the catalysts that make it flow."

"A fascinating concept...It encourages me! I'd like to work with you, but we need to establish an organization that can build on itself with room for any number of aggrieved people to join. Perhaps it should be made up of many independent cells so that it can never be broken up."

"You mentioned that before and I agreed with you then. Each 'cell' should consist of a collection point for explicit information about atrocities that we can use in a publicity campaign. The trouble will be that many people are still too scared to tell what happened to them. Some won't even acknowledge that they're missing members of their own family!"

"Thank you for coming, Carlos...if I may call you that. This meeting has inspired me."

"Thank you for inviting me. We'll depend on you to collect strong evidence of misdeeds from the troubled Tucumán region. *Hasta la vista*, Alicia."

* * *

She was far less fortunate on the way home, picking up a smart, determined tail. To mislead him, she entered a large department store and rode the escalator up to the third floor, where she could look down and see him from floor to floor. She stopped at a cosmetics counter and while pretending to pick out a lipstick, gave the sales lady her name and asked her to call security to inform them that she was being stalked by a man who was then standing at the magazine counter. She had sampled several different colors until a plain-clothes security man arrived and began questioning her stalker. The man objected vehemently to the charge that he was stalking her and the guard brought him over to the cosmetics counter.

"Señorita, are you Alicia de la Rosa and is this the man who has been following you?"

"Yes, Señor, he followed me for several blocks. I made unusual turns, but he stayed behind me and followed me into the store. He stalked me from counter to counter and up three floors on the escalator."

The man objected, but was taken away. Alicia quickly left the store and made it home safely. With pounding heart, she wondered how long it would take before they realized that Alicia de la Rosa was not the Angélica Diaz they were seeking.

The phone rang and she answered, "Senor Bartholomew's office, may I help you."

"You sure can," Kevin answered.

"Bartholomew! I'm so glad you called. I've been followed ever since you left and just had a nasty scare." She went on to tell him about her encounter.

"Have you been to see Raúl about the pistol?"

"Yes and the instructor said he made me into a good shot."

"Well, that should make you feel less frightened."

"Bartholomew, I can't just shoot someone on the street for following me around!"

"You're doing the right things. Word will ultimately get back that you're not the woman they're trying to find. With all this happening much of your survival depends on being identifiable as Alicia. Please go to the Embassy...don't call, go there and ask to see the Ambassador. Tell him that you need him to get you a Spanish passport in the name of Alicia de la Rosa, born in Barcelona. Give them a birth date a month later than your own. Explain to him that if they ever corner you during your travels, your existing passport could be your death warrant."

"What if he refuses?"

"Nobody refuses Alicia. You have to be persuasive."

"Where are you?"

"I'm in São Paulo and am leaving for Buenos Aires in an hour. Have you spoken to your father?"

"No, I telexed him and asked him to pay me a visit and bring my little boy with him. I also asked him to convince my suegra to come and help me with the baby next January. My problem is that I don't know where I'll be. I'm think I'm too vulnerable to stay here."

"Is it that bad?"

"I can't go anywhere without being shadowed! Even with the gun, they could so easily grab me and take me away."

"Perhaps you should marry me...they're less likely to detain an American and Señorita de la Rosa will also not be having a child out of wedlock."

"Is that a proposal?"

"Technically you'd be committing bigamy...we may have to think of a better plan. Perhaps we could let the word out that we've been married all along and for tax or other reasons, you kept your maiden name. That would also explain why your belly keeps getting bigger. Besides, it would pass as chic in intellectual circles—Chopin and George Sands."

"You're being silly while you know that I'm desperate and scared."

"I'll hurry home at the end of this week. How's your committee?"

"I met with Vargas this morning at that table on the beach. He's brilliant...a physician from Segovia," and she explained his situation. "Like me with Fernando, he can't find his wife. He has a very measured approach to achieving our goal, but his objectives are in the stratosphere."

"Keep your eyes peeled...if you have to, shoot one of those bastards. Raúl will cover up for you...they're trespassing on his territory. Got to go, they're calling my flight. Adios."

Hearing from him had given her a real shot in the arm. She was satisfied with her progress toward becoming Alicia. Her love for Fernando had always seemed unfathomable to her, and losing him in such an unexpected, brutal way, shattered her confidence—not that she had any before she met Fernando. She had to avenge his loss to go on. The Gringo seemed ordained to lift her to the level she needed to do it. He'd been so utterly helpful that she'd have to be callous not to recognize the relationship that was building between them. She didn't quite know how to reconcile that with her vows to Fernando.

* * *

Dutifully, Alicia went to the Spanish Embassy and asked for an appointment to see the Ambassador. Being a lady's man, he fit her into his next morning's schedule. She put on her most terrified expression as she told him of being stalked and conjectured as to what would have happened if they'd caught and searched her…finding her passport with a different identity.

"Since my safety here now clearly depends on being Alicia de la Rosa, I have to have a passport that says so…else I'll have to find another country to hide in."

"This is highly irregular and we almost never do it, but I don't see why it would matter to us whether your name is Beron or de la Rosa, so this once I'll tell our passport man to prepare one for you. Take your passport down to him and tell him precisely what it should say."

"Thank you so very much, Ambassador. You may have saved my life today."

"Think nothing of it. When Kevin gets back, let's have dinner together."

An assistant guided her downstairs to the passport department and told the manager to check with the Ambassador about Miss de la Rosa's needs. He interviewed her briefly and filled in the proper names and dates on an application form, which she signed, paid a fee and was told to pick it up at the reception desk at four.

* * *

On her way home, she stopped at a local food market to buy vegetables, fruit and milk. As she was checking out, a scruffy man tried to grab her purse. She spun around and swiped him across the face, forgetting that it contained a hard metal pistol. The effect was dramatic as her stroke tore his cheek, causing it to bleed. Shocked, he began to run away.

She yelled, "*Stop. Thief.* His bleeding face was a dead give-away and he was brought down by a burly pedestrian just a few paces outside the market. With everyone's attention on the villain, she quietly slipped away through a back door and breathlessly called Raúl from the apartment.

"Raúl, forgive me...there were two scary incidents today." And she described them to him.

"The guy in the department store had Argentinean papers and the security guy sent him here. We scared the daylight out of him and he cracked...he was after a woman called Angélica Diaz who looked a bit like you. I told him to call his boss for me. I gave him a hard time, belittling him for pursuing the wrong person...that you were Alicia de la Rosa, from Spain...a special guest of the Ambassador and advised him to call off his dogs. He apologized, but that may not mean much. They lie to us all the time.

"The other guy may not be theirs. We have him in the holding tank. My guys say he looks like a common thief. I'll let you know tomorrow."

"Thanks a million Raúl."

"Nothing's too much for my friend Kevin."

Damn it, the fear of being caught was wearing thin and she took a warm bath to relax and took a nap, leaving the alarm set for three thirty. She was dreaming intensely as she surfaced and took a deep breath, made up her face, dressed in her pantsuit to walk to the Embassy. The passport was ready and she returned along a different route to have a cappuccino. No one stared at her and she was sure that she'd not been followed. However, the fact that she had to be so vigilant brought her much closer to the possibility of having to use her pistol.

CHAPTER SIX

Kevin had an uneasy feeling on his way from the airport to his Buenos Aires hotel. The vigor with which agents had pursued Alicia in Montevideo surprised him. What on earth could they think was so important about apprehending a pregnant mother in her mid-twenties? He had thought of, but now dismissed any idea of calling her.

His first meeting was at the naval headquarters with the captain responsible for modernizing the frigates and destroyers Argentina had bought as surplus from the U.S. Navy. They were out-of-date, World War II vessels requiring modern steering engines, windlasses and winches manufactured by his company.

His visits to the captain had been so frequent that they issued him a permanent security pass to enter the building unescorted. On this occasion he was surprised to be met by two MP's insisting on escorting him. The captain came out of his office to greet him looking perturbed.

"Kevin, these officers want to know if you are harboring a young woman from Tucumán in Montevideo."

"With due respect, Captain...how does this pertain to my business with you?"

"These men say they have a right to receive an answer, since they have a warrant for the arrest of that Argentinean citizen."

"Well, then the answer is 'no'. My only recent visitor was a Spanish person."

"Could you identify your visitor, please?" One of the MPs asked.

"Not that it's any concern of yours officer, her name is Alicia de la Rosa. She's visiting her personal friend, the Spanish Ambassador to

Uruguay, but since his Embassy is full of expatriate Spaniards fleeing Argentina, I agreed to let her stay at <u>my</u> home."

"Sir," said one of the MPs, "our people saw you on the same ferryboat as this Tucumán woman."

"Officer, I frequently ride that ferryboat when the shuttle flights are full. On my last trip, I talked to none of the passengers. What does this woman look like, what is her name and why do you want to arrest her?"

"She has black hair, is of slight build and average height and we think she's about four months pregnant. We want to talk to her about a bribe we think she paid to a crook who said he knew where her husband was incarcerated."

"There must have been twenty or thirty women on the ferry matching your description. At four months, many women hardly show signs of pregnancy."

"What does your visitor look like?"

"That's really no concern of yours, but since the captain and I are long-time colleagues, I'll tell you. She's a slender five-foot, seven-inches, has auburn hair, wears fashionable, colorful clothing, has a vivacious personality and is as sharp as a whip. I'm no expert on Tucumán, but the customers I visited there, have tastes several shades more conservative than those of Señorita de la Rosa. You must be barking up the wrong tree."

"I'm inclined to agree. Gentlemen, would you please excuse us, we have important technical business to discuss," the captain finally cut them off.

Looking disgruntled, the MP's left.

"Captain, I didn't want to antagonize them, but Miss de la Rosa was harassed by Argentinean agents in Montevideo. They are obviously on a fishing expedition. They can't even properly describe the person they're looking for. To be honest with you, I was offended by being interrogated here in the privacy of your office. We are proud of our customer service standards. I've always gone out of my way for you. This kind of treatment is not conducive to continuing that kind of relationship."

"I am very sorry, but these are extraordinary times."

"Captain, it takes extraordinary imagination to suppose that an American, serving your defense needs, would secretly harbor a Communist sympathizer. I resent being associated with such nonsense. I must insist that you use your rank and influence to have your security boss call off his dogs!"

"I'll make sure that they stop pursuing you."

* * *

Kevin had three more calls to make in Buenos Aires, two of which were within walking distance from the Navy School of Mechanics. He took circuitous routes to make sure that he wasn't being followed and wasn't bothered on either call—one of which was to the General of the Air Force.

His last call was on the way to the airport and he took a taxi. As they approached his destination at the airline's maintenance base, the driver mentioned that they were being followed. Kevin asked to be dropped off at the main entrance and quickly disappeared inside. His meeting was with the head of cargo handling equipment for Aerolineas Argentinas and after they had completed their business, Kevin asked if he had any trucks going to the seaport soon.

"Yes, we transfer a lot of cargo to and from the port. What do you have in mind?"

"I need a ride to the ferry terminal."

"Let me see what we have scheduled." After checking with an assistant in a nearby office he announced, "We have a van taking some prepared food to the four o'clock ferries to Uruguay. We do the catering for them from our kitchens. You can hitch a ride with the driver. He'd like the company, I'm sure."

The trip to the ferry terminal was uneventful and Kevin slipped aboard the Montevideo ferry from the baggage loading portal as the food was being transferred. He spent the next three hours in the wheelhouse with the crew, who knew him as a regular passenger.

After they docked, he stayed onboard until all the passengers had disembarked and he could pass through Immigration and Customs without delay. There was nothing suspicious in the nearly empty disembarkation area and, since he had only one suit bag and a briefcase, he walked home; once again using a circuitous trajectory.

* * *

Alicia had expected him to arrive hours earlier on a shuttle flight and was frantic by the time he made it home. He'd been on her mind constantly as she struggled to rationalize their relationship, and her new personality. Alicia craved him, while Angélica wanted to keep her distance.

It all evaporated when he walked through the door and she flung herself at him and kissed him passionately, "Bartholomew, what happened? I've been waiting for hours!"

Surprised at first by her emotional greeting, he began describing the scene at the naval office.

"I can't believe they'd try to use 'Colonel Lopez' to deceive me. One thing is clear...you permanently have to change into Alicia to survive."

"Does that mean I have to do absolutely everything to be in character with Alicia, even if Angélica disapproves?"

"Yes, everything...*Sí, todo*! Otherwise you'll expose Alicia to great harm."

"Are you ready for what that could mean to us?"

"I think so, but it won't be easy."

"At this moment I'm not afraid?"

He held her so he could see into her eyes.

"We have to move gently...it requires life-long commitments from both of us."

"*Si Señor, siempre*...always," she whispered.

He embraced her and softly traced her lips with his fingers before kissing her so lightly, it almost tickled her. With both hands holding his head, she gently pulled his lips onto hers and began kissing him with great passion.

He returned her kisses with growing intensity until they approached the point of no return. She accommodated him until their intimacy became too much for her and she pushed back crying.

"Bartholomew, I can't go falling in love with you yet! It frightens me so to think what it will demand from us. We still have much pain to bear, but the joy I feel will overcome my fear. Please be patient...it will take time for me to give myself to you."

CHAPTER SEVEN

They were hungry and concocted a meal out of what she had in the pantry.

"Does it bother you that I'm pregnant?"

"Yes and no. It reminds me of Fernando. In our situation where we don't even know if he survived, I can't let that bother me. Being pregnant heightens your sensitivity which makes it more thrilling for both of us."

"I have never felt so uninhibited about intimacy. Alicia is liberating me."

"What happened today and yesterday, says that they're serious about arresting you. It has to be something I don't know about yet. What could it be?"

"One of two things: They don't want me to talk about what I know, or, they suspect me of being a leftist ideologue."

"Is there anything in your background to support the idea of you being a fanatic socialist?"

"I belonged to a charity that collected money to buy food and help the poorest people in the community. I studied psychology and in some of our civics classes, the Marxist rebels barged in to take over the classroom and preach their revolutionary gospel to recruit new rebels. They'd threaten the class so much that, by a show of hands, they'd get everyone to agree to join them. I never signed up, nor did I have anything to do with them."

"Well, I'll be damned."

"You told me not to tell you about my life before Alicia."

"If that's all you did, it should just be a matter of time before they'll forget you. I still don't like the odds of staying here until that happens. There are too many agents snooping around. Are you ready to disappear for a while?"

"Where to?"

"How about Chile...or the United States? It would be easier for me to carry on my business from Chile."

"I've never been in Chile. The nearest place to us is Antofagasta, which I hear is awful. What's it like in Santiago?"

"It's big and noisy. Half of Chile's population lives there, so it's an easy city to get lost in. It's also run by a military Junta and there's a nightly curfew from midnight until dawn, called the 'Toca de Qaeda.' If we have to disappear for a while, I fancy the area around Puerto Montt. It's directly across the border from Bareloche. There are beautiful lakes, forests, volcanoes and mountains. We could go riding or take white water raft trips. There's a beautiful town called Puerto Varas on Lago Llanquihue where we could stay. This early in spring, the nights are still cold and there's lots of snow on the mountains."

"It sounds *muy romántico*. When do we leave and how long can we stay?"

"We've got to get out of town right away. I'll see if there are seats on tomorrow's LanChile flight to Santiago. You must get your Spanish Club man, Vargas, to hold the fort for you. Don't spoil the chance of getting important information for your campaign. I won't bring you back here until they've stopped looking for you."

"How will we know?"

"Raúl will tell us."

"Bueno, I'll talk to Carlos and get him to keep working without me."

"Alicia, don't tell anyone where we're going."

"How will I keep in touch with my papa?"

"There's a fishing fleet in Puerto Montt. They use our transmission gears. We'll use their Telex to send messages to your father through the printing company in Montevideo."

"Bartholomew, I'm so lucky to have you to protect me. You hold my life in your hands."

"There's an excellent Tango club here. Would you like to go dancing? They have an awesome Bandoneón player."

"I'd love to go, but will it be safe?"

"I refuse to let those bastards dictate my life style. Take your pistol with you."

* * *

They dressed and took a taxi to the club in the port neighborhood. He tipped the concierge to get a table right at the dance floor. They didn't even wait to be served before getting into dancing the tango. There were good dancers on the floor and they took note of their more dramatic routines to try in their own fashion. Alicia was particularly limber and seductive after their intimate interlude and danced very close and suggestively. They were oblivious to their surroundings as they lavished affection on each other in gesture after gesture. This was the furthest thing from hiding away they could have done and they loved it.

He ordered Brazilian Caiperinias to enjoy the ambiance of the club. The music was terrific and they danced their feet off.

There was a full moon on the way home and he asked the taxi driver to drop them on the beachfront a block away from the apartment. They were walking arm-in-arm as they rounded the corner to turn toward the apartment. Suddenly, a man with a revolver in his hand confronted Kevin. In a broad Lunfadro accent, common to Buenos Aires' mobs, he said menacingly.

"I knew we'd catch you sooner than later. Walk ahead of me!" he commanded and shoved his revolver into Kevin's ribs.

As they approached the corner, Kevin abruptly yelled *"Watch out!"* ducked and looked across the street.

The man with the gun instinctively followed Kevin's lead and looked to see what was across the street. In that instant, Alicia fired three shots with her pistol at point blank range. The gunman went down with blood pulsing from a wound in his neck just behind his ear.

They ran to their building to call Raúl. His duty officer answered. Kevin told him about the attack and that they had shot the Junta agent.

"Colonel Vildoza said we should immediately notify you if this happened. The man is down on the corner of Ejido and Cabollati. We didn't stay to see how bad he was. He had a revolver in my ribs when the Señorita shot him."

"What did you say your name was?"

"Kevin Bartholomew, officer."

"Oh, yes, Señorita de la Rosa's friend! I was her instructor at the firing range. We'll attend to it immediately."

About a half an hour later Raúl Vildoza called and asked for Alicia. "The man you took down was an Argentinean agent all right. You did a remarkable job. He had a forty-five caliber revolver in his hand. By the time my men got there, he was dead. This was the boldest move they've made yet. So, I think you should think of moving somewhere safer, Señorita."

"Raúl, without your help, Kevin Bartholomew would have died tonight. I could not have defended him without the pistol and your training. Where am I to hide?"

"Tell him to take you to California."

"Tell him yourself. He's right here."

"Bueno, Raúl. They tried to interrogate me in Buenos Aires today. I denied seeing any woman from Tucumán, but acknowledged that Alicia de la Rosa, visiting the Spanish Ambassador, was staying in my apartment. They obviously didn't believe me. Will you be kind enough to arrange for one of your drivers to pick us up at ten to take us to LanChile? We hope to catch the Santiago flight at noon."

"That would be my pleasure. What else do you need?"

"May I borrow one of your nine-millimeter Beretta pistols, with papers of course, for, say...a month?"

"Do you know how to handle one?"

"I trained extensively with them."

"The driver will have one for you. Kevin. <u>Vaya</u> <u>bien</u>."

"*Gracias, Amigo*, make sure that word gets around that we've left for Los Angeles."

* * *

Alicia's quick thinking and accurate shooting astounded Kevin. He couldn't have dreamt that she would respond with such devastation to a situation he was responsible for. He was a fool of have taken them to the Tango Club, and he said so.

Alicia cut in.

"Save me the macho travail. You created 'Alicia' and now you have to live with her. Shooting that bastard was a pleasure. Don't thank me. The consequences scare me. They'll never forget Angélica. Cops don't like cop-killers.

"It wasn't your *fault* that we went dancing. I loved it. Dancing like that was something I only fancied through the fog of my inhibited upbringing. Our intimacy this afternoon was tantalizing. Alicia terrifies me. How can I crave you when I just lost my beloved husband? He meant everything to me!" she sobbed, falling into his embrace.

They kissed and as his intensity increased, her breathing became audible. She reached down to fondle him gently. As he grew harder, she loosened his waistband and unzipped him to have full access.

He undid her dress and pushed it down over her hips to expose her stomach and thighs. His hand moved down between her legs to find her warm and very damp.

She groaned softly as he touched her and began gently exciting her. She raised her pelvis towards his hand and hardened her grip on his erection. He could hardly stand more and knelt down to gently excite her orally.

"Before I go any further, I need to know what it meant to you to shoot that agent today. You saved me from certain death."

"Losing you after what I've been through would have been too much and I shot him without giving it another thought."

"It made me understand why we have to stay together. I'll be there for you, no matter what happens.

CHAPTER EIGHT

Thanks to Raúl's help, the flight to Santiago was uneventful. He had them delivered directly to LanChile, bypassing all the red tape.

Santiago couldn't be described as a beautiful city, but it had a distinct character which made Alicia feel comfortable, except for the visible presence of police and soldiers. At least, here they weren't pursuing her.

They stayed in a snug bed-and-breakfast inn with a pleasant, thoughtful proprietor who greeted Kevin as her long-lost friend. While he did his business with the national oil company, the airline and the military, their host vividly described and showed Alicia photographs of the destruction the Communists had wrought in their three-year tenure under Salvador Allende. What began as a relatively benign regime escalated into an unbridled rape of democratic and economic institutions, which had once been the pride of Latin America ...a democracy dating back longer than any country on the Continent? Chile had physically been ransacked, leaving its economy in shambles.

The Inn proprietor took Alicia to the academically-acclaimed, Catholic University of Santiago to explore the possibilities of completing her degree in psychology there. She was thrilled by the promising prospects.

Kevin took her with him on a visit to one of his marine clients in the port of Valparaiso and explored the delightful seaside town of Viña del Mar with her. They stayed overnight—for once in a relaxed, calm atmosphere—in which their relationship could bloom and begin to dispel her ethical inhibitions about intimacy.

"I never expected to feel this way about a man, this soon and feel like pinching myself to prove that it's real. I want it to go on and on and on—and then I'm overcome with remorse for neglecting my son and Fernando's family."

"You would have been dead if you hadn't 'neglected' them, so don't feel guilty yet. As for finding each other, I prefer to view that as divine destiny...I can't explain it any other way.

"To help you feel better about your family, I've arranged with my friends at ENAP, the national oil company, to let us use their Telex to communicate with your father via the printer's Telex in Montevideo—to make it look as if we're still there. We can also stay in contact directly with Raúl and Carlos Vargas via the Spanish Embassy."

In her first message to her father she informed him that they had gone elsewhere and to postpone his visit to Montevideo. In his reply he said that the pursuit of her university colleagues had slowed, as there were fewer left to interrogate. They had heard nothing more about the fate of Fernando. He was presumed dead.

Vargas reported that nothing had changed in Montevideo; that Spanish citizens continued to pour out of Argentina and that there was now also a clamor from Argentineans trying to escape to Spain, much to the dismay of the Spanish government.

After a few more days in Santiago, they left for Puerto Montt. As a precaution, Kevin bought tickets to Punta Arenas, knowing that the flight made a stop in Puerto Montt. An hour into the flight he went to see the head stewardess, explaining that his pregnant wife was feeling poorly and that they'd like to get off at their next stop and continue onto Punta Arenas on a later flight.

Alicia's head was full of ideas to complete her studies at the Catholic University in Santiago.

"What I like about Santiago is that the people there are more cultured than in Argentina—they even speak something like Castilian Spanish. I felt at home along the coast at Viña del Mar...It is so much like the Costa Brava."

"That's my reason for bringing you here. It's a better place for you to live and it's not as far away from Tucumán as Barcelona," Kevin explained.

"Chile just seems more civilized to me," she emphasized. "Señora Moreno, at the pension, was kind enough to take me to the psychology department. I could get my Master's in clinical psychology in three or four semesters...that is, if I can register before the summer term in February."

"Would you really like to do that?" he asked.

"I think so, but it depends on whether you can operate as easily from Chile as from Montevideo."

"I'm not the one going to university," he remarked "Are you saying that you want us to live together permanently?"

"I want to be with you every day of my life. Your plan—which made sense to me—was for me to return to San Miguel to practice as a therapist. If I'm to be faithful to the vow I made to myself and to my Suegro, that's what I have to do." she concluded with less than a happy tone.

"Let's make that decision after our time here in Patagonia," he said to postpone a painful decision.

"What do you think will change in Patagonia?" she asked.

"Nothing...we'll just know more about each other," he answered evasively.

"You suggested from the start that we shouldn't pry into each other's earlier lives. I don't know why that was so important. It left me knowing almost nothing about you. Since you're the architect of my makeover, you know me down to my soul. That's a bit unfair, isn't it?" she challenged.

"When we started, I had no idea what would happen. I didn't want to burden you with my problems. How could I have known that we'd fall in love?"

"Do you really love me, Bartholomew?"

"I've never felt so strongly about anyone, it scares me. When you shot that man in Montevideo and said that you 'enjoyed shooting the bastard', knowing what it really meant to you to kill someone, the realization of it made me confront my true feelings."

"I've known from the moment you talked to me on the deck of the ferryboat that you see right through me. It's going to be the most difficult thing in my life to live away from you for years, perhaps even decades. You must promise me that we'll frequently have time together."

"I don't mean to be insensitive, but right now you have to start acting like a woman in distress desperately wanting to get off this plane."

* * *

When they landed in Puerto Montt, the hostess immediately came to help Alicia off the plane and to arrange for their baggage to be taken off. They went into the terminal ahead of everyone and Kevin stood watching to see if anyone disembarked with discernible anxiety. Kevin spotted his man, the instant he exited the plane. He was trying to push ahead of the other passengers and Kevin quickly took Alicia through the customs area into someone's office.

"Stay here while I take care of this situation. Keep your pistol handy, just in case."

Their pursuer entered the terminal, frantically looking around the baggage claim area. Kevin stayed back in the corridor to be out of the man's line of sight. Having searched in vain, the man returned to the departure area looking round nervously before spotting the phone booths outside the small terminal building on the arrival side. As he entered the nearest one, Kevin came from behind to stick his Beretta into the man's back, commanding him to back slowly out of the booth with his hands up.

"I warn you, make one quick move and you're dead. Now, with your hands held high, slowly turn to face me."

As he turned, Kevin lifted the man's revolver out of his shoulder holster.

"Now turn around and walk slowly back to the terminal," Kevin commanded, as he pulled off three shots into the air with the man's gun. Two armed guards rushed out at the sound of the shots.

"Officer, handcuff this man. Be careful, he's armed! I'll keep him covered."

The guard complied and the second guard stepped in to cover the man.

"Señor, come with us, please," the first guard asked Kevin.

He followed the guard to the guard station and handed him the man's revolver.

"Who is this man and who are you?" asked the guard.

"I believe he is an Argentinean agent. I'm Kevin Bartholomew, an American businessman."

"Do you have a license for the automatic you're holding?"

"Indeed, here it is."

"Why was the agent after you?"

"You'll have to ask him. I don't know. A week ago I was interrogated by an Argentinean official and accused of aiding a woman to escape from Argentina. They confused my fiancé for that woman."

"Where are you going?"

"Puerto Montt"

"Where is your fiancé?"

"She's in an office down the hall."

"Will you bring her here, please?"

"Not until you've searched, identified and taken this man away."

The guard examined the agent's papers, which probably were false, and asked him what he was doing there. He replied that he was on his way to Punta Arenas and got off the plane to make a phone call. When asked why he was carrying a concealed weapon he replied that he was a professional investigator. However, since he didn't have a license for the weapon, the guards held him for further questioning. With the man out of the way, Kevin went to get Alicia and briefly explained what had transpired.

"Officer, this is my fiancé, Señorita Alicia de la Rosa, from Barcelona."

"*Buenos dais Señorita*, sorry to inconvenience you, but something irregular happened that we have to check on. Where do you live?"

"I don't have a permanent residence at the moment. I was born in Barcelona, lived there until recently and have been traveling since. I like your country and may want to move here. In the meantime my contact in Latin America is the Spanish Embassy in Montevideo. The Ambassador is a family friend."

"What is the purpose of your visit here?"

"Mister Bartholomew and I are engaged to be married and we are thinking of perhaps buying property in Patagonia."

"Thank you. May I see your passport, please?" He looked at Alicia's Spanish passport and handed it back to her.

"And yours, Sir, may I see your passport too?" He examined Kevin's passport.

"I see no reason to inconvenience you further. You may leave, but we would appreciate a phone call from you tomorrow, please."

They were of two minds about staying where they had been pursued, or going on to another destination. They decided to explore Puerto Varas and Kevin rented a car.

On the way out of Puerto Montt they stopped at Kevin's fishing fleet client. They made small talk and socialized until he could comfortably ask to use their Telex. Kevin quickly typed a message to Raúl, advising him of what had happened.

The twelve-mile drive to Puerto Varas was picturesque. Kevin pointed out the German character of the houses and gardens.

"Much as in Rio Grande do Sul and Santa Catarina in Southern Brazil, the climate here attracted many German settlers. The families were mostly dairy farmers. You see that yellow church up there on the hill? It's an oak-wood copy of the Marienkirche in Germany's Black Forest. That tall volcano in the background is Osorno," Kevin pointed out.

"It's so beautiful here along the lake with the snow-covered volcanoes on the horizon. Can we stay here tonight?"

"I know the owners of a working ranch up here where no one could find us."

"Great, I love to ride. Bartholomew, why won't they leave us alone? I'm no menace to them here and they can't read my mind."

There was a tourist information booth from which they called the ranch. They asked Alicia about her riding experience since they catered to experienced equestrians. Her answers amazed Kevin.

"When you said you 'liked' riding I thought you may have been a part-time Gaucho in Tucumán, but dressage, jumping, hunting, point-to-point racing in Spain, puts you way above my league. I know how to ride a horse, but none of that fancy stuff!"

"They said they needed help to get the cattle out to pasture after the long winter. That sounds like your meat and potatoes to me...rough terrain, long endurance, slow, fast and dashing moments," she said to comfort him.

The ranch lay in a breathtaking valley and had a lake of its own. The buildings were classic Black Forest structures. The owner and his family ran the place with occasional seasonal hired help. They were invited to come to the corral to select horses and mules.

"You each need a sure-footed horse and a pack mule for the next few days. We'll be camping most of the time and your mule is to haul your provisions and some horse feed," Roberto, the owner, explained.

"Roberto, we've been on the move for a while and will need riding boots, hats, slickers and whatever else," Kevin explained.

"Come to the tack room. There's plenty to choose from. Don't be modest about the size of your horse, pick big ones. My son, Pedro, will help you.

Dinner was basic family fare, served in the traditional manner around a large table with everyone dishing up for themselves. In honor of their arrival they were served excellent red wine. The dinner conversation, with the whole family present, was at a surprisingly high intellectual level.

As with most landowners in South America, they showed disdain for socialism and were grateful to Pinochet for ridding the country of Allende's Communist rule. After only three years, they said, Chile was clean and orderly again.

They chatted for a while after dinner to the accompaniment of two of the children singing songs while playing a guitar and a mandolin. After a respectable time, Alicia and Kevin turned in.

They had a nice room in the bunkhouse with a queen-size bed and its own bathroom and shower.

"This place reminds me so much of the rides Fernando and I went on into the de Aconquija Mountains behind San Miguel. Many of the peaks stayed snow covered even in summer while the valleys stayed verdant and heavily forested. Those were our best years and it breaks my heart to think what may still be happening to him—I almost hope they've killed him. That's why I have to go on, for the sake of my children, if not for Argentina. Do you understand?" She asked.

Kevin responded.

"Yes, I do, but here we are talking about long-term stuff while we could face death tomorrow. How in hell did they know that we'd be on that flight to Punta Arenas...unless it somehow came from Raúl! He's the only person who knew where we were going."

"Jesus, I never thought of that!" Alicia exclaimed "You could be right. From now on, we have to keep him in the dark."

"He may not like that and could retaliate...have us arrested for carrying firearms with false registrations," Kevin pointed out.

"But we have legal papers."

"Legal to him, but to nobody else. He could say we stole his weapons. In any case, since your pistol killed an agent, he could play that card against us."

"I get it. So why don't we stay in touch, but give him misleading information and send back his weapons with proper thanks, explaining that we'll no longer need them where were going."

"Not bad for an amateur and a girl at that!"

"Don't put me down old man! I can beat you anytime."

"You mean like now," he said as he grabbed her and began tickling her.

They rolled onto the bed in laughter until she sat erect astride his waist with her hands pinning down is arms.

"I'll show you what Alicia's imagination can do to the mighty Bartholomew," she bragged as she lowered her face to kiss him so lightly on his lips, he could barely feel it. He struggled to respond and kiss her back, but she kept her distance each time he raised his head. She unbuckled his belt and pulled it out of his pant loops to tie his left wrist to the bedpost. Then she removed her own belt to tie his right wrist to the other post. Still sitting astride him she leaned forward to resume her tantalizing kisses while unbuttoning his shirt to begin exiting him with her tongue, moving down gradually toward his stomach. She lowered his waistband until his trousers held his legs captive and slowly lowered his zipper. Then she began teasing him until he was erect and took him between her lips titillating him with her tongue until he was rolling his hips in heightened anticipation. This was so different from what he imagined Angélica—with her Catholic convent education—would be capable of, that it enhanced his sensation. When she lowered her face to envelop him completely, only to withdraw repeatedly, he was ecstatic, squirming with delight. She had complete control and pleased him in a way more honest and forthright than he had ever experienced. She did it with such elegance and passion that he recognized it as Alicia's way of challenging the inhibitions instilled in Angélica.

*　*　*

They were up early to prepare for the day's cattle roundup and joined the family in the kitchen for breakfast.

"Roberto, you most likely hunt. What rifles do you use?"

"We have three. Pedro has a high-velocity Savage, which has terrific flat range. I'm still old fashioned and use an eight millimeter Mauser. My wife is fussy and uses the Drilling she inherited from her father."

"On the ride today, would Pedro mind if I took along his Savage?"

"He takes it with him whenever we go into the mountains. There are lots of cougars here...one never knows. You can carry mine on your horse if it would make you feel comfortable. Why? Is it important to you?"

"In the past weeks Alicia and I have been confronted several times by agents of the Argentinean regime who were under the impression that Alicia is on their most-wanted list. The more we explain that it can't be, since Alicia isn't from Argentina, the harder they've pressed us. Yesterday, here at the airport, one of their agents, armed with a revolver, confronted me. I had to restrain him and handed him over to the airport security police. The leadership in Buenos Aires is nervous and prone to go to extremes. On the remote chance that they follow us here, I'd like to be prepared."

"You're right about the Argentineans being trigger happy. As you know their border is very close to us and they seem to come across with impunity. If it makes you feel secure, I don't see why you shouldn't carry a rifle. However, it takes training to use the Savage properly. After breakfast we can shoot a few practice rounds."

Kevin was a light breakfast-eater and used the time to phone the security police at Puerto Montt. The man he had apprehended and disarmed was an Argentinean agent and had been turned over to the immigration police, who were taking him to Santiago for questioning.

Everyone was busy saddling their horses, packing up the mules and making sure they had everything they'd need. Roberto and Kevin walked far enough away not to cause a disturbance and went through the routine of familiarizing Kevin with the pump-action, Savage rifle.

"Let's see what you can do. You see that white mark on the rock up there on the ridge?"

"The rock with the bluish object on top of it?"

"Yes. See if you can hit the white mark."

Kevin aimed and shot the bluish object clean off the rock, instantly reloaded and hit the white mark.

"That's good marksmanship!"

"Thank you for the compliment."

Johan Wassenaar

They rode out for several miles and split into two groups when they encountered Roberto's cattle herd. Kevin was assigned to lead the pack mules ahead to the high campground with Analise, Roberto's wife, as his guide. Alicia, who stood out as an excellent rider, asked to be a herder with son, Pedro, and Roberto.

They rode in silence as Kevin adjusted to the art of handling a string of mules. It was difficult to gauge how the mules would react to their frequent encounters with hornets' nests, but he soon got the hang of it.

Analise dropped back to ride with him. "Where are you from, Kevin?"

"I grew up in California and have lived in South America for business reasons these past ten years."

"Where is your base?"

"I haven't really had a base since I've been single. I have an apartment in Montevideo and a number of special places I stay at in Santiago, Buenos Aires, Rio de Janeiro and São Paulo."

"What is your relationship with Alicia?"

"I met her in Montevideo where she was the guest of the Spanish Ambassador. His Embassy was suddenly full of people fleeing Argentina, so I offered her my apartment to stay in. I travel a lot, so it was convenient for me."

"She's pregnant, isn't she?"

"Yes, she's due in January."

"Your child?"

"No, her marriage ended sadly."

"Why do you love her so much?"

"Is it that obvious?"

"I can almost smell it."

"She's a remarkable woman with extraordinary talent."

"That's an evasive answer...I won't pry."

They were riding alongside a rapid-flowing river in the center of a wide valley between conifer-forested mountain slopes, above which loomed the steep rugged cliffs of the Andes. About an hour's ride up-river they turned off onto a trail along a tributary creek where the forest came closer to the much steeper stream. There were meadows every so often in gentle depressions where the forest had drowned and grassland had taken over. They began encountering small herds of Red Stag and Blackbuck.

"We now see Vicuñas again on the higher slopes—since they made it illegal to hunt them."

"How far up are we going today?" Kevin asked.

"In about five kilometers, the valley branches and there's a large bowl with good grazing. That's where Roberto thinks we'll let the cattle graze for the next month."

"How do you protect them from cougars, bear, and so on?"

"None of the predators up here are really large enough to go after cattle, but we ride up here almost every second day for one reason or another and have two trained Alsatians we leave to guard them," she explained.

The trail was getting progressively narrower and Kevin had to pay attention to his mules. He rode in silence and his mind wandered back to the puzzle of how the Argentineans knew where they were and why they kept after them. There could be no doubt that the information was coming from Raúl. He was the only person who they'd kept informed about their whereabouts. Since he had Telexed Raúl from Puerto Montt to tell him about the incident at the airport, Raúl would know that they were somewhere in the Lakes district. If he was spilling the beans, the Argentineans would be out looking for them. Bareloche—where they were holding Isabel Peron under house arrest—was just across the border, so there had to be a concentration of force there to guard her. He'd called the airport security man from the ranch and it certainly was possible for a smart sleuth to trace the call. He had to assume that the Argentineans would sneak across the border get at them. Perhaps the death of the chap in Montevideo was the reason they were so aggressive.

To be on the safe side, he decided to do a reconnaissance loop above the campsite.

They reached a stream crossing and let their mounts and mules have a drink. Kevin took advantage of the stop to question Analise, "How far are we from the border and if you wanted to sneak across where would you cross the Andes?"

"The border's about five kilometers to the east as the crow flies and there's a steep pass above and to the left of the campground. I'll show you on the map when we get to the campsite. It's the first negotiable pass south of the highway crossing at Bareloche. I've done the climb and it took me at least three hours. The summit's about three thousand meters above sea level. I wouldn't risk going up there right now with all the uncertainties in Argentina. I heard you talking to Roberto this morning and it makes no sense. You do business in Buenos Aires—even lived there—they must know you."

"Much of my business there is with their Defense Department. Some of their senior officers are my personal friends, and I'm an American citizen. Their quarrel is with Alicia. They believe she's someone else...someone who knows something they don't want the public to know," Kevin explained.

"Strange times we live in," she said sympathetically. "We've had our own problems here. The Communists came and confiscated everything in sight. They were going to turn our ranch into a commune. They weren't your everyday, home-grown socialists. They were Marxists fanatics imported from Cuba, Colombia and Peru. Many of them were just plain gangsters, in for the rape and pillage of it. In two short years Chile's farm production dropped so low, it couldn't feed its own citizens. There was no foreign exchange left, foreign banks wouldn't lend us money and the people began starving. The frightful thing was that our macho men just crawled under their beds, leaving it to the housewives to step out onto their balconies and porches each night to bang together pots and pans until our cities were just one great big pandemonium. There were too many of us to be scared and our men crawled out to begin doing something about it. That's when the tide turned. Now those pillagers have nothing to do but complain about their food service in jail."

Kevin hitched the mules and unloaded them. It was hard work, and he was soon dripping with perspiration. There was a creek flowing through the campsite. He stripped down and bathed, put on his boots and trousers and attended to the horses.

They organized the campsite, pitched the tents and were seated, having a beer, when the cattle drivers arrived.

He could see intense enjoyment in Alicia's expression. She had ridden in an environment she loved, on a responsive horse, with companions she could relate to.

She greeted him with enthusiasm, "Bartholomew! You missed a magic ride! I've never been on a horse as clever as this one. He can round up steers all on his own, I swear."

She slid down the side of her saddle as he tied up her horse and threw herself into his arms. "Look at all the work you and Analise have done already! Kevin, can't we just stay here forever?"

"I hope so, but first, I have one more job to do. If I'm not back here in three hours, have Roberto and Pedro come looking for me up near the pass. You mustn't come with them. You would make it too dangerous for them."

"You know something you're not telling me. Please don't go. I'd die if I'd lose you too."

"You must stay calm and keep what you know to yourself."

With that Kevin mounted and rode up the trail towards the pass.

* * *

He figured he still had two hours of full daylight and a half an hour of twilight to go and rode quickly. He was soon above the tree-line the trail became so rocky, his pace had to slow. As they approached the apex of the pass near the border, he veered off across an alpine meadow to a mangled clump of ancient cedar trees where he tied up his horse, removed the Savage from its saddlebag and climbed the escarpment to the left of the pass. He found a rock formation where he could hide that gave him visibility over both sides of the pass. He found it ironic that someone had found it necessary to plant an Argentinean banner at the summit. He sat down, scanning the opposite side of the pass with Roberto's binocular.

Roughly an hour into his vigil he spotted two mounted men ascending the pass from the Argentinean side. As they approached, he could see that they were in uniform with bandoleers over their shoulders. He held his breath as they approached the border and cocked his rifle in readiness. They stopped short of the border where one of the men took out a World War II vintage radio phone. The other soldier unwound and held a fairly long, wire antenna. Kevin concluded that this was their last chance to communicate before going out of range. After what seemed like a long wait, they stowed their radio equipment and led their horses onto Chilean soil. He watched them carefully walking their horses down the winding, rocky trail and climbed down to retrieve his horse.

He had no sooner walked his horse back to the trail when it whinnied and their horses answered. He quickly backed up his horse behind a large bolder and had turned half way around when two bullets struck the rock, narrowly missing him.

He crouched and looked through his binocular at the downhill trail where he saw the soldiers' horses standing with their reins dangling. There was a terraced rock ledge to the right of the horses where he spotted the top of one of the men's hat. With his rifle ready, he watched patiently until the man rose up to look upslope over the ledge. He took careful aim at his head and fired. The man disappeared instantly and Kevin continued his vigil. Their horses were getting restless and he took aim at the ground at their hooves and fired. The effect was electric as they reared and bounded off down the trail. He continued his vigil, looking with the binocular at the site where he'd shot at the first man and then scanned to the right of it up to where the pass saddle merged into the almost vertical cliff. He was about to scan back in the other direction when he spotted the other soldier climbing the face of the cliff. He was without his rifle, but had a revolver in a holster. Kevin wasn't sure what to do. Then he realized that if the man made it to the top into radio range he would call for reinforcements. He aimed with great care and shot him through the head. The man fell into the ravine below.

Now Kevin had to move quickly to retrieve his horse and ride down the hill to where the soldiers' horses had stood. He saw the man lying behind the ledge, still bleeding and finishing him off with a shot through the head.

With adrenaline pumping, he vigorously rode over the rough terrain to catch up with their horses and drive them ahead of him. They were still bridled, but had stepped on the reins and broken them. After a while, they just fell in behind him and followed him into the camp.

Roberto was standing waiting as he rode up. "I found these horses—by looks of their tack they belong to someone's cavalry."

"What did you do with the bodies, Kevin?"

"Left them where they were when they shot at me."

"Are they in Argentina?"

"No, they're in Chile."

"What do you propose we do?"

"Wait until your job up here is done, accidentally lose the Savage, and notify the Chilean police of the stray horses."

"What about the two dead men?"

"You'll probably never hear about them again. They trespassed into Chile past their own prominent border marker, so the Chilean Army won't care about them. The vultures will take care of the rest."

"What about their next of kin?"

"What about the next of kin of all the innocents they're making disappear?"

"Jesus, you play hardball!"

"They chose the weapons. Until they leave us alone, they'll pay dearly."

"What are you going to do now?"

"Just keep going until they tire of attacking us."

"What should we do?"

"Turn in the horses when we get home. Please try to understand, Roberto, those men were sent to assassinate us. They would have shown no mercy. They found out where we were from a double agent in Uruguay. If one of your Communist land-grabbers had tried to shoot Analise, you would have killed him. In my inner soul I am as much a Christian as you. What happened today will haunt me for the rest of my life. I have to believe that God will forgive me."

Dinner was somber. By the end of the evening, in large part due to Analise and Alicia's diplomacy, everyone accepted what had happened.

Inwardly, Kevin's mind was in turmoil. He finally escaped to walk on his own down to the river and perched on a large bolder to vent to his feelings.

Alicia found him there, sobbing uncontrollably.

"Why me God? I'm not a monster. Alicia, what I had to do was monstrous."

CHAPTER NINE

Kevin couldn't sleep and as soon as it was light enough, he saddled up and rode back up the trail. His objective was at least to recover the dog tags of the soldiers he had shot. In that way he could perhaps make it easier for their families to accept their loss. After he reached the alpine level he sharpened his vigilance considerably. Fortunately, his horse was incredibly sure-footed, allowing him to ride heads-up. He stopped just short of the top of each succeeding slope to scan the next slope with the binocular. He found no sign of human life until he reached the body of the first soldier.

With gloved hands, he carefully searched the soldier's pockets for identification papers, but found none. He reached up to his neck and found the thin chain with a crucifix broken and his dog tag missing.

Alarmed, he looked around even more thoroughly and carefully scanned each rock and bush he could see with the binocular. On high alert he tied his horse to the same clump of ancient trees he'd used before, and cautiously climbed down the ravine where the body of the other soldier had fallen. It was rough going with only a slight chance of finding the body. At each level of descent he stopped to use the binocular. He must have climbed a hundred feet before he came across a boot and in the gully below it he found the body, stripped bare of any identifications. Once again, the dog tag had been taken.

The climb up to his horse was agonizing. He was exhausted, deeply concerned and full of fear that he was being watched, even though he could find no sign of anyone in the area.

He rode down as far as the first wooded creek and stopped to let his horse drink. Suddenly, his horse neighed and a horse in their immediate vicinity answered. Kevin froze, drew his Beretta pistol and waited. He heard the sounds of someone cautiously navigating the moss-covered fallen tree trunks on the forest floor and crouched to be less visible. The sound continued, when, suddenly, Roberto appeared.

"Good God, Roberto, I could have shot you!"

"I didn't know it was you. Why are you here?"

"I hope you'll forgive a moment of sentimentality. I felt compelled to identify those soldiers to let their families know what happened to them."

"Were you successful?"

"No, someone got there before me and stripped them."

"I have their dog tags here with me. What do you want to tell their mothers?"

"Oh, why didn't you tell me, Roberto? We could have done this together."

"I wanted to, but you were so determined to leave them. Alicia literally begged me to do this. She convinced me that you wouldn't be able to live with yourself without closure. This way, she said, you'd be able to make peace with your creator. I can't tell you how happy I am to find you here. Now we can truly be friends."

* * *

Alicia could hardly control her relief when she saw what had happened. Over breakfast they decided to report the incident to the border security officials of the Chilean Army. Roberto and Kevin were exhausted and Pedro and Analise agreed to ride out to make the report. For reasons she wouldn't reveal, Alicia persuaded Analise to let her go too. On her way out, she collected Kevin's Beretta, her small pistol and a sum of money.

On the ride down to the ranch she had ample opportunity to talk to Analise. "How far away is the nearest sporting goods store?"

"There's one in Puerto Varas, but the really good one is in Puerto Montt. Why? What do you need?"

Johan Wassenaar

"I need to have them replace the barrel of a small hand pistol."

"Yours?"

"No, one I borrowed in Montevideo and want to return."

"You couldn't have worn it out <u>that</u> soon."

"No, I killed a secret agent with it before he could kill Kevin. I don't want it traced back to me."

"You two are amazing. Most people would have been dead by now. What Kevin did last night probably saved all our lives."

"My heart bleeds for Kevin. He didn't have to get into this mess."

"Can't you see he's in love with you?"

"As much as I love him, but there's little future in it for either of us."

"Why's that?"

"The Argentinean Junta, in their rush to clean out the insurgents, condemned many innocent people to torture and their graves. They murdered my husband for no reason at all and then tried to kill me. He was from a respected, upper-class family and was an architect with no political ambitions. I have to avenge his death before I can go on with life."

"Does Kevin feel the same way about the death of his partner?"

"I don't even know who she was. He won't talk about it."

"You'd be better off just going with Kevin. Leave the bitterness behind you."

"I would if I could."

They turned their horses loose in the pasture and prepared to leave in the ranch pickup truck for Puerto Montt. Alicia found a rut about the right width, placed the hand pistol across it and asked Pedro to drive over it. It bent the barrel, rendering the pistol useless.

Their first stop was at the Military Depot in Puerto Montt. Analise told the officer in charge about the shootout, describing the approximate location of the bodies and acknowledged that the horses were at their ranch.

"They came across the border and shot at one of our guests. He defended himself with one of our rifles."

"Was your guest from Argentina?"

"He's an American businessman from California."

"Where is he now?"

"On the ranch, up in the mountain pasture."

"We'll need to talk to him."

"You can do that when you come to fetch the horses."

"Do you have any idea of the identity of the Argentineans?"

"Yes, we took their papers for safe-keeping. You can have them when you come."

Their next stop was at the gunsmith. Alicia showed the owner her demolished pistol and asked if it could be repaired.

"Yes, Señora, but we'll have to replace the barrel."

"How long would that take?"

"That's a popular make. Let me see what spare parts we have."

He came back with a smile, "We still have one in stock. We need to repair a few other parts. Would tomorrow be soon enough?"

"Wonderful! I also need to buy a nine-millimeter automatic like this one," she said as she put the Beretta on the counter.

"The closest thing I have is a German Luger."

"Does it use the same bullets?"

"Yes, both use standard NATO ammunition. We also have special-purpose rounds."

"I'll buy the Luger now and come back for the small pistol tomorrow. Could you kindly package the Beretta up for shipment with the pistol?"

She settled her account and left the store with the Luger.

"For a farm girl from Tucumán, you certainly know your way around!" Analise observed.

"I grew up in Barcelona. I never liked San Miguel. It's a narrow-minded, mean town where everybody's business is everybody else's. I lived there for the sake of Fernando."

"How do you reconcile your devotion to Fernando with your obvious affection for Kevin?"

"It's a constant struggle. I can't tell you how desperate my feelings for him are, but the child within me is Fernando's."

"He can adopt it and you can go on together."

"That's one solution—there are several others—Kevin must decide."

"Aren't you being a bit subservient?"

"No, we've agreed that Argentina will never be a civilized country until it mourns the people it has devastated. Political persuasion doesn't matter; each successive government becomes indifferent to the aspirations of its people. They allow egocentric, corrupt, people to take power. The rich country over those mountains deserves something better than chaos and poverty."

"That's a huge ambition."

"Not really, there are so many scores of people being violated now in the crudest possible way that it's bound to come out. When that happens, Argentina will learn from its shame."

"Isn't that overly optimistic? Down here people have always been afraid to talk. They fear reprisal."

"Like you said, the women here turned the tide against Allende's abuses; the mothers and grandmothers of the victims will rise up in Argentina too. I, too, want Argentina to cry for me."

"How will you make that happen?"

"By prosecuting the perpetrators."

"Are the judges impartial enough to rule fairly?"

"Time will tell, but even if they're corrupt, the evidence will be there for all to see."

"If these people are made to 'disappear', where will the evidence come from?"

"That's the hard part. I hope the tales of the suffering of their kin will provide the bases for future investigations."

"That could never happen under a totalitarian, military regime."

"They don't last for ever. They become arrogant and shoot themselves in the foot."

"What will Kevin do all those years, or tens of years?"

"That's why <u>he</u> has to make the decision."

"You really don't hide from the naked truth. Maybe that's why I like you. If you don't mind me clucking like a hen, you ought to stop riding. Your pregnancy is too far along."

They rode back in silence to the ranch, each deep in their own thoughts.

* * *

The Chilean border patrol was already at the ranch when they arrived. Pedro had horses saddled for each of the two men and guided them to the high pasture.

They examined the horses and tack of the Argentineans and asked Kevin to take them to where the bodies were. They took two mules with them and climbed the pass up to where it all had happened. Kevin tied the mules to the ancient cedars and led them up to the border and to the knoll where he had sat when the soldiers arrived. He explained how he had followed them and where he and his horse were when fired upon.

The soldiers examined the first corpse, put it into a body bag, loaded it onto a mule and followed Kevin down the ravine to the second body. With some difficulty, the three of them working together, brought the second corpse up to the mules and they began the journey back to the pasture.

Roberto gave them the papers found on the two men, but kept the dog tags. They transferred the corpses to the horses and followed Roberto and Kevin back down to the ranch.

They asked Kevin to write a report, describing the incident and examined his passport. They asked him if there were substantive persons who knew him in Chile and what his business consisted of. Kevin gave them the names of his principal customers, including the top officer of ENAP, an Air Force General and a Naval Admiral.

"What are you going to do with the corpses and what will you tell the Argentinean Army?" Kevin asked.

"The Government will lodge an objection with the Argentinean Ambassador in Santiago about the border violation and return the bodies to him. We will keep the horses for our own use."

"What about the shooting incident?"

"That happened outside their jurisdiction. We don't need to report it to them. Their Ambassador will probably ask how the men died and our people will just say that they attacked someone and were shot."

"Will you identify me? I need to know, because I do business with their military too."

"If you request, we won't identify you. Come down to Puerto Montt and talk to our commanding officer about that."

Analise invited the troopers to stay for lunch. Alicia stayed out of the way in the bunkhouse with Kevin.

"Analise is onto who we are," Alicia began. "From the questions she asked, she must have talked to you. She has great empathy with you. She wanted to know what I planned to do with my life."

"What did you tell her?"

"That I didn't know, since you had to decide that."

"You don't mean that!"

"Yes, any decision about my life will affect you the most. I don't know enough about you to know what to expect. Will you adopt my children and take us to the States with you? Or, am I to go back to Tucumán to do battle on my own? If so, how do we continue our relationship? I think you know that I won't allow you to leave me."

"Until this morning, I had no answers. Our agenda was simply to stay alive. Now I have some reason to hope that we can live safely in Santiago while you finish your studies. We have to have someone bring your son to live with us and we'll need a nanny to look after him when you're not there. It would be nice if your mother-in-law could come and stay when your baby arrives. I'll still have to travel a lot on business."

"What makes you so sure we'll be safe there?"

"The questions the Chilean officer asked. He wanted to know who my closest contacts here were. They include the top men at the national oil company, Admiral Moreno, and the General of the Air Force. There's no love lost between Pinochet and the Junta in Argentina. They're concerned that the irresponsible acts of Videla will rub off on Chile's image."

"How do we avoid having the Argentineans know where I'm living?"

"You can't have any direct contact with San Miguel. Use Telex from here via my company in Los Angeles. Anyone coming here has

Johan Wassenaar

to go out through Montevideo and over-fly Argentina, directly to Santiago," Kevin explained.

"I broke the small pistol so the gunsmith had to repair it with a new barrel," she told him. "That way they can't trace the slugs in the man I shot in Montevideo, back to the gun. I bought you a new nine millimeter Luger and packaged the Beretta to be sent with the repaired pistol to Raúl. I'm planning to write a pleasant note of thanks to him, saying that we're safe and no longer need firearms. I thought of sending it through my father's company in Tucumàn to make Raúl believe that I'm living there again. It could help undermine his credibility with the Argentinean authorities."

"I like your style."

"I'll have to use my real name at the Catholic University to match my transfers and end up with the proper academic credit. I can't practice psychotherapy under a false name."

"What a shame you have to do that. I'll be lost without you. I can't live in Argentina. Not after the shoot-out on the pass."

"Let's make a pledge," she suggested, "that we'll spend at least two weeks each year, here with Roberto and Analise."

"I'll have to see you more often than that. A year's too long for me," he said as he took her into his arms.

The awareness of having to live apart made them seek relief in each other's devotion, Neither of them held back and they finally consummated their commitment to each other by gently making love with intense passion in spite of her advancing pregnancy. He used elegant ways to enter her from behind, to which she responded with extreme excitement. As they lay kissing and stroking each other in the aftermath, Alicia told him about Analise's advice. "She wants me to stop riding. Isn't that going a bit too far?"

"As long as 'riding' doesn't include making love to you, it won't matter too much. You can join the equestrian club in Santiago in the fall."

* * *

There was a knock at the door. It was Roberto announcing the departure of the troopers, suggesting that Kevin follow them to meet with their commanding officer while the iron was hot.

He kissed Alicia good-bye and left in the rental car. The Army base was on the outskirts of Puerto Montt and the troopers were anxious to be the ones to introduce him to their superior.

The Colonel received him graciously and began their conversation, showing great interest in Kevin's business dealings in Chile.

"I suppose in the overall scheme of things, Chile is small potatoes to a firm like yours?"

"On the contrary, industrial equipment demand isn't necessarily related to population size, Colonel. The work we hope to do with ENAP is substantial. We are designing a natural gas liquefaction plant for the gas field near the Straits of Magellan which requires under-ocean pipelines as well as liquid gas marine terminals."

"Why would Chile want to export its gas?"

"Chile needs the income from the gas to rebuild its economy and the gas is too far out of the way—in Tierra del Fuego—to distribute in Chile. To get the gas to Santiago, it would have to be transported by ship in liquid form, anyway."

"What else do you do here?"

"Mines such as El Teniente and Chuquicamata are important customers too, but our next largest customer after ENAP and LanChile are the Chilean Air Force and Navy."

The Colonel's ears perked up at the mention of the military services. "Who do you deal with?"

"Most of the time I work with Majors—Commandante as you call them—Colonels, Captains and Commanders too, but when things get important, my company deals with Admiral Moreno and the General de Aviación."

"Very impressive! What do you know about our Navy?"

"Not as much as I know about your Air Force, which is closer to the USAF. Your Navy is more British-oriented. However, when it comes to deck machinery, pipeline and cable laying machines, we do well with your Navy."

"As a matter of interest, how do you rank Chile against other South American countries?"

"That's not a fair question...I personally have a pro-Chilean bias."

"Why is that?"

"In my experience, the Chileans are honest, sober people who can be trusted. Chile is not as corrupt as Brazil or Argentina."

"What will happen in Argentina?"

"If I knew, I could retire for life. I heard one Argentinean economist say that Argentina only grows when the Argentineans sleep."

"Why are they after you?"

"I'm damned if I know, Colonel. I have as many top contacts there as here, but they came right into the Naval Captain's office and interrogated me about someone I didn't know. You already know what they tried to do to me here. It just doesn't make sense."

"I can't say that I understand it either, except that they aren't really after you. They're after your female companion."

"Why would they go after a Spanish woman from Barcelona?"

"They must think that she knows something damaging to them."

"Interesting! What would you do if she resided within your jurisdiction?"

"If she behaved herself, I'd protect her. If she turned out to be an extreme Marxist in sheep's clothing, I'd hand her to the Argentineans."

"What do you do with Argentinean intelligence agents snooping around in your territory?"

"Once we establish that they are agents, we put them in jail and if they are found to have conducted espionage, they stay in for a long time."

"Colonel, do you know your opposite number on the north side of Santiago—say in the Alameda area near the Catholic University's main campus?"

"Yes, I know the Colonel there. We've been to meetings together several times."

"Would you do me the favor of sending him a message to introduce me?"

"That would be a pleasure."

CHAPTER TEN

To diminish the chance of being followed, they returned by train to Santiago and Alicia stayed at the guest house she liked so much while Kevin visited his Brazilian customers in Rio de Janeiro, Brasilia, Belo Horizonte, and São Paulo.

Alicia found them an apartment to rent with respectable, yet modest furnishings, leased a small car and registered at the university. She attended several lectures and with the guidance of her professor was close to deciding an appropriate subject for her dissertation. They were leaning towards a study of the effects on the psyche of persecution victims.

Kevin returned and they spent the next weekend in Viña del Mar to relax and get to know more about each other. Kevin was persuaded to tell her all about his background, and particularly the grotesque loss of his heartthrob at the hands of the Junta. She began to understand why he shared her passion for exposing their misdeeds. The fact that his motivation to help her wasn't entirely selfless, made her slightly jealous, but also gave her comfort.

Their relationship was maturing into a deep sense of devotion. The decline in her sexual appetite, as she approached childbirth, seemed hardly to matter.

Her father brought her son, Carlos, when he came to visit. Since he and Kevin shared engineering interests, they were immediately comfortable with each other. Having a small child in the house to love and care for came naturally to Kevin, especially with the live-in help Alicia had engaged.

He was seriously concerned about doing his business rounds in Buenos Aires and called his client, the Navy Captain, from ENAP's offices and asked for assurances that would not be harassed again. After checking with the Admiral, the Captain called back to assure him that no one would bother him. He still felt insecure and called his other contact, the Air Force General.

"General, we need to talk about your A-4 modification program. The last time I visited Buenos Aires two MP's interrogated me in a Navy Captain's office with respect to a woman I didn't know. I don't think they believed me, because someone continued to follow me."

"Intelligence is not my responsibility, Kevin, but I'll tell the people here to treat you as they always have."

"That may not be enough, Sir. Could I ask you for a Telex to say that I'm visiting you on an important military matter and to accord me safe passage?"

"Of course, what's your Telex number?"

"My next stop is Santiago. It would be nice if you could send it to ENAP's Telex," and he gave him the number.

In spite of all his precautions, Kevin still viewed his visit with trepidation and discussed it with Alicia.

"My problem is that we don't know what they have on file about me. If the death of the two soldiers is linked to me, no amount of posturing will help. But, I have to go there to do my job. Going now has the advantage that their Navy and Air Force both urgently need my information and advice," Kevin explained.

"What was her name and what did she do?" Alicia asked.

"Who are you talking about?"

"The woman they murdered."

Kevin went pale and his hands began shaking. He breathed in deeply and exhaled several times and then, with a faraway look, slowly began.

"She came to Buenos Aires from Salvador as a tour guide. I met her in a hotel in Bareloche. I found myself drawn to her in a most unusual way. I couldn't take my eyes off her and when the dance band began playing, I asked her to dance with me. She was a superb dancer and her tour group began applauding loudly to spur us on. We obliged them by dancing until we were hot and in need of fresh air. She led me onto a terrace adjacent to the lake. I took off my blazer and she loosened the collar of her blouse. The moon was nearly full and its reflection danced on the ripples in the water. We were leaning on the railing looking into the water and I could see her face dancing with the moon. I still don't know what made us do it, but as I put my arm around her, she embraced me around my neck and began kissing me passionately. It felt as if we belonged together and before long we were making love in the shadow of a gazebo. Neither of us could get enough and when we finally stopped, she rushed away in apparent fear.

"It was bizarre. Neither of us even knew the other's name, yet the way in which we made love was as emotional and intimate as two people bound together. I don't mean to sound irresponsible or promiscuous...it was neither."

"How did you catch up with her?"

"Several months later on a flight from Miami to Los Angeles, I saw her boarding...she hadn't seen me. As luck would have it, the seat beside her was empty and after takeoff when the seatbelt sign was turned off, I quietly sat down beside her."

"How did she respond?"

"Calmly. Without even turning she said that she had wondered when this would happen and introduced herself as Carolina Pierpont. She stopped me from answering and said that she knew all about me, but had felt superstitious about contacting me. 'It had to happen in this unexpected way to be God's will,' she said. Not being quite that spiritual, I was a bit skeptical. But after ten days in her beach house in Malibu, I was a true believer."

"Did you marry her?"

"I proposed, but she didn't want to move that quickly. She said that we'd instinctively know when the time was right."

"What happened then?"

"My job took me back to South America and she stayed in Malibu."

"How did it end?"

"When she felt that our time had come, she flew down to Buenos Aires with a tour group. By then the Junta had taken over and when her flight arrived all hell broke loose. They later said that there was an undesirable person on board. All I know is that they forced her off the flight and when I found her body two days later in the harbor, she had been savagely abused. She was a Salvadoran citizen—next door to the Marxist rebellion in Nicaragua—which left me without leverage to get them to explain what had happened. I've never been so disgusted in my life.

When I saw you on the ferry a few weeks later, I saw in your eyes a companion in misery with the same streak of revenge as I felt. I had to help you at any cost, because I knew where you were trying to go."

"I can't believe that I was that transparent."

"You were. That's partly why I did the taxi routine...I hoped for signs in your reactions that you could make the change to Alicia. I knew if you were bound to Angélica, you'd be killed."

"Did you make love to me to escape the image of Carolina?"

"No, I only thought of you as Alicia. You blossomed in that role...you don't know how attractive you really are. It felt as if our relationship had depth from the moment we met."

"What I remember most was dancing in that hotel," Alicia responded.

"I had never experienced such exhilaration, even if I was scared out of my wits. Must you go back to Argentina this soon? I won't be able to sleep until you're out of there again. I don't trust any of those officer friends of yours. They are subservient to a wicked cabal that clings exclusively to the objective of eradicating any opposition to its ideology...at any price."

"My company relies on me to keep its commitments to all of its customers. At this moment, the Argentinean Air Force and Navy both rely heavily on us to modernize their aircraft and ships."

"Doesn't your company care about your safety?" She asked.

"They are very compassionate people, but outside of Argentina, almost nobody understands what's going on. It's simply too heinous for strangers to believe. Even foreigners living in Buenos Aires don't get it. How could they? No one talks about it and the news media say nothing.

"It will take years, or even decades, before the scope of these atrocities dares to come out. That's why it's so important for people like you to gather up the information to form the basis for court cases in which the facts will publicly be divulged."

* * *

Kevin had a call to make in Lima, Peru and arrived in Buenos Aires on Pan American. In his first meeting, the Naval Captain assured him that he had made it very clear to the intelligence people that he needed Kevin's technical input on a regular basis and to leave him alone.

He used the Telex from the Air Force General to enter their Headquarters and was not disturbed throughout his two days' of meetings there.

He felt far less secure in his travels to his civilian customers, including government-owned enterprises such as YPF, the natural gas company, and the national airline. He kept a sharp eye out for any suspicious followers and stayed in his hotel after dark.

On his last day, he called Colonel Raúl Vildoza in Uruguay from the airport.

"Hi Raúl, how are things going?"

"Well, I never...Kevin! Where have you been?"

"Back in the States...refresher courses on new products and that sort of thing. Have you heard anything from Alicia de la Rosa?"

"Yes, she reverted to her former self and is back safely in her hometown. She sent me the guns I lent you guys. She said she didn't need them any more."

"I'm glad to hear that. I really took a shine to her and will have to look her up. What's the latest you hear about the Junta's shenanigans?"

"People keep pouring through here. Many of them are Argentineans now. They give your friend at the Spanish Embassy fits. This soon after Franco's death, Spain needs a fresh bunch of radical imports like another hole in its head."

"How long will this last?"

"Oh, around Buenos Aires, they have a long way to go. It's still full of radicals...perhaps Córdoba too. I'd say it'll stay at this level for another year."

"Thanks for the update. They're calling my flight. Go well my friend."

Kevin stood back in the newsstand and carefully observed the departure gate for the next International flight. He didn't have long to wait. About ten minutes later, two security men came to the gate and began double-checking each of the passengers' passports and travel documents. Raúl was still on the job.

Kevin left the departure terminal in a catering truck to do his business with the airline cargo people and hitched a ride to the Montevideo ferry as before.

He called the Spanish Embassy from the docks in Montevideo and set up a meeting with the Ambassador and Carlos Vargas, of the "Spanish Club". On his way, he stopped at his apartment to pick up the few personal belongings he had left there. He notified the rental agent that he had vacated the premises and instructed him to end his month-to-month lease.

The Ambassador was as cordial and helpful as ever and quickly brought Kevin up to date with political developments between Spain and the Argentinean Junta.

"We're still adjusting to life in a democracy after all those years under Franco's autocracy. The last thing we want is a flood of rabid Communist revolutionaries fleeing Argentina to take us back to our civil war days. So, I have to discourage Argentineans from seeking exile in Spain, without sounding too harsh. There's an anti-Argentinean bias developing in Spain. Businesses won't employ them, landlords won't rent them living space and the government won't help them."

"Mr. Ambassador, I asked to see you to warn you about Raúl. He can't be trusted. I believe he's actively working for the Argentineans. He damned near got us killed and landed me in trouble with my good customers in the Argentinean Defense Force."

"You're right," the Ambassador agreed. "He does a good job for Uruguay, but he's greedy enough to sell his services to the Junta at times."

"The reason I asked Carlos to be here," Kevin said "is to make sure that nothing has been said to Raúl that would give away the 'Spanish Club'."

"No way," Vargas replied. "We haven't shared anything outside the group, and as the Ambassador originally suggested, we are divided up into separate airtight cells to prevent anyone from getting a complete picture. In fact, we've had two cells that leaked, but not through Raúl."

"Are you getting much useful information that we could use in legal actions?"

"Some...but not nearly enough. People are still too frightened to say much. They're still protecting the ones they left behind. It's hard to blame them. I've reported this to Alicia."

"How many of your members are already in Spain?"

"Only two. There isn't much yet that they can do for us there."

"To use an old metaphor, I hate to leave over a hot cup, but I've a flight to catch. Thank you again for your time and attention, Ambassador."

"How's Alicia?"

"As far as I know, she's doing well."

* * *

The flight to Santiago was uneventful and he saw no suspicious persons en route or onboard. As previously agreed, Alicia didn't meet him at the airport and he took a taxi downtown to the ENAP offices to check on his Telex messages.

There was one from the President of his company addressed to him personally. It began, *"Dear Kevin, it grieves me to inform you that Chuck Savage passed away night before last of a heart attack. That leaves the top spot in International Marketing open. I'm sure you realize this vacancy cannot be left unattended. You have done much for us in Latin America and I know that you would do no less on a global basis. The board and I would like you to accept this promotion. Kindly let me know how you wish to proceed.*

Sincerely,

Phil Gordon."

Shit, how would he explain this to Alicia? He had worked hard to qualify for the promotion, to the point that he felt under-utilized. It would open new vistas for him, but it would increase their distance apart. He would have to base out of Los Angeles and many of his travels would be to the other side of the world. The best solution would be to take her with him, but she was so comfortable with her program in Santiago and her mind was set on practicing in Tucumán—at least until she had obtained enough information. Also, she'd have to brush up on her English, which she should anyway.

Amongst the other messages was one from the Colonel in Puerto Montt giving him the name and phone number of his colleague in Santiago? He added that the Argentinean Army, cared so little about their two soldiers, that they denied them being missing. They just said that Argentinean soldiers wouldn't knowingly trespass into Chile.

He called the Colonel in Santiago and was invited to meet him at their officer's club for lunch.

"I hear that you do business with us and know Admiral Moreno?"

"Yes, on both counts."

"You must know then that the Admiral is probably the officer closest to General Pinochet."

"Yes, I've been with him in Los Angeles and in Washington to introduce him to certain key people in our government. He travels a lot to improve Chile's image in the United States."

"What can I do to help you?"

"I have a Spanish girlfriend who the Argentinean Intelligence people keep harassing for unknown reasons. They came across the border in Patagonia to assassinate us. In defense I shot both the assassins. We want to live in Santiago where my girlfriend is attending the Catholic University and since I travel a lot in my work, I have to find a way to protect her."

"I'm afraid we can't guard her."

"I don't expect you to. However, you keep a close eye on people around here and probably keep track of active Argentinean agents. I also anticipate that you keep a particularly close watch on university students. Could you possibly alert me if your men see any suspicious characters around the psychology department of my wife's...excuse me...girlfriend's university."

"What's her name?"

"Alicia de la Rosa."

"We know about her. The professor told us that the Argentineans abducted and probably murdered her husband."

"Will you help me protect her?"

"If you vouch that she has no political reasons for being here, I'll be glad to help you protect her."

"She's pregnant with her second child and has never had the opportunity or inclination to indulge in politics."

"OK, who should we contact if we see anything suspicious?"

"Please call me or her," Kevin answered and gave him two phone numbers.

Next Kevin called Alicia and asked her to meet him at the private hotel where they had first stayed.

He showed her the Telex from his boss and began translating it, but she waived him off. She didn't know whether to laugh or cry. She wanted the promotion for him, but it precipitated the decision they'd been dreading for so long. Suddenly, they were at the crossroads of their lives and their directions were diverging even wider than they'd imagined.

"Bartholomew, Los Angeles seems so distant to me. It might as well be on Mars. How can I go on without you? I don't think I could stand it! I loved Fernando, but you possess my soul! I'll *have* to go with you. I could finish my degree at our sister university, Loyola Marymount in Los Angeles and if we still feel as passionate about avenging the cruelty of the Junta's men, I could still set up shop in San Miguel for a year or two. By then you'll be able to visit me frequently."

"What about the baby? You're only eight weeks away.

"You can base out of here until next March." She suggested. "If you're so valuable, they'll agree to you establishing a satellite office in Santiago. Besides you'll have to marry me to be respectable in their eyes and to make them feel responsible for me."

"You have a practical mind..."

"Yes, but I still know nothing about your past. For all I know, you have an ex and kids back there in California.

"Come to think of it," she continued "we could use the American media and Hollywood to carry our message, instead of waiting for a broken legal system to mend itself. To force Argentina to look at itself in the mirror of reality, we have to get the rich countries to shame them into it. That highway starts in Hollywood, New York, London and Paris!"

"I guess I had my nose too close to the grindstone to think globally," Kevin responded. "I was still trying to stay alive, while you were on your way to the stars. Tonight I'll take you to a small restaurant on top of that hill to the north of here and I'll bare my soul to you. I will answer every question you have, no matter how painful. Then we'll work together on shaping an Alicia with longer wings—an Alicia I won't have to share with Angélica."

She smiled broadly and kissed him tenderly.

* * *

Kevin's choice of restaurant had a romantic ambience. They served excellent Chilean wine and suggested their special venison dish for the evening. Kevin wasted no time enumerating the key elements of his past. "I was born on a farm in Montana where we raised beef cattle and horses. The winters were long and extremely cold...."

"Never mind the details and academic stuff. Tell me about your real life. Who did you first love and what was she like? What sports did you play? What role did religion play in your life? Who were your best friends?"

I don't remember who my early girlfriends were. I always had many girlfriends. My first love affair was with an older woman. She was heartbroken when her husband ran off with her best friend and leaned on me for comfort. She definitely wasn't inhibited and taught me how to please a woman. She must have had a lot of sorrow to drown, but I enjoyed it."

"What happened to her?"

"She took to playing bridge and it consumed her."

"So when did you really fall in love?"

"I'd answer with certainty if I knew. There are those rare matches like the one I had with the Salvador woman. That, too may have been infatuation, rather than love. I had an affair that came close to marriage with an Anglo-Saxon woman. I've never really lived with one.

"But now it's your turn to tell me about your youth. All I know about you is post-Fernando."

"I'm not too proud of my teens. I had a motherless friend so we mothered each other through puberty. We set each other rather liberal examples and soon lost our virginity. By the standards of our peers, we were borderline promiscuous, sometimes even sharing partners. We didn't learn much in a sexual sense and would probably have done better had we taken up with older men. However, we learned a great deal from a psychological and philosophical point of view, allowing us to mature more quickly than our peers. I knew virtually nothing about love until I met Fernando. After that I only had eyes for him. He taught me how to love and I worshipped him."

"You're right. I believe that living one's life with a particular woman requires it to be a soul partnership; something you have to be willing to kill for." Kevin agreed.

"Is that what you feel for me?"

"I can say 'yes' with humility. The insight to make it work came from you."

"I could argue that point. Who came up to me and transformed me into Alicia? The defining moment for me was that night by the river after you'd killed the two soldiers. That's when I knew I would never stop loving you.

"Have you any offspring?"

"Not that I'm aware of. The only pregnancy I caused ended in miscarriage. She had an ovarian cyst."

"If you love me that much, why am I the one proposing to you? Perhaps you didn't notice when I asked you to marry me."

"Alicia! I didn't mean to snub you. We were talking about living arrangements and things. It sounded like part of a scheme to fit into my changed circumstances. Oh, I *am* sorry. The answer is <u>yes</u>, I'd <u>love</u> you to be my wife!"

"Technically I'm still married to Fernando. We don't know if he survived. But, in your corporate world, I have to qualify as your dependent, whatever it takes."

She went home with fewer questions in her mind, even though she knew that there remained skeletons in his closet much as she still had some that would surface in time.

While they didn't talk about it, he obviously had faith in a higher being, which was of vital importance to her. Angélica had faded into her past as her interests became focused on her new persona—one which would now have to speak English.

* * *

Over breakfast she began her program of involvement in their mutual planning and through skillful questioning quickly gained a full overview of his career prospects.

"Which of your international territories require the most management attention?"

"Europe, by far."

"Wouldn't it make sense if you ran international marketing out of Europe?"

"That idea's been kicked around. We came close to setting up a Swiss subsidiary."

"Wouldn't it make sense to revisit the idea? It could save a huge amount of wear and tear on you—not having to fly all that distance from the West Coast to see most of your customers?"

"We should do a little study and I'll propose it to Phil Gordon."

"He's waiting to hear from you," Alicia reminded "so what are you going to say?"

"First I'll accept the promotion and thank him. Then I'll tell him my plan to base out of here until March, while I find and train a replacement for myself and let my bride settle down with her new baby. Then I'll raise the question of the best place from which to manage our international marketing and tell him that I'm studying the alternatives. He will probably want me to attend their annual management council meeting next month."

"So how do we handle this 'bride' notion of yours?"

"We'll get married where they don't ask too many questions...Reno, Nevada, for instance."

"Is that 'anything to keep Alicia happy'?"

"On the contrary, it's my way of asking you to marry me."

"This time I honestly think you mean it and I gladly accept, Bartholomew."

CHAPTER ELEVEN

In spite of their new-found happiness, Alicia was nervous about the future. She was thrilled about her current academic situation. Culturally her environment was so close to her Spanish roots—her part of Santiago might just as well have been a suburb of Barcelona. All seemed quiet and peaceful, but they both had to remain vigilant, always looking out for suspicious people around them.

That abruptly changed when Kevin received warning from his friendly Colonel that a student, who they suspected worked for Argentinean Intelligence, had been shadowing Alicia on campus. They described him as 5 foot 10 inches tall, with a pallid completion, usually covered with the stubbles of a 5 o'clock shadow, wearing small oval wire-rim spectacles and walking with a limp in his left leg.

This news disturbed Alicia intensely and she found it very difficult to show up for classes. Kevin went to the university gym to monitor several wrestling and martial arts classes. His attention was drawn to an athletic Chilean in his early twenties with superb balance, agility and muscle-tone. Kevin engaged him in conversation.

"I'm impressed with your style and fitness. What do you aspire to?"

"I'm trying to win a martial arts grant to help pay my tuition fees."

"What are you studying?"

"Microbiology."

"How much do you need?"

"The equivalent of about a thousand American dollars.

"Would you be open to serving as an invisible guard of one of your fellow-students?"

"Sure, what do I need to do and what will you pay me?"

"There's a man following my wife. She majors in psychology. I need to discourage him."

"What's his intention with her?"

"I think he's an Argentinean agent who, at least wants to scare her, or in the extreme, wants to hurt, abduct or even kill her."

"What do you want <u>me</u> to do?"

"I want you to watch him carefully until you get the hang of how he operates. If he seems threatening, I want you to disable him and call me at any time on these numbers."

Kevin gave him his office and home numbers.

"How do you want me to disable him?"

"Do something very painful—like dislocating a joint—to disable him until I can talk to him."

"When do you want me to do this?"

"Start observing him tomorrow."

"What will you pay me?"

"If you scare him into cooperating without violence, I'll pay you two hundred. If you have to disable him your fee will be four hundred."

"OK, what does he look like and where do I find him?"

Kevin gave him the description of the man and showed him a photograph of Alicia.

"This is the woman he's stalking. I'll introduce you to her this evening. She'll explain where she moves around on campus. Here's a hundred dollars to get you started. Come with me, I'll bring you back here or take you wherever you need to go."

He accepted the cash and climbed into the car with Kevin. The handsome youth had refined manners and good diction. Alicia was surprised when Kevin introduced him to her, explaining that he would be acting as her body guard. After some conversation they both seemed comfortable and Kevin drove him home.

"Call me immediately after you've got control of the guy. We may need your help again, so let's try to stay in touch. What should I call you?"

"Enrique and here's my phone number."

"Muchas gracias."

"Bueno, Señor."

Kevin kept his fingers crossed when Alicia went to class the next day. Late in the afternoon Enrique called.

"The guy isn't even registered here as a student. All he seems to do is keep an eye on your wife. He's stupid...sits in full view outside her lecture hall when she's in class."

"Perhaps he wants her to notice him following her to scare her before he makes contact with her," Kevin surmised. "Let's put him to the test? Go up to him while he's sitting there. Start a conversation. Be nice and friendly. Ask him what he's studying, how long he's been on campus...that sort of thing. If he responds in a friendly way, offer to buy him a cup of coffee. It would be best to do so near the end of my wife's class to see how strongly he resists leaving his post. If he declines, withdraw to where he can't see you. When my wife leaves the building, if he follows her, come up from behind and greet him loudly like you would a long-lost friend. Stay glued to him and converse in a loud enough voice for my wife to hear you."

"I get the drift, you want me to be such a nuisance that he has to do something to get away from me. I'll stick with him until he gets angry and does something physical. I'll pretend to be afraid...inviting him to rough me up. Then I'll clobber him. Am I on the right track?"

"I like your style. If you can, tell my wife what's coming down. That way she can call me the moment he hits the ground."

Johan Wassenaar

Two class periods later, Alicia called and Kevin raced to the campus. The man was down with a dislocated knee in an empty lab corridor where Enrique had dragged him.

Kevin addressed him.

"If you think you're in pain now, just wait and see what happens if you don't cooperate."

"Please, sir, I meant no harm. What do you want?"

"Who sent you here and why are you following my wife?"

"They sent me here from Buenos Aires to bring her back with me."

"Who are *they*?"

"The military police."

"You have two choices. You can cooperate and I'll get your knee taken care of, or you can resist and you may never see Argentina again. Which will it be?"

"I'll cooperate."

"OK, I work for the American government and know in detail what the Junta in Buenos Aires is doing to its citizens. If they want the continued support of my government, they have to stop harassing people like my wife and me. I'll take you to the hospital and when you can walk again, I'll put you on a flight to Buenos Aires. When you arrive there go directly to General Videla. You will have to insist on seeing him. Say that you have a secret message from the United States government. Tell him that if we have any more trouble with his agents here, we will kill them. Make no mistake. OK?"

"Yes, sir, I understand."

"Enrique, help me get this man to where he can be taken care of?"

"No need for that, you and I can fix it. It will hurt, but only for a short while. Turn him on his back and sit on his chest to hold him down."

Kevin complied and with one strong pull and a twist of his leg, Enrique popped the man's knee back into its socket. He yelled with pain and then held his knee tightly with his hands. They stood him up on his good leg and, with one of them on each side, slowly walked him to Kevin's car.

"Thank you Enrique. You do good work. Alicia and I would like to befriend you. Come by our apartment this evening to collect your reward."

By the time Kevin had secured a seat for him on a Buenos Aires flight, the man was able to walk with the aid of a cane. Kevin used his influence to escort him onto the flight and stood by to be sure that he didn't get off. He then went to see his friendly Colonel to report.

"Colonel, anything you can do to convey the notion to the Argentineans that I may be a CIA agent, would be of great value to me and my wife."

"Are you one?"

"Colonel, a CIA agent never admits to being one."

"I read you load and clear. I'll do my best to spread the word."

* * *

In Santiago, Alicia felt closer to Fernando's parents. She owed them a great deal and knew that taking her children far away would hurt them.

The thought of returning to San Miguel to live, even temporarily, depressed her. She couldn't see herself returning to the confines of Angélica's existence. Her conversion to a pro-active Alicia was becoming ingrained in her.

She still had some distance to go to fit into Kevin's global perspectives, which frightened her. He seemed comfortable in any culture and able to adapt effortlessly to major changes. His friends and allegiances were universal. If he had to, she thought, he could even adjust to living in Tucumán. To stay with him, she'd have to become more adaptable. Moving to Geneva didn't seem as daunting as going to America. Inwardly she knew that it was just nervousness and that she would learn to cope. Nevertheless, it bothered her.

* * *

The atrocious stories about the mistreatment of expatriate Spaniards she began receiving by Telex from Carlos Vargas upset her. Apart from their gratuitous brutality, their methods were so utterly vulgar that it turned her stomach. She hadn't yet shared any of this with Kevin, who was extremely busy stepping in to take the reins in his new job.

One of the cases she thought would particularly interest him was about a Spanish journalist found investigating corruption and human rights violations in Buenos Aires. He was violently harassed to silence him. Fortunately his findings got out of the country before they handcuffed, beat, shot him to death and burned his body to hide his identity.

What scared her most was the prospect of having to listen to graphic descriptions by victims who'd been detained and tortured endlessly, as she imagined Fernando had had to endure. Merely imagining it brought back her anger and solidified her resolve to expose the bastards even if it took the rest of her life to do so.

* * *

The nanny she'd found, handled the household and her little boy, Carlos, beautifully. She came from a large family where she'd had to take care of her baby siblings and knew the routine. She was anxious to learn and Alicia provided her with books to read and helped her study. Her favorite subject was art and she began attending drawing and painting classes. The walls of the rented premises were soon blossoming with examples of her art.

Alicia was getting uncomfortably large as Christmas and the warmer summer weather approached, and she began making plans to take care of her baby. She'd have to miss some time at university and would have liked her mother-in-law to be present to help her for a few weeks. Not that she needed the assistance as much as she felt that her mother-in-law emotionally needed involvement with the offspring of her missing son. This would create a problem, as Mrs. Diaz, a conservative Catholic of the old school, would disapprove of her intimacy with another man.

* * *

Kevin had taken temporary office space next door to ENAP and installed a Telex machine. He had agreed with his boss on the hiring of his replacement for Latin America. His leading candidate was a Chilean engineer who had also graduated from UCLA and knew the company's business areas quite well.

His main concern was where it would be best to establish his base. Gordon favored Los Angeles, but had no objection to a European base, agreeing that it would be to the company's advantage. Kevin could be persuaded either way, which essentially left the decision to Alicia.

To acquaint himself with his newly-gained operations in England, Germany and France as well as Iran, India and Japan, he'd soon have to circumnavigate the globe. He wanted to get it done before Christmas to be back in time for the birth of Alicia's baby.

The reports he was getting from his sales reps in Argentina were disconcerting. The Generals had pulled all the stops in their hunt for "subversives" and a competition between the four "Zone Commanders" seemed to exist on a basis of who could terrorize their populations most.

The Buenos Aires zone, was having unanticipated trouble getting rid of the Montoneros rebels. There were many more of them than they had anticipated. So they put local and federal police, border guards and regional prison authorities all under the supervision of the

Zone Commander, who was a hard-line War Lord called, Suarez Mason. Mason was also given supernumery powers in counterinsurgency matters over the Buenos Aires provincial civilian authorities, which effectively gave him total control over the majority of Argentina's population.

After an extremely harsh campaign, Mason was close to completing the annihilation of insurgents and was changing tactics to unmask any surviving Marxist influences in the labor unions, educational institutions and neighborhoods—effectively a replay of the Spanish Inquisition.

* * *

Neither Kevin nor Alicia felt completely secure after the episode on campus and there was much for them to talk about. To avoid being interrupted he invited her to meet him for lunch at the Prince of Wales Country Club.

The grounds of the club were ever-so-British and they were seated on the terrace of the club house, watching a cricket match in the background. Kevin liked the club. It felt like an oasis of tranquility in the middle of the hustle and bustle of the city.

Alicia greeted him.

"So what's with the formality? I guess I'd better sharpen my skates for a tournament of the minds."

"No, relax. I just felt like having you all to myself for a change."

"Where do we start?"

"Phil Gordon will go either way, Los Angeles or Europe. I don't really care, each has advantages and disadvantages. Take your pick."

"That's like hitting me over the head with a cricket bat. I'll take LA."

"OK, when do we move?"

"I don't want to move until the end of a semester. The next semester here starts in early March. I've been doing some research. At Loyola Marymount in Los Angeles the semester starts a bit earlier. I have a baby to deliver in January and I'd prefer not to travel for, say, four to six weeks. If I qualify for their upper school, it could work. Do I have to decide this now?"

"No, just think seriously about it. Remember, you can't go back to Argentina for at least another year, say late seventy-eight. Also, you shouldn't go until you have the credentials to practice. I wish you'd never have to go, but I suppose that would be selfish of me. I couldn't join you there. The children's grandmother wouldn't accept me."

"How do you know that?"

"She's a strict Catholic and obviously, hoping her son is still alive. I want to be here when Maria is born, but she has more reason to be here than I have. Could you stand me not being here?"

"God, you're generous! I don't deserve you."

"Earn it then, get ready to move by mid February."

"What else is on the agenda? I've something to tell you."

"Before you tell, I want you to know that things are really bad in Buenos Aires," and he told her what he'd heard.

"So what's new?" She said.

"We'll soon hear about new atrocities that affect us deeply. We'll both want to strike out on the warpath and I don't want to risk losing you," Kevin said almost pleading.

"I've been thinking about that too. Carlos Vargas sent me several accounts of torture and murder of Spaniards. They're so gross it angers me beyond reason. They don't care what they do anymore."

"How do we cope so we can stay together?" He asked.

"We have time," she reassured him. "We have two years before I'll be able to set up shop in San Miguel. After six months, I'll bring in a partner so I'll be able to get away to meet you for R and R to help us remain sane. Once we have enough evidence, I'll quit and we'll bide our time together until the Junta goes down and the courts open up for us to help prosecute them. I have to have resolution."

"I'm happy you've accepted living abroad with me and that you plan to limit your time in San Miguel. The rest I can handle, although I think you're optimistic about the resolution part. They'll fight to the grave to keep their misdeeds out of the public eye."

"What do you think will cause the Junta to break up?"

"Rivalry between factions. Videla's crowd is too 'liberal' for the Mason-Massera faction and they'll sabotage Videla. To show their power, they'll over-play their hands and do crazy things that will bring the whole Junta down. In any stable autocracy, the strong man at the center is king, like Stalin, Hitler, Mussolini, Franco, Castro...Once the strong man falters, the whole regime tumbles."

"How long will it last?"

"That's impossible to say...perhaps ten years."

"I wish that I wasn't so pregnant."

"Is it very uncomfortable?"

"That too, but I was thinking how nice it would be to go home and make love."

"Why the sudden affection? There's something bothering you!"

"Yes, Vargas sent me a graphic description of an interrogation and torture which almost made me vomit. I couldn't believe my eyes. It left me speechless and drained me of thought as I read his account of a Spaniard who, by accident, had escaped death in a detention center near Buenos Aires. I kept thinking that's what Fernando must have gone through. It made me realize that I'd have lost my mind if you'd not come along. My family won't understand, but I hope my children will know why I can't stop loving you," she said as she reached for his hand.

"What did Carlos say?"

"Sit here next to me and hold me. It was so awful! The Spaniard was taken by armed men from his place of work. They came without warning; destroyed everything in their way to spread fear and terror. They beat him up and threatened every one with death if they told anyone what they'd seen. They were plainclothesmen without any warrant to authorize his arrest. They left with him lying gagged, hooded and bound in the trunk of their car and took him to a secret detention center.

"There, they physically and mentally isolated him. As an unregistered detainee, he had no official status. In the eyes of the world, he no longer existed.

"The center was designed as a torture chamber. The intelligence men wanted to know the names and addresses of anyone he thought was involved in anti-regime activities. The torture room was euphemistically referred to as the 'intensive therapy' room. It was run by a team of torturers. There was an iron bed, a table, a barrel of water, and a battery-operated field telephone, which they used to generate electric current by turning a handle. There were two sets of wires—one for a hundred-and-twenty-five volts to cause involuntary muscle movements and pain all over the body; the other for two-hundred-and-twenty volts to cause hideously painful contractions that induced vomiting and left deep ulcerations in his flesh.

"He was held naked and blindfolded, tied down to the bed with his arms and legs spread open. He was tortured and beaten by invisible hands, and questioned by anonymous voices that shouted insults and threats at him. There was a 'doctor' present, ostensibly to prevent his untimely death.

"His interrogation started with a 'softening up' session of beating to persuade him to cooperate. Since he had no information to give them, they gave him the 'grill' during which they applied electric shocks to his temples, ears, gums, teeth, breasts and genitals. They finally gave him a 'wet submarine' by immersing his head in the barrel of water until he was about to drown.

"His torture wasn't confined to the interrogation room. He remained bound and hooded, or 'walled up' as they called it, from the moment he was abducted. His handcuffs were permanently left on and the shackles on his legs were removed only when he was taken from his cell. His hood was lifted only at mealtimes. He was not allowed to see the faces of his torturers, nor could he see the rubber truncheon or the electric prod approaching his body.

"They kept him waiting for long periods, hooded and chained and made him sit or lie down on the ground of his cell in the same position from the time he woke up until he went to sleep at night. He wasn't allowed to move, not even turn his head, unless they told him to do so. He was not permitted to talk to anyone.

"They denied him basic needs, such as eating and sleeping. His meal, when he got one, consisted of a boiled drink, some boiled corn-flour, soup without meat or vegetables and perhaps a piece of dry bread. He was fed once every few days. Sleeping hours were irregular. They woke him in the middle of the night and interrogated and tortured him, then returned him to his cell and mattress which they had flooded with water.

"There wasn't such a thing as hygiene in the place. His clothes and mattress were filthy with blood, vomit, sweat and urine. He was seldom permitted to shower; instead, they hosed him down as one in a bundle of prisoners. They marched him to the toilet twice a day as part of a 'train' of men and women in hoods, each one holding the person in front by the waist or the shoulders to avoid stumbling on the way. If he needed to relieve himself between 'train' times, he just had to go where he stood.

"He said that detainees without further use were marked to be 'transferred' and taken away in groups, sometimes sedated, to unknown destinations. All he knew was that the trucks left the detention center loaded with people and returned empty.

"He has no reason to doubt that his release was due to a clerical error."

Alicia was weeping softly as she wound up explaining, "I was surprised at my emotions. It sounds bizarre, but I know of worse treatments. It's just that the setting the man described fit Fernando's abduction so neatly, it made me imagine him having to survive such debauchery month after month or that he may even still be enduring it. I can only thank God that you're here to give me hope and safe harbor."

* * *

The next few weeks rushed by as Alicia worked hard to bring her studies to the level needed to transfer to the graduate school of the psychology division at Loyola Marymount. Kevin was away on his whirlwind tour of all the international territories now brought under his stewardship, leaving it to her to make their Christmas arrangements.

She felt very pregnant and began making arrangements for her mother-in-law to visit her from early January until mid-February. She had to enlist the help of her father to organize her mother-in-law's trip overland to Montevideo for a flight directly to Santiago.

Alicia had made many friends during her stay and they arranged what her American friends called, a "baby shower" at the private inn they liked so much. The thought of soon leaving her friends again, filled her with wistfulness.

She wrote Roberto and Analise explaining their situation and expressed the hope that they'd be back to see them again the following spring.

As busy as she was, she couldn't keep her mind off "Bartholomew" with whom she now shared her entire being. After being Angélica, who was almost prosaic in demeanor, it was exhilarating to be the more intense Alicia.

To add to her longing, Kevin's tour was prolonged by difficulties at the company, requiring him to double back through Los Angeles.

By the time he arrived, overjoyed to be home, he only had ten days left before Christmas to service his Latin American customers. A week later, he planned to introduce his successor to the company's most important customers in Chile, Brazil and Argentina. He had serious misgivings about returning to Buenos Aires.

CHAPTER TWELVE

Elvira Díaz, Angélica's mother-in-law, arrived in Santiago less than a week before the birth of her granddaughter, Maria. She was delighted to see her grandson, Carlos, again, after living with her during Angélica's absence.

The relationship between the two women had been cordial, but not intimate. Spain, during the "hippie" era wasn't far behind Britain or America and the tone of their youth sounded discordant to the matriarchal ears of upper-class Tucumánian grandmothers, who still expected to be addressed formally as "usted" rather than the informal "voz".

Elvira was a kind and generous person, but had a strong personality and a dominant role in her household. Her children treated her with unusual respect and gave in to her wishes whenever possible. At the outset, she was unenthusiastic about Fernando's romantic relationship with Angélica. She favored the daughter of a local elite family. She had misgivings about Angélica's motherless status, having arrived from Spain with her commercial-class father. Her own family members were professionals and landowners with agricultural interests.

Sharp class distinctions existed in rural San Miguel where a relatively small cadre of wealthy people traditionally ruled the vast, poor labor-class.

Over time, she warmed to Angélica when she showed dedication to academic achievement. However, it wasn't until the tragedy of Fernando's abduction struck, that they drew closer to becoming friends and confidantes.

In contrast, her husband, Dr. Diaz, had immediately taken to Angélica and they had become soul mates. While old fashioned, he was a man of great depth and purpose and had the unusual distinction of having a law degree from Harvard, when it was still a rare credential in Argentina.

Both her in-laws had experienced peril and angst after the disappearance of Fernando, when the Junta's men kept searching for Angélica and watching them with suspicion. Their mild political allegiance had been to the Catholic branch of the Perónist movement, which didn't sit well with the military commander of the province.

For significant periods they hadn't know where Angélica was and even after they heard that she was safely in Chile and wanted to be reunited with her little boy, Carlos, they still worried about her.

Understandably, Elvira's meeting with Alicia in Santiago was rather emotional and her joy at seeing Carlos was particularly palpable.

In spite of her private nature, their dialog was spirited and extensive—she had so much to ask and tell. Once things settled down, she began to question how Alicia had managed to escape without physical harm and where the resources had come from.

Alicia tried to explain "There was a man who saw me being followed onto the Montevideo ferry in Buenos Aires and rescued me. The man who followed me worked for that awful 'Colonel' who extorted money from us in Buenos Aires. He wanted to turn me in to claim the reward that was posted for my arrest. My rescuer really knew Montevideo where he had an apartment and introduced me to the Spanish Ambassador to Uruguay. Without his help, I could not have survived."

"How did you to repay him?"

"He asked for nothing. He knew how I felt and wanted to help me avenge the terrible things they did to Fernando."

"Why did he bring you here?"

"We were in peril in Montevideo where we discovered that the Uruguayan secret service was working closely with Argentina. He had business connections here where he thought we'd be safe."

"Who is this saint of a man and where is he from?"

"He's an American businessman from Los Angeles and he has as many faults as any of us."

"This man, does he love you?"

"He must love me—all the things he did to let me survive without losing my mind."

"Do you love him"?

"He did things that people won't understand. They made me want to love him forever."

"Be honest, do you feel deeply for him?"

"I do, Suegra."

"What does that do to your devotion to Fernando?"

"I mourn his disappearance every day and the more I learn about the disgusting things these men are doing to other innocent people, the stronger my resolve is to avenge his treatment at their hands."

"You are a changed woman, Angélica. You are much stronger than I ever thought you'd be. I hope you will use your power wisely. Where is your mentor? I want to meet him."

"He's away on business. We didn't think you'd want to meet him."

"The man who saved my grandson's mother—how can I not want to meet him? If he loves you, he would want to be with you when your baby's born."

"He wanted to be here. He didn't want to offend you."

"He must think I'm an ogre without compassion. I want you to ask him to change his plans. Tell him I won't respect him if he doesn't come home to be with us when your child is born. What is his name? I want to meet him."

"His name is Kevin Bartholomew, he speaks Spanish fluently and I will call him so you can tell him yourself how you feel."

"What does he call you?"

"He calls me Alicia...Alicia de la Rosa."

"Where did he dream up that name?"

"I chose it."

"Here in Santiago, who knows you as Angélica?

"Nobody"

"What's the reason for that?"

"The Junta's agents are still searching for Angélica—we hoped they'll think I'm a different person."

"Why are they still looking for Angélica?"

"Because she shot and killed one of their agents in Montevideo."

"Why did she kill him?"

"He had a revolver in Kevin's back and she knew that they'd murder Kevin."

"Does her conscience bother her?"

"More than you can understand—she had to do it."

"She must really love Kevin."

"At that moment, <u>he</u> became the one who loved <u>her</u>. Before that he just tried to help her as a comrade."

"When did Alicia find out that she loved him?"

"The Junta's agents followed them into Chile over the mountains near Bareloche. He quietly rode out of camp up the narrow pass to the border and waited for the Junta's men to come. They shot at him and he killed them both. Alicia found him by the river praying for God to forgive him. He was a strong man, but she found him weeping. That's when Alicia knew that she could never stop loving him. Madre, forgive me if it hurts you to hear this?"

"That's the first time you've called me 'Madre.' It makes me feel so proud. I've always envied your close relationship with my husband. Perhaps now it's my turn to have that satisfaction," Elvira said as she embraced Alicia.

* * *

Kevin had done the Brazilian circuit with his replacement, Eduardo, and their next stop was to be Buenos Aires. Again, he left no stone unturned to ensure that during the visit he and his colleague would be safe. He spoke to the Captain about the destroyer upgrade program and the Air Force General about A-4 modernization details, informing them of his replacement and his promotion. They were both cordial and assured him that there would be no interference during his visit.

He made a practice of never calling Santiago from Argentina and called home before his flight out of São Paulo. Alicia answered and asked him to hold on for a second, as if she needed to turn down the heat under a cooking pot. It came as a complete surprise to Kevin when Elvira's voice came on the line.

"Señor Bartholomew, I'm so sorry that you weren't here for me to meet you. Could you change your travel plans and come home, please?"

"Señora, Diaz, is it urgent? Is Angélica all right?"

"Alicia is fine, but her baby's due any day now. It could be as soon as tomorrow. I think you should drop everything and come home."

"What does she think about that?"

"We had a long conversation and more than anything, I want to meet you."

"This is completely unexpected, but I like the tone of it. May I talk to her?"

Alicia came on the line. "Bartholomew, she knows the whole story and she opened her heart to me. You must come soon, please."

"OK, I'll change my reservation. It's funny that this should happen just as I was about to go into Argentina. I've had bad vibes all night about going in. I'll call you to confirm. How are you feeling?"

"I'm ready to pop and it's very uncomfortable, but the doctor said everything looks fine, so I shouldn't complain."

"Good, I'll be seeing you soon. *Te quiero.*"

Kevin briefed Eduardo on his need to rush home and ran through their intended program in Argentina one more time.

"Keep your eyes peeled. The place is dangerous because the Junta is still 'cleaning' house. A few visits back, my meeting with the captain was interrupted by two MP's. They began questioning me in a very threatening way. Now I always call ahead to make sure that the coast is clear."

"What do I do if they won't listen to me?"

"Hammer home that you are there to help the military get their equipment in good order and not for any other reason. The Navy Captain and the Air Force General will back you up."

Kevin saw Eduardo off and with great excitement took the next flight to Santiago. Upon arrival in Santiago there was a message for him to call home as soon as possible.

Elvira answered the phone.

"Is something wrong? The message to call sounded urgent," Kevin asked.

"There's nothing the matter with Alicia, but she had an urgent call from your office. I'll put her on."

"Kevin, those bastards took Eduardo off the plane in Buenos Aires to interrogate him. You have to get the Captain to do something fast."

"Who called to report it?"

"The Air Force General's office."

"How are you feeling?"

"I'm getting close. I'm having contractions and they are pretty regular."

Kevin called the General. He came on the line personally. "Kevin, the new chap you hired; has he ever been an activist?"

"Hell no, General, he graduated in Engineering from UCLA and worked for United Aircraft in Connecticut until I hired him. He left Chile long before Allende became a viable political factor. What are you doing to get him released, General?"

"That's why I called you. This Mason guy, running the terror machine here in Buenos Aires, doesn't give a shit about his actions. All he wants to do is embarrass Videla. I tried pulling rank, but with his emergency powers he won't listen to the regular military."

"What if my company got the State Department to intervene?"

"That would get General Videla's attention. Without airplanes that fly, his Junta is done."

"What about the Navy? They depend on us for the refit of the destroyers they bought from the U.S."

"You should call your Captain friend there, if he depends on you guys he'll go to Admiral Massera who is Mason's boss."

"Thanks for the advice, General."

Kevin phoned his Captain friend. "The new chap taking over from me was hauled off Aerolineas on his way to see you and is being interrogated for unknown reasons. Unless they release him forthwith, we'll hold up all shipments to you and will inform Admiral

Massera of our action. My man's name is Eduardo Gil Gomez, he is a Chilean who studied and has lived abroad in the U.S. for the past twenty years. I'll give you two hours to get him released before I put in a stop order."

"I'll go to work on it right away, Kevin. I can't understand why they won't get off your back."

"Call me at my office in Santiago as soon as something breaks, please. Thank you, Captain."

Next he called Phil Gordon and explained what had happened. "Phil, can you get hold of our favorite Senator from North Dakota to persuade him to lean on the State Department to intervene with the Argentinean government? The Videla Junta thought they had a champion in Henry Kissinger, so they'll listen if we complain through State."

"I'll see what I can do and let you know immediately. Is there anything the least bit revolutionary about Gil Gomez' background?"

"No. Ideologically he's a conservative American and much too busy to screw around with politics."

Now all the forces he could bring to bear were at work and all Kevin could do was to wait, hope and pray. However, there was something no less important to him and he rushed home. Elvira met him at the door,

"Kevin, I'm so glad you came! In God's own strange way, it may have saved your life. I hope your new man will survive, but I can see that you are strong and resourceful and will find a way out. Come and see. Alicia will need to be taken to the hospital soon," she led the way to the bedroom where Alicia sat up in bed.

"How are you doing? Getting close?" he greeted and kissed her.

"I'm so glad you came. My contractions are much worse than they were with Carlos. They're more painful and last longer. Thank

God you didn't go on to Argentina. They were obviously prepared and waiting for you."

"Does the doctor know about your condition?"

"Yes, he expects me to be ready to go in by early evening."

He and Elvira kept each other company at Alicia's bedside with Elvira getting up each time there was a contraction to hold Alicia's hand and encourage her. As the mother of four, she'd had ample childbirth experience.

To Kevin, the process was more distressing. It was obviously exhausting and painful to Alicia. He was almost relieved when Elvira and Alicia jointly decided that it was time to go to the hospital.

They admitted Alicia to a previously-reserved room and the nurses took over, leaving him on his own in the waiting room.

There was a phone and he called his office to see if anything had transpired in Buenos Aires. The Captain had called back to confirm that he had informed the Admiral that deliveries would stop unless Gil Gomez was released unharmed. Phil Gordon had forwarded to Kevin a copy of his Telex to the Senator asking for State Department intervention.

If he was a smoker, Kevin would be lighting one cigarette off the previous one. Finally, a nurse came in to tell him that the birth process had commenced and that both mother and child appeared to be fine.

He could wait no longer and walked down the stairs to a staff cafeteria for a cup of coffee. To his surprise Elvira was there too and joined him.

"Alicia told me a great deal about you and, much as I mourn the loss of my son, I welcome you into our family and into my heart."

"That is most generous of you—we hardly know each other."

"That is where you're wrong. Thanks to Alicia, I can see deep into your soul."

"Why do you call her 'Alicia' and not 'Angélica'?" Kevin asked.

"They are different persons. Alicia is the one with the will to survive and to find resolution for the senseless murder of Fernando," she replied.

"I'm glad you understand the difference," Kevin said.

"'Alicia' was your idea, wasn't it?"

"Yes, but she had to make it happen."

"What are you planning to do with your lives?"

"Alicia is going to Los Angeles with me next month to continue her studies at Loyola Marymount University so that she can practice as a therapist in San Miguel."

"San Miguel is not a place where you could live. It's far too parochial and provincial."

"I don't think it's the right place for Alicia either."

"Then why does she want to practice there?"

"She would like Fernando's children to grow up knowing the traditions and culture of their father. She reveres you and her suegro and doesn't want to become estranged from you.

"Also, and this is something you have to keep to yourself, she hopes to use patient-therapist confidentiality to obtain information from those who innocently suffered at the hands of the Junta, so she can prosecute them some day."

"Why would she want to be that dedicated?"

"We both believe that Argentina will never reach its promise as a civilized society, until it views itself in the mirror of reality and curbs its extremist attitudes."

"That will be a monumental task and use up both your lifetimes."

"There will be legions of terror victims to fuel a huge movement. In the end, no political system will be able to stand against it."

"This is fascinating. I didn't expect you to be that much of a philosopher. I begin to understand why Alicia is so enamored of you. Let's go and see how the baby's coming."

Maria Elvira de la Rosa was born an hour later and displayed through the window of the birthing center for her elated grandmother and Kevin to admire. She saw a creature of great beauty, while he saw a little shrimp of Homo sapiens.

He went down to the ever-present flower shop on the ground floor to purchase a dozen red roses to present to Alicia as soon as they were allowed in to see her.

Even if it wasn't his offspring, it marked a highpoint in their tormented existence together and they kissed each other with tenderness.

* * *

Fretfully, Kevin returned to his office worried about Eduardo Gil Gomez' detention by the Junta's "Mafia". There was a Telex from the Navy Captain acknowledging his message that all shipments would be held up unless his company's representative was forthwith released unharmed. The Telex was copied to Admiral Emilio Massera.

An hour later, Phil Gordon called to discuss the matter further and said that the State Department had sent a message to the Argentinean Ambassador in Washington to demand the release of the company's employee.

It wasn't till the next morning that Eduardo called to give Kevin the news that he was free and all was well. Eduardo was a stoic and while they sought to drive fear into his heart, he maintained his dignity until his release. Fortunately, his incarceration never went beyond the airport immigration office.

The incident was enough for the company to withdraw its representation from Argentina until safer conditions returned. In the end, there was a virtual embargo on military supplies from the United

Sates as the Junta prepared to fall on its own sword with its ill-conceived occupation of the Falkland Islands.

* * *

Alicia was released from hospital a day later to a happy home as their relationship with Elvira deepened and Kevin began taking a more active part in little Carlos' life.

That short period in Santiago before their departure for Los Angeles probably marked their happiest time together. They weren't constantly made conscious of sinister threats and the awkwardness in Kevin's relationship with her in-laws had dissolved. He developed genuine affection and enormous respect for Elvira who championed his cause so enthusiastically it fell just short of making Alicia feel uncomfortable.

Alicia was thriving intellectually in her studies as her personality gained strength from her deepening philosophy. This aspect, more than anything thrilled Kevin.

His own career was expanding in leaps and bounds as he worked his way into the global marketing opportunities and concerns of his company, which was also advancing rapidly in its technical and industrial reach.

As Chile was hardly at the geometric center of the company's business interests, Kevin had to travel longer and more often than their family life could comfortably sustain, and they all looked forward to their move to Los Angeles.

CHAPTER THIRTEEN

They rented a house on a bluff in Playa del Rey not far from the Loyola Marymount campus, Kevin's office and the Los Angeles International Airport.

They contemplated buying a house and to make life easier from a legal standpoint he proposed quietly getting married in Las Vegas. At first Alicia objected.

"What happens, if by chance, they find Fernando alive?"

"I don't think we'll ever know what happened to him. The Junta doesn't issue death certificates, you know. Perhaps you could look upon a Las Vegas wedding as an interim solution to be followed by a proper ceremony later."

"While on the subject of legalities, my student visa and arrival documents here are all in the name of Alicia de la Rosa which means my social security card will be that way too. Hence I have to register as Alicia at Loyola Marymount. That means Alicia de la Rosa will be my professional name."

"That can only be to your advantage if you still want to go off to practice in Tucumán. Your father says Bussi is very popular amongst the people of influence in San Miguel's. They wield a lot of power locally and for your own safety your professional persona has to remain far removed from Angélica Diaz. You haven't thought of changing your name to Bartholomew, have you?"

"No, that just doesn't sound like me. But then, as Shakespeare said 'a rose by any other name...'"

"What about the children? I have to adopt them in case you get wiped out in Tucumán. God, how I wish you didn't have to go back there."

"You should adopt them, but I owe it to Fernando's family to maintain their familial identities. His father, whom I love dearly, would be mortally offended."

"Sweetheart, that chain has already been broken! Maria is a de la Rosa! You have to think of the choices they will someday have to make. You can't have children, who essentially grew up here, finding themselves not able to get a job, because they're not citizens. They must at least each have a green card."

"Much as I love you, I can't do that to my Suegro," Alicia stood her ground.

* * *

Bewildered at first by the fast pace of Southern California and its affluence, Alicia soon fell into her own comfortable pace.

That pace, she soon discovered, was significantly faster than that of her peers in the psychology department. They seemed less motivated than a small cadre of expatriate students mostly there on scholarships with strong desires to succeed.

Her advising professor, an enthusiastic Latino from Puerto Rico, went to great lengths to get her signed up for the best courses for her purpose and helped ease the transition into English language instruction.

She joined several clubs on campus and soon had a coterie of friends with interests compatible with hers. It didn't take long before they sought her out to tell about her hideous experiences in Argentina. For a Catholic institution, the irony was that Jewish students, with a lively interest in the holocaust, were most adamant about inviting her to speak about the torture and mass murder of innocent "antisubversives" in Tucumán by another totalitarian government. The talks began drawing the attention of small academic publications and then grew into coverage by a broader range of mainstream periodicals. There was inherent danger in this kind of exposure and they reluctantly had to turn down the invitation of the New Yorker Magazine to co-author an article. Throughout, Alicia meticulously remained aloof of any political discussion and focused strictly on the suffering of the people and its effects on their psyche.

They always looked forward to their monthly "date", which invariably wound up with them tearing each others clothes off by the time they got home. In spite of their heavy schedules and Kevin's extensive business travel, they reveled in heir relationship which only grew stronger with age.

Due to runway expansions at Los Angeles International Airport, they were evicted and bought a larger home in West Los Angeles.

* * *

Their main sources of displeasure were Carlos Vargas' monthly Telex reports of newly-recorded atrocities and the occasional threats Alicia received from students on a campus with large numbers of Latinos. There was a period during which the threats were strong and persistent enough to move Kevin to secretly have her guarded by a classmate.

Having moved back to Spain, Vargas still managed the "Spanish Club" in Montevideo. His catalog of vile deeds perpetrated by the Argentina was meticulous. For Alicia's eyes only, he'd subtly classify them according to the guilt of the victims. This was according to their agreement to focus only on cases that involved the persecution of innocents, since those would have the greatest public impact. They didn't want to sound like shrill revolutionaries, which unfortunately, many of the victims had been.

His worst incident concerned a young Spaniard living in Uruguay who was taken by an interrogation detachment of the Uruguayan Army, known as the "Anti-subversive Operation Coordinating Organization", who handed him over to the Argentineans. His taped recollections were transcribed by Vargas as follows:

"They put me in various rooms, with my wrists handcuffed behind my back. I was blindfolded—bleeding from the blows struck by the Uruguayans—when a new wave of blows began. This went on for about half an hour before they took me to the top floor and stripped all my clothes off. They handcuffed my wrists behind my back and threw buckets of water all over me. Then they attached wires around my waist, thorax and ankles.

"They hooked a chain to the handcuffs and pulled my arms up as high as they would go without dislocating my shoulders. It was the most intense pain I'd ever felt. I was left hanging about a foot above the floor. The pain was so bad, I couldn't tell how long I was left there before they came and lowered me so that my toes almost touched the ground. By extending my toes I could take just a little stress off my arms, but as soon as my toes touched the ground, I felt an electric shock. I can't describe the agony of those shocks. The soles of my feet were so burnt that it formed layers of hard skin, which later peeled off. The shocks made me lose control of my motor senses and I vomited and defecated simultaneously.

"I felt the electricity rising up in my body. The parts where the wires were attached, felt like they were being torn from my body...first the feet, then the legs, testicles and thorax. They tortured me for five days, making it worse each day, finally they inserted wires into my anus and penis.

"As excruciating as the physical pain was, what disturbed me most were the torturers sitting around, drinking, laughing and making insulting remarks. Judging by the severity of torture, one could swear that I had hidden the plans to make an atomic bomb, but all they wanted from me were the names of Uruguayans living in Argentina who opposed the Junta. Ironically, I didn't know a single Uruguayan living in Argentina."

Kevin could feel the anger rise in him as it did when he discovered Carolina's body at the docks in Buenos Aires. He could only imagine how Alicia felt. They just sat clinging to each other, mentally renewing their determination to expose the perpetrators. It made it clear again to them those circumstances beyond their control was robbing them of the opportunity to live a normal, comfortable life.

* * *

The time came for Alicia to choose a subject for her thesis and she chose a case drawn from the "Dirty War", which few Angelenos were aware of. Nevertheless, her choice raised hackles amongst certain faculty academics who suspected her of having a left-leaning political motive. Her advising professor, who had more knowledge of circumstances in Argentina, finally had to come to her rescue. What he didn't know was that she planned to use her own experience in her case study.

"I think you're crazy to use yourself as your guinea pig," Kevin advised. "How can you objectively analyze your own emotions in the way that an impartial therapist would?"

"That's precisely the strength in my idea. No one can imagine what it feels like to have your innocent husband dragged off and mutilated by a band of evil vultures, unless you've lived through it. You don't see me walking around with peculiar twitches or other behavioral traits resulting from trauma...do you? So there's nothing to prevent me from analyzing my emotions rationally."

"I worry about what reliving those moments under a microscope may do to your demeanor. Reliving trauma can be more hardening than the original jolt."

"I know that. That's why the thought of going back to Tucumán to sit there like a sponge, absorbing the dreadful sorrows of victims, is such a daunting challenge to me," she protested as she burst into tears and buried her face in his chest. "Kevin, be there for me, your love is all that keeps me going."

CHAPTER FOURTEEN

Alicia's graduation was a major event for them and was celebrated in memorable fashion. Her father, Sergio Beron, came from Argentina and Kevin invited all their friends and colleagues to a reception in their garden. As a surprise, he arranged for a small Flamenco group to perform on the patio and engaged a caterer. With the enthusiastic help of her father they decorated the patio and family room lavishly.

She had style and dressed just right for the occasion, bringing out her charm, vigor and enthusiasm. Boosted by the satisfaction of receiving her Master's degree with honors, she looked absolutely radiant.

Kevin welcomed their guests while the caterer passed out fluted glasses of Champagne and he then brought them together with a brief opening address:

"This is a very special occasion for us to see you all gathered here in California to honor the achievement of a very courageous woman, whom I am privileged to call my wife. Alicia de la Rosa has proven her resilience to adjust to vastly different circumstances more frequently in her young life than most people can expect to face in their entire lives. Her recent metamorphosis from a Spaniard in rural Argentina, to a high-achiever in an American university, while settling into family living in a very different culture with two young children, is something to be admired. Let us all drink to Alicia, for winning her Masters in psychology, Cum Laude."

Every one drank the toast as Alicia's professor took the stage and in Spanish thanked her for so convincingly vindicating his belief in her. There were several more accolades from her father and the president of Kevin's company.

A bit haltingly, Alicia thanked them.

"I hope my English will be up to this occasion. I've been overwhelmed with kindness ever since arriving in this country of abundance. It made me realize anew how high other countries have to reach to attain your level of civility. I pray that the heart of Argentina will someday be as open to its citizens as yours. Before that can happen it must learn to mourn its thousands of innocent victims. I would not be who I am, without the selfless generosity, at great personal peril, of Kevin, my 'Bartholomew.' *Yo le debo mi Alma a voz,* I owe my soul to you." she said and hugged him.

Drinks and hors d'oeuvres were served, the Flamenco group began performing and the reception was in full swing. An hour or so later, people began drifting away.

Many close friends stayed on, including the Flamenco guitar player and a pianist friend of his. Alicia's professor had brought an Argentinean friend along with a Bandoneón and they began playing Tangos on the patio.

Smiling from ear to ear, Alicia steered Kevin to the "dance floor" to relive their magical evening at the Tango Club in Montevideo. They danced with incredible intimacy…she leaned backwards until her hair touched the ground…they used every step and routine to dramatize their performance, until they were oblivious to those around them…just responding to their mutual desire to please each other. Their friends' applause finally brought them to reality, much to the satisfaction of the musicians.

The party ended when Los Angeles policemen arrived and politely asked them to tone it down.

The evening was a fitting way to reward an ambitious achievement. It showed clearly in the expression on her father's face.

* * *

They now faced that inevitable moment when Alicia would have to return to Tucumán to practice as a psychotherapist. To mark the end of their idyllic period together, Kevin took the whole family on a vacation to a ranch in Colorado. The ambience at the ranch drew Kevin and Alicia back to the Andes near Puerto Varas.

The respite gave Kevin the opportunity to get to know Sergio and since their age difference was only ten years, they felt part of the same generation. Their main topic was the attitude of the folks in Tucumán, which deeply concerned Kevin.

"Don't you find it strange in an industrialized country like Argentina, to be living in a small Andean city with virtually no middle class?"

"Yes, the plain below the mountains is rich agricultural land. What's unique about Tucumán is that it has no winter. The temperature hardly ever goes below freezing, so almost all plant species flourish there. Similar to your San Joachim Valley, it's dry and sunny most of the year, yet there's tons of water from the mountains for irrigation. In that environment, well-capitalized farmers thrive."

"But the San Joachim," Kevin pointed out "we have supporting industries such as farm machinery manufacturers, food processors, etcetera, to support a middle class."

"That's because the San Joachim has the huge American market on its doorstep. Tucumán can't support an industry like that. It has to go abroad to sell enough produce to attain efficient production. We're very efficient sugar cane growers, but as long as countries subsidize their sugar beet farmers, we can't sell as much as we can produce. So we have to grow other crops with high perceived value...as the French do with wine and Persians with Pistachio nuts. In what we call Argentina's 'Garden of Eden', unusual crops flourish, but it takes specialized corporate farmers to succeed commercially. So, we end up with well-heeled farmers employing masses of low wage laborers.

"Poverty, lack of education, spiced up by a hoard of dissidents selling utopian Communism to the destitute, makes for an explosive brew," Sergio explained.

"What do you think of Alicia's plan to set up a psychotherapy practice in San Miguel?"

"It's foolish of her to go back there after what they did to Fernando."

"Why?" Kevin queried.

"People down there don't question authority...they simply assume that Fernando, and Angélica too, were guilty of something. If she showed up after evading the Junta all this time, they'll kill her," Sergio predicted and went on to explain. "She'll have go there as a repentant person wishing to be accepted by the elite of San Miguel. That will mean blending in with their view that the Junta did well to restore law and order in Tucumán. The least glimmer of opposition to their authority would put her life in jeopardy. Even after they've gone, the local leadership will adhere closely to conservative doctrine."

"That's why she changed herself into Alicia. She'll be arriving as a new professional face from America."

"They'll see right through your charade. Too many people know her. I hate to say this, but you're being naïve. She'll have to go back as the same old Angélica, except for a professional name change, or else she could say that she remarried a fellow called de la Rosa. It would be more effective if she went as Alicia Bartholomew, the wife of an influential American. That would keep her out of the hands of Antonio Bussi who is partial to Americans. You should adopt the kids so they can go there on U.S. passports."

"What do you know about Bussi?" Kevin asked.

"You have to realize that the people you did business with there, represent less than ten percent of the population. That's a small community—everyone knows everyone. I've attended many social events with Bussi. Our conversations were about the demand for sugar mill equipment as a bell-weather for universal cane sugar demand. He's nobody's fool and wanted to improve the economy of the province. The civic leaders in San Miguel stand behind him. Part of the problem is that Angélica and her in-laws supported the socialist Perónistas, which goes over like a belch in church," Sergio wound up the conversation.

* * *

As a final touch to their experience together in America, Kevin and Alicia took a ride on their own up to the Continental Divide. The trail was rocky and steep, passing through pine forests until they reached a glacial lake at the tree line.

From then on the views were spectacular. They followed a canal just below the ridge of the mountains assuming it had been built as a water race for a mine. When they came to a saddle in the breach of the ridge and could see westward into the distance, they realized that it was diverting water over the Continental Divide to the western slope of the Rockies.

They returned through a high Alpine valley with lakes terraced in loose moraine, cascading down to lower elevations. It was such a beautiful sight that they stopped to eat lunch.

Kevin told her about his conversation with Sergio, dwelling on his final suggestion that she go back as Mrs. Bartholomew with her kids bearing his name and American passports. She was about to state her objections, when the hail started falling so hard they had to seek shelter behind a huge boulder.

"You have to think hard before you reject your father's recommendations. Like an invisible observer, he's been close to the center of power in Tucumán. They think of his stay as temporary...an outsider there to serve them. That way he hears a lot of stuff few folks know much about."

"What's wrong with me just being Alicia de la Rosa?"

"He says too many folks will recognize you as Angélica. I also think that Carlos' accent will be a dead giveaway."

"I still think they'll leave me alone if I do something they need badly enough."

"He disagrees...your in-laws don't have pull...As Perón supporters, they're viewed as socialist daydreamers. Antonio Bussi's the man who'll have your fate in his hands. He is supported by the elite in San Miguel. You'll have to win his confidence by acting the part of supporter, buttering up the town's civic leaders. You'll have to play the two-faced game of being his friend while preparing to put him in jail."

"While it goes against my grain, I can see my father's logic. You'll be the legal guardian of my children and I'll be Señora Bartholomew. That would make life easier."

The hail turned to snow and they resumed their thrilling ride from the thirteen thousand foot level to the ranch. The cloud formations were spectacular, swirling and plunging them in and out of bright sunlight.

"It's hard to believe, but at the turn of the century, there were so many gold diggers up here, that mule trains came here every day to bring in supplies and take ore down to the reduction plant in Georgetown. One could sit here by one's fireside and read a daily newspaper!"

"As usual, you're letting your imagination run wild."

"Speaking of wild...in my imagination I'm a sex-starved miner seeing this lost woman on horseback riding into my camp. She smiles at me and asks if I could spare her a cup of tea, spiked with a touch of whiskey to keep out the cold. I bow and help her off her horse to lead her into my humble shack. Suddenly, I lose control over my senses and take her into my arms. She comes willingly and kisses me passionately."

"OK, even I get the hint," she said as she slid down from her horse.

There's something exciting about making unbridled love out in the open to the person you most adore. They relished every moment as they pleased each other in fanciful ways they had never dared try.

There was so much feeling pent up in their hearts, they had to go to extremes to experience enough passion and intense pleasure. They lay, completely spent hugging each other.

"Dad's right, you have to be the father of Fernando's children."

"What about having some of our own too?"

"After what you just did not me, that question may be redundant."

CHAPTER FIFTEEN

Reluctantly at first, Alicia began organizing her return to San Miguel, first searching for a suitable professional partner with whom to share the burden and provide for regular escapes from Tucumán.

Her professor at the Catholic University suggested Elena Mendoza, a woman who'd attended school in Argentina before transferring to Santiago. She had just graduated with a Master's degree and had focused her training on the treatment of trauma victims.

Alicia immediately phoned her.

"I'm calling from Los Angeles. I just graduated in circumstances similar to yours. I'm interested in starting a post-trauma depression relief practice in San Miguel de Tucumán and would like to share the practice with a strong partner. Since I'm told you lived there once, would you be interested?"

"What did you say your name was?"

"I didn't. My professional name is Alicia de la Rosa."

"Alicia, may I ask why you're particularly interested in post-trauma stress disorder situations?"

"I figured the 'Dirty War' would leave behind a lot of serious depression cases to work on."

"Did you experience such trauma?" Elena asked.

"Yes, they murdered my husband," Alicia answered.

"I am sorry to hear that. They took my brother and his wife," Elena added.

"Where and why did it happen and where were you?" Alicia inquired.

"I was visiting my boyfriend in Punta Arenas. They were arrested in Bahia Blanca, south of Buenos Aires...God only knows why they were taken. She was pregnant too. "Why did they take your husband?"

"We never found out why," Alicia replied.

"So what's your purpose in counseling the traumatized—you're not into playing Florence Nightingale, are you?"

"Before I answer that, what's your purpose, Elena?"

"One, I feel sorry, especially for the women; Two, I'd like to know what happened, and; Three, I'd like to get even with the villains."

"Since you're being up front, I'll level with you." Alicia responded, "I swore an oath to avenge Fernando's death. Like you, I too feel compassion."

"What kind of routine do you have in mind? I liked some aspects of living in Tucumán—except for its rainy season and the fact that its people were up-tight. I'll need to come up for air frequently. Besides, my boyfriend just became my husband and lives in Santiago."

"Mine lives in Los Angeles. I too will need lots of R and R. How about alternating months, doubling up for one week at each turn?" Alicia offered.

"That could work. What about money?" Elena asked.

"We bankroll and share the profit, fifty-fifty," Alicia suggested.

"When do we start?" Elena asked.

"We were waiting for the ant subversion activity to die down. My father still lives there—you may remember he's from Spain—and says they're pretty well done with arrests and interrogations in San Miguel," Alicia explained.

"Now I get it. You're Angélica Beson! We had outrageous fun together. Let's meet in Santiago in a month's time," Elena proposed.

"Great, thanks a lot. Please call again soon."

The arrangement between Alicia and Elena jelled and they moved forward to establish the firm of *de la Rosa y Mendoza, Psicoterapeutas*. They decided to meet in Santiago the following week before going to San Miguel, which Alicia still viewed with unease, despite her father and Dr. Diaz' assurances that they wouldn't be harmed.

Alicia reviewed their plans with Kevin for about the tenth time.

"I don't think you ought to put all your eggs in one basket. Leave the children here with me until I have completed adopting them and have American passports for them. The fact that Maria's passport is in the name of de la Rosa, while her sibling is a Diaz is sure to draw attention when you least need it," Kevin argued.

"Elvira is so looking forward to having them stay with her...but, I suppose that can wait. What are your travel plans for the month?"

"Phil Gordon called one of his major management meetings next week. People from all over will be here in LA for the better part of a week. Several of my chaps are coming so we'll be having meetings of our own. Once that's over, I had hoped to stay home for a while. It's going to be strange to be without you. I've never enjoyed a lifestyle as much as ours. By the way, I've been counting the days. Shouldn't you have had your period by now?"

"Damn you, I should have known you'd remember. I think I'm pregnant!"

"At least now I can be sure that you'll come home to me."

"Is that all you can think of saying?"

"No, I'm delighted. It's like the frosting on the cake of loving you."

"I'll miss you terribly."

* * *

As if to remind Kevin of the dangers facing his wife, Alicia's professor delivered a Telex from Carlos Vargas. It described the accidental kidnapping and shooting, the previous January, of a seventeen-year-old Swedish girl in Buenos Aires by a lieutenant of a notorious task force at the Navy Mechanics School, ESMA. A Spanish survivor reported that the girl had recovered well from her wound, and in talking to her, he had found her to be mentally sound. The abduction of a young, innocent, Swedish citizen caused the Junta great embarrassment and developed into an international disgrace. To prevent her from divulging details of their atrocities, they shot her in cold blood.

Kevin's representatives in Buenos reported that Massera's "Task Unit" had kidnapped and probably murdered two French nuns, which seriously angered the French government.

Of more immediate concern to him, was the threat of war between Argentina and Chile over the Beagle Channel islands off the tip of Tierra del Fuego. The dispute had been hovering for most of 1977 and the first half of 1978. This could make it impossible for Alicia and her partner to operate out of Santiago. Fortunately, at the last moment, Pope John Paul II intervened and settled the dispute.

Kevin had difficulty rationalizing Alicia listening daily to patients talking about unspeakable horrors that had befallen them, while maintaining a benign social presence in a community largely supportive of the Junta. Yet, it was essential that she do so.

"We have to be careful how we approach this psychotherapy venture," he cautioned in his next phone call to her in Santiago. "You'll have to make yourself politically invisible by socializing with the elite and swallowing hard when they show their support for the Junta."

"Yes, that's why I need Elena as my partner. I couldn't pull it off alone. I need those three weeks away from Argentina each eight-week period."

"Let's keep our communications through San Miguel strictly personal and do the difficult stuff through our company office in Santiago. Either you or Elena will be in Chile all but one week out of each month. Take any sensitive material you develop to Santiago. Leave nothing incriminating in San Miguel. I'll send you my idea of a set of code words we can use in emergencies in normal-sounding conversations from Tucumán."

"How are the children?" Alicia inquired.

"I put Carlos in pre-school. He loves it—all the pretty little girls. His English is improving in leaps and bounds. Maria's beginning to walk and we've had to take everything off the coffee tables. She's very bright. I wish she was <u>my</u> daughter."

"To all intents she is. I'm so glad you like their company."

There had been rumblings about Kevin's company being taken over by a competitor.

"What's the gossip about the merger?"

"I hope to hear soon."

"I miss you dreadfully."

"Likewise, I'll call again tomorrow."

"Please do. We're leaving the day after tomorrow for Tucumán. Can you believe it...LanChile now has a direct flight to San Miguel from here!"

* * *

Alicia found Elena a joy to work with. Their interests were so close that standing in for one another should pose few problems. They had very similar training and their preferences with regard to schools of thought in psychology were quite similar. Neither of them was from Tucumán, but they had experienced living there together as two inseparable, motherless teenagers. They both were broad minded, intellectual and curious. They shared a desire to help emotionally distressed people and saw the possibility of an unusually strong demand for their services in the angst-ridden community of San Miguel. What really bonded them together was a mutual desire to know specifically what had gone so wrong to transform Argentina into a fascist state in which the lives of people had become freely expendable.

With misgivings they prepared to make their first trip to San Miguel, wondering how they would gain the support of the hard-line ruling class of Tucumán.

Elena posed a scenario.

"What if we found strong latent demand for our services amongst the military personnel? You can't tell me that a young conscript, stuffed into a uniform and given a gun to shoot down people in cold blood, won't experience severe depression in the aftermath!"

Alicia conjectured.

"I've thought about that too. Imagine a physician, trained to save lives, being asked to supervise torture proceedings to avoid culpable deaths! How does an obstetrician feel after delivering babies from mothers, he knows are destined to be put to death so that their offspring can be given to childless cronies of the Junta?"

Elena added.

"The need to have patients from the world of officialdom is nothing but self-protection. The wife of a Commander who swears that she has experienced great relief from being treated by us, would help gain us protection from those in power."

Alicia knew that they were rationalizing to hide their fear of going where she had experienced senseless brutality, knowing that she could still be in harm's way.

* * *

Their flight to San Miguel was in an older-vintage airplane that barely cleared the Andes Mountains northeast of Santiago. The direct route from Santiago to Tucumán traversed the Andes range at its widest point between Chile and Argentina, which resulted in a most interesting, but moderately rough flight. They passed by an enormous volcano, which the pilot pointed out was the third highest mountain in the Andean chain—over twenty-one thousand feet high. The sight was magnificent. The pilot also pointed to Aconcagua, the south face of which they could see some distance away, mentioning that it was the highest mountain in the Western Hemisphere.

Alicia had to acknowledge a feeling of nostalgia as they neared the edge of the mountainous escarpment bringing into view the vast plain stretching east of San Miguel, brim full of sugar cane fields and expansive lemon, orange, and avocado orchards. This had been her home for years and the sight of the city below brought back treasured memories of many high points in her life, the most important one being Fernando.

In dramatic contrast to metropolitan Buenos Aires, the atmosphere in the interior of Argentina was relaxed, with a small-town feel to it. It had always surprised her how closely the middle class in San Miguel was interlinked to each other through marriage, cousins and long-lost childhood friends. It wasn't uncommon to hear talk of someone married to a cousin of a husband's uncle's wife. If you needed a doctor, dentist, architect, teacher, banker, mechanic or lawyer, invariably there was someone in that wide "family circle" to turn to. The phone-book effectively became a reference of last resort.

Here people "come home" twice a day. They go off to school or work at 8 in the morning and return home at 1 o'clock to eat their main meal of the day. In the best Spanish tradition, a siesta follows until about 4 or 5 when they go back to work and the children return to school. Everyone comes home around 9 o'clock for a light diner snack and to sleep.

In their younger days, she and Elena would hang out on Fridays and go dancing on Saturdays. Hanging out would seldom start before midnight with a pizza and last until 5 or 6 in the morning. There was always someone with a guitar and they would drink wine, beer or Fernet...a hard-liquor mixed with Coke. They'd hang out playing music, flirting, making love, or just talking, before going home to catch up on sleep and be ready for Saturday, the dancing night.

They would go to one of several clubs after midnight and dance the night away. It always seemed romantic to them to return home after sunrise.

Sunday was the day of the "asado", similar to a beef barbeque, accompanied by a simple green salad. For appetizers they'd have "empanadas"—similar to stuffed Pita bread.

The whole Diaz family—from grandparents to aunts and uncles— used to get together for the Sunday asado. Everyone ate lunch, took their siesta or sat around chatting. The younger set would start a soccer game. Older folks would take a walk. Sometimes they'd all go to the park and have ice cream. She would always go to bed with a warm fuzzy feeling Sunday nights.

Alicia wondered how the trauma of torturing people into telling on their friends, had changed these familial, friendly customs.

* * *

Her in-laws and father were at the airport to greet them with enthusiasm. Almost immediately Alicia ran into the conflict of which name to use. Elvira and her father had become accustomed to "Alicia" and had accepted Kevin as her life-partner. Dr. Diaz still stumbled over her change in image and it would obviously take time for him to adjust to a much more robust daughter-in-law. To her, nothing in their relationship had changed and she continued to address him as "Suegro", Spanish for father-in-law.

They had gone to great lengths to make her feel at home by repairing the damage the troops had done to her house and restoring the furnishings and garden.

"Xavier at the stables has been asking about you almost weekly since you left. He's been riding Tonterías several times a week and has even ridden him in one cross-country race. You must go out there to see him," Elvira suggested.

She found her father-in-law in deep thought in his study and sat down with him for a private talk.

"You have changed a great deal," he said. "You are much stronger and more assured. Elvira told me about Kevin and how the two of you helped each other stay alive. I am deeply grateful to him, but I can't get over the loss of Fernando."

"Fernando will always be in our hearts," she assured him "which is why I remain committed to the covenant I made with you to avenge his disappearance. But first, tell me, did you sue that crook, Villalobos?"

"No, I thought I'd let sleeping dogs lie. The whole ambience here had changed. Everyone blindly followed the Provincial Commander."

"How did that reflect on your career?"

"Under Antonio Bussi, there was no career for an Advocate. What he said was the law. I still do what Attorneys do, but nothing big. Had I been a conservative member of the elite, I'd do better now, but they all know that I supported Perón, which makes me persona non-grata."

"You used to get along with everyone, even the town's elite. What did you think of Bussi?"

"Politically, he wasn't bad. He even acquired a following amongst the poor people for creating jobs. But, as an Army General, he was ruthless. However, he did the job they gave him more quickly than the Commanders to the south of us. Apart from some unusual cases, there have been no political arrests here since Bussi left at the beginning of this year. After he gave the farms the Communists had confiscated back to the landowners, they all supported him. Bringing that ruined land back into production created jobs and helped the local economy."

"My partner and I want to set up a strong psychotherapy practice here, and would like to have some of the elite—especially women—at the core of our practice. That way, we won't be viewed with suspicion by the people in power. They don't have to know what we're up to—we're only trying to relieve the pain of the victims who still suffer from the effects of severe trauma."

"That's not why you came back here, is it?"

"Let's not talk about that. What you don't hear, you can't repeat."

"What are you going to do with the children?"

"They're with Kevin in Los Angeles. Carlos is already in pre-school. They will come here often. I want them to be as bi-cultural as possible. That's the wave of the future."

"Will they remain Argentineans?"

"We don't have much reason to be proud of Argentina right now. It is becoming the world's pariah. Carlos can someday choose what he wants to be. He was born here. Maria was born in Chile to a Spanish mother called Alicia de la Rosa. She is getting an American passport and both kids are being adopted by Kevin, so they can become American citizens."

"Well, that doesn't leave me much to argue about. I just want you to know how concerned I was about your safety and how nice it is to see you well and happy. I suppose I'll have to get used to having a Gringo in the family. Without him you wouldn't have survived. Elvira thinks well of him and she's usually right."

"Suegro, you mustn't think of it as a betrayal of Fernando. Kevin only came to me because he saw how scared I was. If <u>he</u> noticed it, the agents of the Junta and their Uruguayan helpers would have noticed it too. He had to stop me from being so obvious, so he changed me into Alicia. Once he had me in a safe place, he saw how much I wanted to fight back. That's what he wanted also, so we teamed up."

"What did <u>he</u> have to fight for?"

"He was in love with a Salvadoran woman who guided tours from America to Argentina. He wanted to marry her and she finally accepted. They were to meet in Buenos Aires. The Junta's men got to her first. He found her mutilated body in the harbor near the ferry-dock.

"Suegro, he <u>knows</u> Argentina like the back of his hand. He has worked in South America for <u>years</u> and knows many powerful people, even in *our* military."

"I <u>am</u> sorry. Now I begin to understand."

"It will take you a long time to understand what happened between us. He literally owns my soul, Suegro."

"Then I must befriend him."

"That would make me happy; I'm pregnant with his child."

CHAPTER SIXTEEN

Alicia and Elena rode into town in the little car her father had loaned her to look for space to rent for their new practice. Several of the Realtors remembered her as Angélica and immediately welcomed her home. They each had different ideas of office space to lease and just the mention of what they planned to use it for, stirred excitement.

"If ever there was a time we needed post-trauma therapists, it is now. Women in that role will do well here. So many of our troubled ones are women," the first Realtor said.

Then she asked, "Why do you use the name of Alicia de la Rosa?"

"That was the name I used to get into university after I left and so it became my professional name," Alicia dissembled.

"That's probably a good idea. You know what they say about familiarity breeding contempt. A shiny new name won't hurt."

After a morning of viewing their options they decided on an office apartment with a balcony on a quiet street, two blocks from the civic center. Each of them would have their own office with a reception area between the two and a small kitchen alcove, with a toilet leading from it, in the back. They signed a one-year lease with an option to renew it annually.

They began planning an open-house reception to help attract their first clients and to stimulate word-of-mouth referrals.

Alicia persuaded Dr. Diaz to give her the names of wives and mothers who he knew had suffered at the hands of the Junta. They were able to contact and invite a number of them to their open-house. Some of them were still afraid to appear in public, but agreed to stop by on their own for private discussions.

From her father she obtained a list of officials who had had a hand in the ant subversive campaign and invited their wives.

As a precaution, Elena, who was less known in the community, went to see the city police to tell them about their intended reception. The officer on duty asked many questions about its purpose including a description of the people who had been invited. When he heard the names of wives of senior officials, he approved it.

The time for the reception was set for four o'clock at the tail-end of siesta on the following Tuesday. They worked hard to get everything prepared for the event and used the Diaz family as their critical audience to practice their presentation.

Even before the reception they received a number of calls from interested people wanting to make an appointment. To their surprise, there was a soldier amongst them.

His appearance drew their attention to the immediacy of their venture and they set to work creating an appointment scheduling and management scheme.

Underlying all the excitement, there remained a sinister sense of danger. Alicia couldn't dispel her killing of the Junta's agent in Montevideo and Kevin's shooting of the two Argentinean soldiers in Patagonia from her mind. If that ever came to light here in Tucumán, her life would be over.

* * *

Coming on top of her constant fear, the hectic week of activity, left Alicia with great desire for peace and solitude. She drove out to the stables where Xavier was delighted to see her. He couldn't find enough good things to say about her five-year-old Andalusian grey called, *Tonterías*… "nonsense" in English. They saddled up and left in high spirits for a long ride into the foothills.

Xavier was a very private man and kept mostly to himself. He was an excellent trainer as well as riding instructor and had helped her win a number of ribbons in horse shows. While they were good comrades in the saddle, they knew little about each other's lives. She knew that he too had come from Spain…albeit from the far south-western part around Seville. From his build, she always fantasized that he may have been an amateur bullfighter.

They rode in silence, giving Alicia a chance to let her thoughts wander. She was happy that she had cleared the way with her family for Kevin. She passionately wanted him to feel a part of it. It felt strange, after living in Santiago and Los Angeles, to suddenly be transported back in time to a rural life style, steeped in tradition with leisure ways and old-fashioned values. There was much to enjoy about it, but it also put her patience to the test with its slow pace and many rituals. She would find it difficult to live here permanently.

On the positive side, Tucumán lay in a wonderful setting with many refuges. A ride in Los Angeles' Griffith Park was certainly no match for losing oneself in the foothills of these ranges. They were at least as spectacular as the ones they visited in Colorado.

Everything down below now seemed far-off and insignificant to her. She had no fear or concern about those she loved most. Up here in the heavens she felt just as close to Fernando as to Kevin. She had Fernando's children to show for it and felt oddly poetic about carrying Kevin's child within her. Her cause for pursuing the terrorists for restitution now seemed self-centered. If she was chosen to help expose them, there had to be a higher purpose.

While Alicia was living in Los Angeles, a group of courageous, elderly women referred to as the "Mothers of Plaza de Mayo" had formed spontaneously as grandmothers of abducted young people began each Thursday to protest at the Plaza de Mayo in Buenos Aires. It caught the authorities off guard. They couldn't very well be seen harming defenseless elderly women in broad daylight. Alicia and Kevin had decided to keep their distance from the "Mothers", since it could spoil their plans to independently obtain culpable evidence of wrongdoing. They had to remain silent until the Junta had lost power.

By the time Alicia and Xavier returned to the stable, her thoughts had come full circle, focusing again on her main task of mining for evidence.

She was anxious to talk strategy with Kevin, but it would have to wait until she returned to Santiago.

* * *

Kevin was busy dealing with his multiple visitors, while keeping an eye on the children and their nanny. She was competent, able to drive Carlos to pre-school and back and do the grocery shopping. He made a point of being home in the evenings at bed time to read to the children and comfort them in the absence of their mother.

While Phil Gordon's meeting was ostensibly to update management about the company's new business opportunities, it began sounding more like a preamble to a possible later announcement of a more fundamental nature.

On the penultimate day, Gordon selected Kevin and a small group of marketing people to meet separately with him. They were sworn to secrecy before he began questioning particular people about hypothetical business impacts, should certain competitors be amalgamate with the company. Representing the foreign markets where the company had most of its competitors, Kevin received many of the questions. From where he sat it seemed that there would be a breakup of the company, with different pieces merging into different competitors.

Gordon beckoned Kevin aside.

"I feel awkward about all this secrecy. In sharing some of this with you, I'm obligating you to the same degree of confidentially.

"As a public corporation, we are bound to consider an offer to merge with two or more companies. Effectively, they are trying to match up parts of our company with different competitors to strengthen the financial appeal on both sides of the transaction. It's the old story of maximizing shareholder value. The largest match-up joins our marine, mining and oilfield enterprises with one of the world's biggest mining equipment manufacturers with huge market shares in the your stomping grounds. You know that business and its political ramifications better than anyone in the firm. I'd like you to join me for dinner tomorrow evening with the CEO and a few other members of that company. You'll find the President very knowledgeable about the mining business."

"OK, where do we meet?"

"Let's start at the Beverly Hills Hotel at seven. That's where they're staying."

"Fine, I'll see you at seven."

Kevin was glad to get out of the office to get home in time for his daily phone call to Alicia. He'd become increasingly concerned about her safety and wished they could speak more openly.

"So how's the redeemer of the emotionally distressed this evening?"

"She's anxious to hear from her knight in shining armor."

"Is the mother of all things still out to find fault with you?"

"Not so far. I'm busy trying to befriend her replacements. But tell me about Carlos and Maria, I miss them."

"They're growing so quickly, soon they won't know who you are...only kidding, they ask about you all the time."

"I went for a magnificent ride into the mountains with Xavier today. I wish I could have substituted you for him. I would have slid down the saddle into your arms like in Colorado. That part of you I miss most of all."

"Is that a symptom that you're basically a nymphomaniac, or didn't they cover that in your classes?"

"No, but they told us what the consequences were. Your child is definitely growing in me."

"Is it a 'him' or a 'her' and what's its name?"

"Santiago."

"Speaking of Santiago, it is likely that the company will be transformed. If so, our interests in Chile and Brazil would be enormous. I wouldn't be surprised if they sent me back there."

"How lovely, could we meet there soon? I have things to tell you about my 'mother.'"

"I'll let you know tomorrow. Good luck with your grand opening."

* * *

At the private dinner Kevin was questioned extensively about his most productive contacts in the mining industry and the economic conditions in various mining countries. In particular they wanted to know the latest news from Chile.

"As you know, Allende nationalized the mines in seventy-one without due compensation for the capital and technology it took to develop them. Pinochet poured oil on the troubled waters and then merged all the established copper mines into Coldelco, a single national company. New mines are still free to be developed with private capital" Kevin began explaining.

The visiting CEO, overhearing their conversation, butted in.

"Overall, what do you think will come of Chile?"

"It'll be run as an autocracy to institute major economic reforms before being turned over to an elected government," Kevin answered.

"Do you believe that nonsense?"

"As a matter of fact, I do. Remember, before Allende broke his promise to Parliament and installed a Communist dictatorship, Chile had been the longest-standing democratic government—since 1833—in South America."

"That's interesting! We're so easily tempted to view the travails of Latin American countries as 'banana republicanism.' What goals have they set themselves?"

"Chile wants to build businesses in which they can attain a dominant export market share and import the stuff they can't make economically. They no longer want to build cars inefficiently under heavy protective import tariffs. They'd sooner abolish import tariffs and put their money into industries where they can be major exporters—copper, other minerals, forest products, fisheries, high-margin agricultural commodities. They are basically implementing a Milton Friedman free trade plan."

"You speak well of them."

"Not really, all of South America, Chile included, is infuriatingly simple-minded. Not that we are that much better—we just have such overwhelming resources, we succeed more often, sometimes even spectacularly."

"How long did you say you lived in South America?"

"Fifteen years."

"We'll need someone down there who's really on the ball. It could become our most important market."

CHAPTER SEVENTEEN

Alicia and Elena's open-house turned into an exciting event. More people came than they had expected. What pleased them most was the cross-section. There were prospective patients from every walk of life.

Elena acted as principal spokesperson and began by talking about her training in Santiago to earn her master's degree in therapeutic psychology.

Alicia added her own American credentials.

"Elena and I had a common desire to help alleviate the pain of post-traumatic stress disorder here in Tucumán. We thought the women of this community would appreciate having female psychotherapists to turn to."

Elena began explaining what psychotherapy was and how it evolved as an important step in helping traumatized people return to a normal life.

"You have probably all been depressed and asked yourself 'why am I depressed.' Usually, something happened that upset you severely. When that something shocked you such that you couldn't bear to think of it again, you may have experienced trauma. We are here to help you get over the effects of that trauma which may be so strong that you stop functioning like a normal person. Our job is to figure out what went on in your mind when the trauma occurred. Then we help you get over your depression, mood swings, sleeplessness, repeated bad dreams, and so on."

Alicia continued, explaining.

"Shock makes one feel unsafe—you don't know who or what to trust...you feel strange, even 'crazy.' This usually happens in a life-threatening situation...someone dies and you're left feeling helpless. You have flashbacks or dreams in which you relive the experience...or you purposely avoid anything that reminds you of the experience. You're easily upset and worry a lot.

"We spot your adjustments and help you recognize and avoid more dangerous situations. If the adjustments don't go away after weeks or months, or get more pronounced, you will need our help. Depression, anxiety, and dissociation are nasty effects to deal with and if you ignore them, they will make your life, and the lives of those around you, miserable—marriages break up, children get neglected, people even try to kill themselves."

Elena took over.

"You and those close to you first have to understand how you got to be so disturbed, what effect it has on you and those who care about you. You and they must be made to realize that it's a sickness which anyone subjected to extremely stressful conditions, can get. We help you resolve your anger, shame, or guilt. Then we teach you how to cope with your memories of the shocking event. Your bad memories may not go away completely, but we can help you make them tolerable.

Alicia stepped in to conclude their lecture.

"We need not tell you that your treatment will be absolutely confidential. We're only interested in finding out enough to treat you. The event which terrorized you is not necessarily important to us. Our job is to figure out how to cure you."

There were many questions from the audience—more than a few relating to the horrors of the ant subversive campaign. Interestingly those remarks came from both perspectives—the perpetrators' and their victims'.

At the end of the day, they were satisfied with the results. The apparent demand for their services was greater than they had imagined. It seemed possible that it could require both of them full-time. Neither of them wanted to become that heavily engaged.

Newly-wed Elena had committed to not be away from her husband in Santiago for more than four weeks at a time. Alicia wasn't sure how she could manage more that four weeks at a time in Tucumán, with Kevin and her children so far away. It all depended on where he could establish a new home for them.

"You know," Alicia theorized "it won't be easy to pinch-hit for each other here. These people will bond with you or with me and won't like being shunted off from one to the other."

"Well, that's just too bad. This will be highly stressful work and without regular respite we'll burn out. When it's all over, I still want to have the mind-set to enjoy life."

"You're right. They'll just have to adjust."

* * *

Alicia could hardly wait to tell Kevin about their successful opening. She was anxious to hear where their future home base would be. Sitting in San Miguel de Tucumán, Los Angeles seemed very far off to her as she waited for the phone to ring.

"Kevin, I've been dying to hear from you."

"How did your open-house go?"

"We scored big on attendance. What's more, they responded intelligently to our presentation and we now have a bunch of appointments for initial consultations."

"That sounds good! What kind of folks showed up?"

"A sampling of people from across the spectrum; some big wigs, lots of small-fry, rich and poor, old and young, mostly females, a few males and even a soldier. Our problem may be too many patients. But tell me what's happening with the company? Will we have to move?" She said anxiously.

"Nothing is certain...what I know, has to be kept between us. A deal is in the making," he said and sketched out what he had learned. "I'm sure that they will offer me the southern hemisphere marketing job. South Africa, Australia, Brazil and Chile are their best growth areas."

"Does that mean we might wind up in Santiago?"

"That's almost too much to hope for, but it's likely."

"Alicia, you seem anxious. What's the matter?"

"I miss you and the children...things Angélica knows nothing about. Living here makes her crawl out of her closet."

"Don't talk like that. To succeed the woman in that new office has to be none other than Alicia de la Rosa!"

"That's what scares me; it could eat me alive. There's so much here waiting to be done and most of it's not easy. I would feel less angst if you were closer to me."

"I'll do what I can. But, you didn't answer me? There's something eating away at you. Is it Angélica?"

"Kevin I'm scared! My only relief from the daily grind, which frequently has dreadful content, is horseback riding in the foothills with Xavier. Riding with him makes every inch of me feel like Angélica. He was much closer to Fernando than I had known and reminds me so much of him that, in my mind's eye, I could mistake one for the other. Angélica didn't become responsible until she fell in love with Fernando. She doesn't understand Alicia's passion for you and discounts it as irrelevant to life in Tucumán. I swear she could seek solace by transferring her love for Fernando to his close friend, Xavier."

"Oh dear, how intense is this feeling?"

"It gets stronger, the longer I stay here in a place which Alicia basically doesn't like or respect."

"When next can you rotate out?" Kevin asked.

"Elena interrupted her honeymoon to come here and should go out first. That will keep me here for another three weeks. How about meeting me in Santiago? I'd like to go with you to the ranch in Patagonia. I'm really on edge without you. To be Alicia consistently, is more than I can manage."

"I can't get there sooner than three weeks from now. Try not to be so frightened...rather think with pride and confidence of what Alicia has already accomplished."

"Please come soon, Kevin!"

* * *

Alicia received her first appointment early the next morning. He had been a soldier and was discharged because of what he described as a nervous breakdown, leaving him unfit for military service.

"What happened to push you over the edge?"

"I was trained by the signal corps in radio communications. I knew nothing about interrogating people and wasn't prepared to torture and mishandle prisoners. They assigned me to a unit at a secret holding center in the gymnasium of the shuttered National University here. Their treatment of the inmates shocked me. My comrades made fun of me for being a sissy and I only lasted a week. To teach me a lesson, I was ordered to join a firing squad to execute prisoners, whom they said, had no further value for them...Using their terminology they were 'marked to be transferred.'"

Alicia used reasoning and intuition to sort out his emotions. She carefully repeated detailed imagining of his trauma while calmly making him feel safe so that he could master his distress. She gradually worked up to the shooting of prisoners by starting with less upsetting events, one piece at a time, in the hope of desensitizing him. She had a problem detaching herself from the fact that Fernando might have been one of the prisoners being put to death.

"Considering the emotions you felt when you saw how people were tortured, could you not bring yourself to see relief in them being killed. In your role as executioner you could be viewed as being merciful," Alicia tried to down-play the key source of his trauma.

"I thought of that too, but it didn't work for me. Think of the grief I was causing their kin," the soldier answered.

"If you hadn't done the shooting, others would have. So why take all of the blame?"

"I saw a firing squad hesitate once. Their commanding officer came up shouting in anger, drew his sidearm and shot three of the prisoners in the back of the neck. Nobody hesitated after that."

"Who was the commander?"

"General Bussi."

"It's obvious to me that you had no choice, and you must stop crucifying yourself for something you couldn't stop?"

"I'd feel better if there was a way for me to make restitution."

"Someday, that may be possible, but for now let's work on reducing your pain. I'll work with you for an hour, twice a week. Come back on Thursday morning at the same time. To be effective we should keep what we do confidential. Bueno?"

"Sí Señora."

Alicia sat dead still for minutes after he left to gain control of her rising anger mixed with empathy for the handsome, masculine soldier.

Several appointments in a much lighter vein went by and she was at peace with herself by the time siesta arrived. She and Elena met and decided to hire an appointment secretary.

* * *

The next morning Alicia saw Elena off on her flight, complete with notes to archive in Kevin's Santiago office, and went off to ride with Xavier. This time, they towed the horse trailer to El Mollar in the foothills west of the city, which offered exquisite terrain for horseback riding.

Their trail took them along a pristine river in a valley rich in vegetation, wild life and birds. They stopped to eat lunch in what appeared to be a campground.

Xavier began describing.

"This was one of many hiding places the Marxist rebels used when the Army came to take back the province. These hills are full of places like this. They'd hide here during the day and launch their attacks on the troops at night."

"How many of them were there?" she asked.

"That's hard to say. They came from Chile, Uruguay and Brazil. I heard some of them say they came all the way from Peru. The Army was well-directed and probably killed most of them, perhaps two or three hundred."

"Did the rebels have strong support in San Miguel?" Alicia asked.

"The radicals believed Trotsky's theory that socialism has to be established throughout the world by a non-stop revolution. They were fanatics, sounding like bunch of pumped-up evangelists promising the poor, a carefree, abundant life if they'd follow them. They had strong support from farm labor unions and promised to confiscate all the farms and give them to 'the people' to run. They actually did take some of the farms and gave them to the workers to run," Xavier said.

"How did the workers do?"

"They made a mess. None of them knew how to run a farm."

"Xavier, after these rebels were taken out, how many more civilians, would you say, were killed in Tucumán?"

"You were here and saw what was going on. Nobody knows—I'd say they probably 'disappeared' about five hundred people," Xavier said.

"Where were you when all this happened?" She asked.

Johan Wassenaar

"I was hiding in the mountains. On many of my rides with other people, including Fernando, we ran across left-over rebels still hoping to come back. They were anxious to talk about their ideals and why we should support them. They didn't attack us and allowed us to leave freely. So I figured the men of the Junta would suspect us of being rebel sympathizer. They caught many of the rebels and tortured them to tell who their supporters were. Under torture, people will say anything to stop the pain. I was afraid they would use my name," Xavier explained.

"Did they?"

"I don't know, but I always had the feeling that they used Fernando's name."

"Was that the reason they arrested him?"

"Not the only reason. Fernando was more liberal-minded than most of his peers. Intellectually, he was more curious. Perhaps Military Intelligence considered him to be a socialist," Xavier concluded.

"Was it a crime to be a socialist?"

"I don't think you understand how arbitrary the whole process of 'ideological cleansing' was."

"I know exactly, but why? What's the sense of murdering as many innocents as guilty people, if, with a little more care, the innocents could be spared?"

"I think the hard-liners saw the chaos as an opportunity to get rid of their worst political enemies. I can understand that attitude. Peron's regimes had a history of corruption and political instability."

"At least he was democratic," she defended.

"I guess some of us Spaniards have short memories. 'Colonel' Perón was one of the coup leaders that ousted the constitutional government in forty-three. If anything, he was a shit-disturber who organized mass protests to make him famous enough to win the election in forty-six. He formed the General Confederation of Labor and nationalized industries left, right and center. If it hadn't been for Evita, I don't think he would have been popular enough to last. Three years after she died, a Junta had to take over and exile him to Spain," Xavier set the record straight.

"If I remember my history correctly," Alicia fought back, "the governments during the sixties got nowhere; the economy suffered and terrorism from the ERP and left-wing Montoneros, got out of hand. I don't think anyone can deny that Perón won the election in seventy-three. That's why I think of him as a democrat," Alicia rationalized.

"That win didn't matter. He died less than a year later, leaving us in a terrible mess with Isabel in charge. That's when the Revolutionary Army of the People really began showing up in these mountains. They came armed with Ché Guevara's philosophy that Latin America was ready for revolution. 'All it needed was a small dedicated corps to begin armed action, and the masses would follow.' They used their cousins, the Workers' Revolutionary Party, and with the Chilean and Uruguayan Communists, formed something they called the Revolutionary Coordination Junta and took over large portions of Tucumán and Salta provinces."

"I remember that, because it put us at the top of the military's list to be 'liberated'," she agreed.

"Yes and how! They sent the Army's top General up here to kick the Communists out and he really went to town. We couldn't ride up here for ten months while they unearthed them," he exclaimed.

"The problem, it seems to me," she said "was that they didn't know when to stop. When the Junta took over the government, they just kept going and instead of fighting terrorist rebels, they began terrorizing their own citizens. I can see no sense in them destroying Fernando!"

"I totally agree. Before we get too serious, let's ride further up into the mountains."

It was a wonderful recreational experience to ride in the beautiful hills and by the time they'd trailered their horses back to the stable in San Miguel, Alicia felt rejuvenated and ready to face her difficult task ahead. She had gained a lot of respect for Xavier and warmed to him as she learned more about him. In her youth she had dated him a few times and they had made love. As she remembered, he was one of her "hot" ones.

The first week in business had taught her a lot and her confidence level was growing. As the tension diminished, her mind shifted to her children and Kevin, who she devoutly missed. It was comfortable here amongst family and friends, but she longed to be with her own. Oddly, she missed Los Angeles. It was the most progressive, diverse and adaptable city she'd ever lived in. Its vitality constantly astounded her.

CHAPTER EIGHTEEN

The restructuring of Kevin's company was settled. He was co-opted to serve on the steering committee to draw up plans for the three-way consolidation.

To him, living with Alicia in Los Angeles had been like a dream. He enjoyed Santiago, too, and knew how much at home Alicia felt there. He explained all of this to her in their next daily call. She responded with an audible sigh of relief.

"You don't know how hard I prayed that you would wind up with your headquarters in Santiago. The situation here is turning out to be hectic and commuting to Los Angeles between four-week sessions would have been impossible. Suddenly, that full day of travel each way will now become a two and a half hour flight. I also like the idea of using Santiago as an escape hatch if things get too hot here. When will you be able to move?"

"I hope to get down there to do some scouting in a month's time. The ultimate move may have to wait for several months. But, that's unimportant. Tell me, how are things going?"

"On the whole, I think we're ahead of schedule. I didn't expect such a high level of interest. I have a notion that the term 'Post-trauma Therapy' got their attention. I hope so, because it allows us to concentrate on patients with more serious needs. Elena took off for Santiago and will be relieving me about the time you said you'd come to Santiago. I hope we'll have time to do something special together."

"You know, I've been thinking. For the next several months, I'll be very busy with the organizational chores here in Century City. Perhaps it would be better if I brought the children with me and took them to stay with Elvira for a while where they will have time with you. Instead of going down to Roberto's ranch for a mini-vacation, we could go on our own pack-trip into your mountains. That way I'd have the chance of getting to know your father-in-law."

"That's a good idea. Give me time to think about it. I want to make sure that it won't complicate my professional situation here. They gossip a lot, and bringing you into the picture may confuse them."

"We could vacation in Tafi Del Valle and go riding where you go with Xavier and beyond. That way, only a few people need to know about my visit."

"I would love you to come here. It would help me feel less divided. When I'm here on my own, I often wind up feeling like Angélica. Your visit here would help me to associate more of San Miguel with you."

"Is it that bad?"

"It tears me apart. I had a good life here. They had no right to take it away from me. You saved me and made me see a whole new way. I so want to be true to it and to you. But, when I'm living here, I can almost smell the past. When Xavier began reminiscing about their times together, Alicia felt like an intruder into Fernando's legacy."

"There's no reason to feel conflict between your devotion to me and your love for Fernando. You're not responsible for his disappearance and I share your sorrow over losing him. I'm part of you."

"That's not the point. Angélica owes no loyalty to Kevin and if left to her own devices, could do dreadful harm to Alicia's relationship with him. She has a provincial outlook on life. She doesn't understand that the Marxist rebels would have destroyed Argentina had the Army not prevented it. When the ant subversive campaign began, she won't accept that the soldiers couldn't tell a Communist conspirator from a funeral director...That they made up for it with brute force trying to get the rebels they captured to tell them who their supporters were...That they knew nothing about persuasive techniques to get information and just beat everyone they arrested until they told them the names of some 'conspirators'. To stop the beating, the victims just told them any old names which made the numbers of 'suspects' soar, making the number of rebels look falsely huge. So the soldiers got tougher, making the number of 'suspects' grow even faster, until the vicious cycle spun out of control. This concept is just not within Angélica's grasp.

"Thank God, it ended here sooner. Sometimes I just don't know what to think anymore. I already know that there will be trauma patients from both sides of the conflict."

"We knew all along that it would be difficult, but in the end it will come down to the immoral cruelty the Junta inflicted on its citizens. There is no way to justify its torture and brutal slaughter of thousands of innocent people."

"I so wish you could be here. Why do we have to live separate lives? Is this God's way of punishing me?" she asked as she began losing her composure and put the phone down.

* * *

Alicia's Monday dawned with a full schedule of consultations booked in advance.

Her first patient was a woman about her own age, who had been abducted and sent to the "secret" detention center in Famaillá where Fernando was last seen. This prototype of secret detention centers was located in a small deserted rural school. It held up to forty prisoners and became the model for other secret centers used during the "ant subversive" operation.

The woman complained about experiencing recurring nightmares causing her sleepless nights.

"What do you dream about?" Alicia asked.

"It's always the same dream," she responded. "I once saw them bury a naked prisoner alive. They left his head poking out and stamped the wet earth tightly around his body, leaving him there for two whole days. After the first day, the poor man began yelling from the painful cramps in his legs. The cell I was in was so close that we could hear him crying out all night long. That's what I dream about—that and about him being executed by a firing squad."

"Did you see the firing squad shoot him?" Alicia asked.

"In my dream, the officers use hand guns. I can see no ordinary soldiers—the General fires the first shot."

"Where do they do this?"

"Behind a munitions building in the trees, after lunch."

"How many people did they kill?"

"I can't see. Two or three."

"Are you sure this is only a dream?"

"I dream it, but I also saw them do it twice."

"How did you get out of there alive?"

"I was useless to them. After two weeks they drove me to the edge of town and dropped me by the roadside."

"Were you tortured?"

"Everyone was tortured, some more than others."

"How did they torture you?"

"They took my clothes off and beat me with wooden paddles until my buttocks were on fire. Then they poured cold water over me, tied my arms and legs and threatened to shock me with electrodes while they questioned me. I couldn't see any of them. They put a hood over my head."

"What else did they do?"

"Just to show whose boss, they raped me."

"Were you tortured often?"

"I was lucky. They saw that I knew nothing and they ignored me. I got less food, but it gave me hope."

"So, your real trauma was the torture of that man, and the executions?"

"Yes, I think it will haunt me all of my life."

"When you got out, how was your life changed?"

"My friends shunned me; treated me like a criminal. My boyfriends avoided me. It made me feel like a prostitute—a soiled person."

"What about your family?"

"I knew they loved me, but they had reservations. It was as if I had cancer or something."

"Can you come back here for regular therapy starting next week?"

"Yes, next Monday, the same time?"

"*Bueno*. How would your parents feel about talking to you with me in a special session?"

"I don't know. They are skeptical about psychological treatment. I'll ask them."

* * *

Alicia's appointment secretary drew her attention to signs that their practice could be under surveillance. From her position at the reception desk she could see across the street and had noticed a nondescript man leaning against a lamp post until just before someone entered the building or just after someone had left when he would stand erect to make notes in a small note book or sometimes cross the street as if to address or confront the person entering or leaving. However, so far there had been no complaints from their patients. As an extra precaution the receptionist took it upon herself to question arriving patients in oblique fashion about their ease of access to the building and the stairwell leading to their consulting rooms. She found no evidence of any form of obstruction. Yet the man continued his watch.

Alicia had just wound up an exploratory consultation with the wife of an Army officer who was distraught about her husband's change in personality after he was forced to participate in the torture and execution of prisoners. According to her, he began treating her disrespectfully and losing his patience with their children more often. Alicia saw this potentially as a valid case that could help her get in with the military hierarchy and had invited her back for therapy.

The receptionist's news seemed that much more jarring against the backdrop of her sympathy with the officer's wife.

The more she thought about the new threat, the more anxious she got, until she simply had to excuse herself to seek help. Without thinking, she drove out to the stables to seek Xavier's counsel. Her mood was dramatically less secure than that of Alicia and she could feel herself slide into a response more like that of Angélica.

"Xavier! I'm scared to death. There's someone watching me. I know what happens when they interrogate people! You have to help me, please!"

Instinctively, he held his arms open to welcome her and without hesitation she embraced him, looking up to plead for his protection.

"Easy now. Calm down angel...tell me what happened."

Haltingly she told him about the surveillance of their practice.

"Please, find out what they're after...I have to know!" She said clinging tightly to his body as he embraced her in return.

"Relax little one, it may just be some bureaucrat from the city trying to assess your business."

"Do you really think so...Oh, I so hope that's all it is. Please hold me, I'm so dreadfully scared."

He tightened his embrace and as he looked down into her fear-stricken eyes she pulled herself up to kiss him. It brought back memories of their brief romance when she was too young to give it meaning and he responded by kissing her with surprising passion.

They grew bolder, had to sit down on the nearest bale of hay and were soon helping each other shed clothes. Their excitement grew to frantic proportions as he went down on her until she grabbed him and guided him into her. Their intercourse grew almost desperate as he turned her over and entered her from behind. She shrieked with delight encouraging him to quicken the pace until they erupted in uninhibited orgasms.

Lying limply on the hay bales he assured her that he would use his influence to determine why they were watching her.

"Come back here tomorrow evening and I'll tell you what I've learned."

* * *

She pulled herself together to keep her lunch date with her in-laws.

"Suegro, do you have any idea how many people were taken in Tucumán?"

"In the war to expel the Marxists in seventy-four, –five and -six, they killed at least a hundred and fifty rebels. I don't think they took more than five hundred civilians during the ant subversive campaign—that's about one person out of every hundred people. Why do you ask?"

"There are signs that we're being watched down at the office. Xavier says it could just be someone from the City trying to assess our business. What do you think?"

"I would say that they have a political motive and that it's someone from the intelligence branch trying to get some idea of who your patients are. The person watching...is he armed?"

"I don't think so. He's not in uniform and mostly makes notes in a little book."

"Your patients...do they have a particular characteristic?"

"No, they come from all walks of life and many of them are related to officials or are soldiers themselves."

Johan Wassenaar

"Then I wouldn't worry too much. Just make sure to keep an eye on them. But tell me, how is your program coming along?"

"I'm mainly interested in the suffering of innocent people. There can be no excuse for their murder—not that I don't also see the death of the others as a crime, it's just that Fernando's death must have real meaning for me."

"I admire your struggle and hope you'll succeed. It has great meaning for me too. Things are getting better now, but until the Junta ends, there's no hope of reconciliation."

"Are you ready to meet Kevin?"

"How can I not be ready? I'd have to be blind, not to see what he's done for you. Is he coming soon?"

"In about three weeks. He doesn't want to be noticed in San Miguel. He says it will draw too much attention to what I'm doing. So, we plan to go into the mountains around Tafi del Valle and ride through the high, open grassland. He says he wants to see the Inca ruins at Quilmes. He's bringing Carlos and Maria to visit you and Elvira. He also wants to spend time with you."

"Will I like him?"

"I think so. He's a passionate man with great ambition."

* * *

She kept wondering about Xavier the whole next day. Even in her role as Alicia she couldn't find that much wrong with seeking his sympathy in her moments as Angélica and promoting its development into a sexual interlude. It had come quite naturally to Angélica considering her prior affair with him and his close association with Fernando, which, in her mind, made the two virtually interchangeable with one another. Alicia couldn't condone her conduct and almost panicked at the thought of how she would explain it to Kevin.

However, that had to wait until the surveillance matter was resolved and she looked forward to her meeting at the barn with Xavier.

He was waiting for her in the living room of the bunkhouse where he lived and had made obvious preparations to receive her, such as wearing a clean shirt and being freshly shaven.

"Sit down and let me get you a drink. What will it be?"

"Thanks, a beer would taste good right now. So, what did you find out about the snoop looking over my shoulder?"

"He works for the Feds and keeps tabs on the legitimacy of small businesses to make sure that they're not used with a political agenda adverse to the regime."

"So, how do I handle the situation? Our practice involves sick people of all kinds, including family members of key administrators."

"To you it may look even-handed, but to them, they'll be wondering about patients who are related to their victims. I wouldn't put it past them to track those kinds of people and even to interrogate and scare them off."

"Oh my God, that could have dreadful consequences. I have patients on both sides of the fence who were seriously traumatized and all my hard work to bring them back to some state of normalcy would instantly be washed away were they interrogated. Please, is there something you can do to prevent that from happening?"

"I'll try, but don't expect miracles."

"Xavier, please stop them. I can't bear the thought of seeing my life's work go down the drain...and if that happens they will probably kill me too. You must stop them, please!" she said in panic as she hugged him purposely.

"Stay calm little one, just give me time to arrange things...I'll have to take risks which I'd normally avoid." He replied as he put his arm around her to comfort her.

She came willingly and began kissing him with great urgency. He picked her up and carried her into his bedroom to resume their sexual exploration of each other.

* * *

Elena returned and Alicia brought her up to date. She had signed up twelve deserving patients for regular treatment and many more irregular clients. Seven of the regular ones suffered from trauma relating to the "Dirty War".

They sat down to review each case in detail to agree on the best treatment for each. Elena had regained her verve and was anxious to go to work when Alicia broke the bad news of being watched.

"Just when one thinks things couldn't be worse, they get worse. So what are we to do?"

"I've got Xavier working on putting a cork in their bottle."

"Xavier, your trainer! Shit, I remember when we both made love to him. He was a hot one."

"He found out who was watching our office and why. Now he has to stick his neck out a long way to get them to quit."

"Why would he go that far for you? As I remember, he was quite vain about his looks and how people perceived him."

"He was a very close friend of Fernando's."

"Yes, I remember him telling me that he planned to introduce Fernando to you so we could play a round as a foursome."

"Is that what he said? Fernando would never have gone along with that sort of thing!"

"Look it wasn't easy for me to get into living here again. I was shocked by some of the things our patients told me. It made me furious all over again. But, then the professional in me came to the rescue and I could see things more objectively. I admit that I look forward to my time off and having Kevin and the children here with me next week."

"Kevin's coming *here*! Isn't that like waving a red flag at a bull?"

"No," Alicia explained. He's bringing my children to stay with their grandmother. He and I are going into the mountains to stay on a private ranch. He'll be invisible to San Miguel's townspeople. Besides, he did business with a number of our influential land owners in Tucumán and in itself, seeing him here won't raise too many suspicions. We just don't want my professional name linked to him."

"I still think it's a risk we could do without," Elena concluded.

"If you knew what he did to keep me alive you'd feel better about him visiting me. He's on a first-name basis with the Air Force's top General and has powerful connections in the Navy. He came back to Argentina more than once during the worst part of seventy-six. He knows how to keep his nose clean."

"If he's so great, why do you carry on a relationship with a guy like Xavier? I know what he's after and you will probably give it to him."

"If he can stop the guy with the notebook, it may be worth it."

"With a man like Kevin on your team, you really surprise me."

They worked together for the week to make Elena familiar with their patients and to handle the growing load of first-time consultations, which they were still providing at low rates. It was becoming obvious that their generosity was being exploited and that they would have to charge higher fees. For truly needy cases, they could always make exceptions.

Much to their relief, after the third day of Elena's stay, the surveillance man stopped coming.

On average, about half of their patients were "Dirty War" casualties and their insight into what went on in the secret detention centers was rapidly increasing. With it came the profound challenge of inventing the proper therapeutic treatments for them. Their experiences were too horrible to appear in any textbook.

Without being calloused, they had to adapt to hearing the terrible details without being provoked. Their response became like that of an emergency physician in a triage center.

* * *

Kevin arrived unexpectedly on a private plane of one of the mining companies in Chile. He'd been to Chuquicamata and had run into a colleague who was on his way to Jujuy. Kevin accepted eagerly, since Maria posed a logistics problem for him.

When he arrived unannounced at the Diaz' front door, Elvira was overjoyed to see her grandchildren. Seeing the affection in her greeting, Dr. Diaz responded warmly to Kevin. There was much to talk about and they asked many questions, but he longed to see Alicia and soon persuaded them to take him to her. She was involved in a consultation with Elena and he was asked by their receptionist, who had no way of recognizing him, to take a seat. He waited patiently until the end of their consultation when he could hear the receptionist announcing that she had a visitor. Her surprise at seeing him was more than gratifying. She fell into his arms and kissed him with abandon.

"Oh Kevin, you sneaked up on me! I didn't expect you until tomorrow. Come, you must meet Elena," she said, dragging him through the doorway.

"This is the savior you've heard so much about," she introduced Kevin.

There followed the kind of polite conversation that occurs when minds are set on other things. He couldn't wait to be with her alone and urged her to take him home with her.

Even in the car, he began touching her as she drove with purpose and by the time they were indoors, he had her half undressed. She came eagerly to him and they made love passionately on the carpet in the living room. It began with delicate foreplay. They couldn't do enough to show their affection and climaxed repeatedly until they both lay limp on the floor.

"You've no idea how much I missed you. The house seems empty without you, in spite of the children demanding my attention. I didn't know how to imagine you here. All I could see was your face," Kevin confessed.

"What I missed most was your advice and encouragement. This has not been easy duty, but I'm getting used to it now. In the end, they're all just ordinary people with the usual weaknesses, no matter which side they're on. The trauma to the perpetrator is just as real as that of the victim. That's where I get confused sometimes and crave your advice."

"You are incredibly brave and enterprising. Few people would understand what you're doing. Maybe only doctor Diaz will know. To me, the premise always comes down to the dignity with which we treat each other. Argentina is not alone in having to learn how important that is."

"Let's just forget all that heavy stuff for now. I have you all to myself for as long as you can stay. On Monday we're going off with Xavier to the Calchaquí Valley high up above the forests with three of the best horses you've ever seen. We'll be staying with good friends on a ranch."

"Can we take Carlos? Ever since our trip to Colorado, he's so hyped-up about horses."

"Here comes Mister Hilton Hotel. I guess we can do that for Carlos—Xavier would like it. He was so close to Fernando. I'm so happy that you've bonded with Carlos."

"Speaking of hotels, how's the baby doing?"

"Everything looks fine. I think it's a boy. I want to call him 'Santiago.'"

"Are you sure that it's OK to do all that riding?"

"Sure, it'll be fine for another month or two."

"Say, we had better go. Dr. Diaz seems anxious to talk to me."

"Can I make a suggestion?"

"Go ahead."

"Call him by his first name, Arnoldo. He's not that much older than you."

"Next you'll be calling me 'Old Man'"

"After what you just did to me, that day's still a long way off."

* * *

Kevin was right. Dr. Diaz was eager to have a conversation with both of them and invited them to join him in his study. The first thing Kevin noticed was his 1944 Harvard Law School degree on the wall behind his desk. He went over to look at it and remarked in English, "Would you mind if we spoke English and if I addressed you as 'Arnold?'"

"Not at all, but I thought you were fluent in Spanish."

"I am, but I thought that you and Alicia would welcome a chance to practice your English vocabulary...that's just a joke. It would make it more difficult for people listening to understand us."

"I wanted to talk to you about why Argentina has so many social problems," Dr. Diaz began. "I often wondered why its style of government and approach to personal relationships tries so hard to tell people what to think; why it stifles individual choice and personal responsibility; why it loves authoritarian hierarchies; why it remains so strictly Catholic and frankly, snobbish. It is, after all, a constitutional republic.

"But then all of Latin America shares that problem," Dr. Diaz went on. "We modernized in the twentieth century, but our fundamental attitudes, beliefs, and sentiments, born of three-centuries of Spanish rule, didn't change that much. In spite of institutional boundaries between civilian and military segments, our military continues to reflect the society from which it came. Many non-Latinos blame the military for this."

"And why shouldn't they," Kevin asked "if military intervention in politics ends up being predatory and corrupt, usurping constitutional government and looking like permanent enemies of the people?"

"No the problem goes deeper," Dr. Diaz continued. "Don't forget our constitutional arrangements enshrine a powerful chief executive who is relatively immune to opposition from the elected legislature and the courts. We place political power in the hands of one or few leaders—in the way the Spanish ran things from the top."

"What you're saying is that this heritage makes it acceptable to do things without democratic consent of the governed. So it's OK to seize and maintain power through military intervention?" Kevin questioned.

"I'm not defending it, but that's been our history. It became our custom to change power not just by elections, but by coups, revolts, revolutions, strikes or heroic acts."

"Yes," Kevin agreed. "Argentina's democracy isn't rooted in successive waves of people, such as ours is in the States."

"Yes," Arnold agreed "we lack a mature political culture; one that guarantees civil supremacy over the military and outlaws the use of force."

"So, what are we fighting for, if it can't be changed?" Alicia asked.

"That's a good point." Kevin answered. "In my opinion, the Junta went too far this time. What they've done, can never be swept under the rug. The Mothers of the Plaza de Mayo have begun building that resistance. When they first demonstrated in front of the Presidential Palace, no one dared support them. People wouldn't even acknowledge when their own children disappeared. They were too scared to say anything when they saw young people and even children being taken away. The 'Mothers' kept gathering every Thursday at the Plaza de Mayo. Even the brutal murder of two of their founders didn't stop them. Now it's beginning to snowball."

"I agree with Kevin, that the shock of the 'Dirty War'—the fact that so many innocents were murdered—will live in Argentina's memory until it searches its soul to avoid having it happen again. It isn't a one-sided game of 'them' and 'us'. *We* are the enemy, *all of us*," Arnold added. "To take effect permanently, everyone has to know what happened—how abject brutality was made commonplace. That can't happen until the Junta leaves office."

"When will that be?" Alicia asked.

"No one knows. I would guess three to five years."

"That's still a long time for a mother of children to be perched on a sack of dynamite," Alicia protested.

"That's not all, my child," Arnold added. "It may take several more years for constitutional government to clear the way for charges to be brought against military officers. The publicity will help, but the public won't believe it until it's recorded under oath in a court of law."

"Suegro, I'll be old and gray by then!" Alicia complained.

"By the way, since we have proven that we communicate well with each other in English, keep doing it. It will reduce the chance of being overheard," Kevin reiterated.

"Right now conditions are relatively peaceful."

"Don't be too sure," Kevin cautioned. "Some of the wealthy land barons here think they're Napoleon and are quite capable of doing their own horrid deeds."

CHAPTER NINETEEN

Argentina's future didn't seem important as Kevin, Xavier, and Alicia set out towing a stock trailer seventy miles up the mountain pass to the mile-high Tafi Del Valle.

They climbed up along the Sosa River and gradually the forest thinned and turned from green to wild, drought-resistant, vegetation. Their destination was a ranch situated in a subtropical wilderness with high area forests and a wide variety of seasonal flowers.

Given its rich natural resources, the political plight of Argentina at that moment seemed absurd.

* * *

The ranch was reminiscent of the one Alicia and Kevin loved so much in southern Chile. The family members were all involved in running it.

Alicia was assigned to help start green horses, little Carlos to help feed baby goats and Kevin to join the stable crew. By siesta, they were essentially part of the family.

Alicia looked forward to the luxury of a nap, which she'd had to forego most of the time in San Miguel. Kevin's biological clock didn't come with siesta provisions and he made a nuisance of himself.

"You'll wear me out," she complained. "I'm still sore from yesterday."

"At least I know that you weren't playing around in all your leisure time."

"You're getting fresh again. Remember what happened in Patagonia?"

"Is that a threat or a promise?"

"This time you do the driving," she volunteered and held out her wrists to be tied.

He teased her mercilessly until she was writhing and then gradually brought her to just short of her boiling point, before releasing her. She kissed him wildly before firmly guiding him into her. It took a long time before they climaxed.

"Oh God, I love you so. Please don't die on me?" she whispered.

"You're the one who has to stay alive. I hope we're not underestimating our enemies. Please maintain your image of total impartiality."

"That's easier than I thought. I find myself having as much empathy for the soldiers and soldiers' wives who come to see me, as I do for their victims. In fact, some of the victims aren't real victims. They went to war with Argentina and got killed."

"It's time to go riding. Get your things while I hunt for Xavier. He's a fine man and a good friend to have, but to be on the safe side, don't confide in him."

* * *

Xavier laid out their riding plan.

"We'll start up the winding road to the high valleys and spend the first night near Amaicha Del Valle. Then we'll go into the Quilmes valley and spend the night amongst the ruins before returning along a fabulous cross-country route I know of."

"Those ruins are supposed to be an archaeological marvel. I've been told, they clearly display how complex the Inca architecture had become," Kevin pontificated.

"It must have been an impressive citadel," Xavier agreed. "It held back the Spanish for more than a century. Sadly, they were uprooted and marched all the way to Buenos Aires. Only few of them survived."

Overhearing their conversation Alicia cut in.

"I can see that you guys don't know much about the Incas. Since I studied their history and know how much garbage has been printed about them, let me give you a running commentary as we go along.

"What's the road like to that first village?" Kevin asked Xavier.

"It's a dirt road up a steep pass called the 'Little Hell's Pass.' The town lies in the high valley beyond the pass. It's just a native village...very primitive. The first day will be a hard ride. I wouldn't take Carlos along, if I were you."

"What will we do with him while we're away?"

"The Herrera's volunteered to look after him," Alicia answered.

"When did they do that?"

"At lunch," she replied. "I knew you'd be crazy enough to want to go all that way on horseback."

"Is that too far for you?"

"No." She answered with an attitude, "It's just silly to ride all that way when we could go there so easily by car."

"I thought we came here to have fun and get away from civilization...have some peace of mind for a change." Kevin countered.

She responded with resentment.

"What peace is there for me in this God-forsaken country where I don't even know who I am?"

"Would you rather stay quietly on the ranch?"

"No. With both you and Xavier around, that would be worse."

"Alicia, what's the matter? I've been dying for a chance to be together with you again. That's what we both said we craved."

"When you're here with me in purgatory, I see double. Alicia loves you, but Angélica won't let a foreigner into her heart. To her you are an intruder."

"How long has this been going on?"

"Since I began riding with Xavier. That's when Angélica first came to the fore. She resented you for stealing my heart, which belonged to Fernando and Tucumán. She prefers Xavier. He's part of Fernando's legacy and her friend."

"Had I known, I'd have taken you to Patagonia."

"That would have been a band aid. I would still have to confront her daily, back here."

"That problem will take time to solve. In the meantime, let's see how Carlos is getting on."

"You really care about him, don't you?"

"Yes, he's a wonderful little chap with heaps of talent."

"You're not just biased, are you?" She asked.

"Would that make you jealous?"

"I wake up in a cold sweat at times, dreaming of losing your affection."

"Why is that?"

"You only know Alicia. You've never spent time with Angélica. She can be unprincipled and doesn't feel obliged to repay you for your incredible magnanimity to Alicia. I'll try to make life easier by letting Alicia handle your crazy ride."

* * *

The ride up to the ruins went through spectacular, open, high country. Xavier guided them onto a trail commonly used by ranchers. They trotted until they reached the Little Hell's Pass which switched back and forth up the steep mountain slope and stopped at the summit to rest and water the horses. It was late afternoon when they rode into small native village and set up camp for the night. Their conversation had been constrained on the ride and they turned in rather early.

The second day's ride to the Quilmes ruins was less arduous. It went through country reminiscent of an Arizona desert with lots of cactus and drought resistant plants. Even the topography resembled that of Arizona with spectacular terra cotta, wind-eroded cliffs and mountain ranges. The scene at the ruins was even more so, complete with Yucca trees shaped like candle sticks.

The terraced foundations of the citadel lay cradled in a bowl against the barren, rocky Alto del Rey Mountain where the Quilmes defended themselves with arrows, stones and catapults from two high fortresses at the north and south ends. Dry-stone walls surrounded the citadel and were thick enough to serve as causeways.

Alicia explained.

"This was an important place in the Pre-Columbian Inca culture. It was one of their most sacred valleys on the continent."

"Then, why aren't they still here?"

"That's not funny. Since you're a smart-ass engineer, it would perhaps capture your admiration when you see the network of irrigation canals, dams, ditches and water reservoirs they built. It rivals those designed by Leonardo da Vinci!"

"What's with the animosity? I know that they were talented, brave people, but they were also given to pagan ideas of brutal conquest. My point is that their civilization lacked the breadth to survive. The only reason it took so long for the Spanish to defeat them, was not that they were invincible, but more likely because someone in Spain theorized that there was gold in this valley."

Alicia protested angrily.

"The Spanish didn't have to march them eight hundred miles to Buenos Aires."

"The Spanish only did what Incas customarily did with their vanquished," Kevin countered.

Alicia decided to break the tension.

"Why are we arguing? These people lived here for five centuries and created a sophisticated, all-encompassing civilization, remarkably advanced for its time. Their demise is a loss to all mankind."

"I'm sorry, Alicia. We must be tired. Let's see what we can find around here to eat."

They found a tourist campground with some amenities and a place where they could take care of the horses. There also was a small cantina, still open after the tourist season, where they could sample the local Indian cuisine.

They spent the afternoon walking through the ruins, enjoying the expansive views from the stepped citadel.

They made a small campfire beside which they spread their bedrolls and sat down to talk, but the atmosphere remained confrontational.

* * *

On their way home, they went cross-country through a spectacular pass bypassing the ancient village and leading directly to the Sosa River. It was very rough, steep terrain and they were glad to reach the forested banks of the river where there was good grazing for the horses and an excellent campsite.

Once they were settled and had a fire going, Xavier began explaining the origin of the site.

"The Marxist Revolutionary Army came down the mountains along rivers like this one and hid in the dense vegetation while they prepared to invade Tucumán and Salta provinces. This was one of their favorite sites."

"How big was the rebel army?" Kevin asked.

"There were fewer rebels than the Army expected to find. There probably wasn't more than four hundred '*Companheiros*', as they called each other. But, they were well trained by the Russians to infiltrate lightly defended places. Then they started campaigns in the towns to spread their Trotsky propaganda. They used Ché Guevara's speeches...he was their folk-hero."

"Are you suggesting that they were less than sincere?" Alicia asked.

"Like all politicians, they just wanted power. This wasn't the first time that power was seized through revolutionary uprising. The whole idea formed the basis of Guevara's platform."

"How do you know so much about them?" Kevin asked. "Almost no one in Buenos Aires even knew about the Communist takeover of Tucumán and Salta."

"Isabel Peron's government didn't want to encourage the spread of the revolution and kept it quite," Xavier answered. "My career has been to ride up here in the mountains as a guide or as a Gaucho. I know these valleys very well and stumbled upon the rebels many times. They knew that I was familiar and tried to befriend me. I kept my distance, but they were armed and some of them looked fanatical, so I just did what any Samaritan would do and continued on my way," Xavier explained.

"What kind of help did you give them?" asked Kevin.

"Small things...like where to cross the river safely, where to get fruit and things to eat, and so on."

"Did they ask you where the Army was?"

"Yes, but I didn't know."

"Did they swear you to secrecy?"

"They didn't have to. I made it obvious that I was private."

"The military...did they seek your help?"

"They stopped me from time to time, but I just played dumb. When they started coming after civilians, I left town."

"Did you meet any of the top rebels?"

"They didn't wear their ranks on their shirts, but later when the 'wanted' posters began appearing, I recognized a few of their faces. I later heard that they'd all been caught and executed in Buenos Aires and Córdoba."

"Who told you?" Kevin asked.

"The owner of the ranch...my employer. He had friends in the military."

"Did your boss have any idea why and where they took Fernando?"

"Fernando was a civilian. He wasn't a prisoner of war. My boss knew nothing about that side."

"Do <u>you</u> have any idea why they took him?"

"Fernando was open in his dealings with people. When we ran into rebels, he'd introduce himself. I never mentioned my name. The Army caught many of those guys and tortured them to say who their sympathizers were. They might have given them Fernando's name."

"But, he didn't collaborate with them, did he?"

"No, they just used his name to stop the torture. They couldn't leak the names of their Companheiros. That would have been dishonorable."

"What more do you know that you haven't told us?" Alicia asked.

"I keep no secrets from you, Angélica, but there are two things I didn't tell you."

"And what were they?" she asked impatiently.

"First, I didn't tell you that most of the trail we rode over the mountain today was once an Inca road. I didn't want to steal your thunder, but right where you are sitting, is as far to the east as the Incas probably ever came. They were mountain people. Like me, that's where they felt safe. I share your admiration for them. They built stone buildings like no one had ever seen and ran an empire of many millions without a written language. Modern Argentineans have a long way to go to be as good as they were."

"What was the other thing you didn't tell us?" Kevin asked.

"The last time I stopped here, a few years ago, this place was littered with rebel bodies. They'd been ambushed by the Army. It was a hot day and the bodies were bloated. I didn't linger to count, but there must have been more than ten of them. From the cartridge casings, up above where the soldiers had been, I could tell that they had used one or two thirty-caliber machine guns. By the tracks they left, they had no more than six horses. It must have been an efficient operation. I was surprised. It showed that Videla and Bliss had come with crack battalions and were serious about quickly defeating the rebels."

* * *

After their discordant, long ride, they were happy to be back in the comfort of the ranch and Kevin could seriously address Alicia.

"We have to talk about our future together and our living arrangements. Your unfriendly manner on this ride...pushing me away whenever we were in Xavier's company, pissed me off. It felt as if you had led him to believe that our relationship was casual and non-binding...that there was room for romance in it for him. I haven't come this far with you to see you throw in the towel and revert to being Angélica. That would be the kiss of death for you. Alicia has to learn to discipline her weak sister ego or you will have to leave Tucumán for good."

"Please don't be so angry with me. I didn't hide the fact that Angélica presents me with a huge problem. When she takes over, you just don't matter to me...she only cares about her own gratification. I also warned you that she could hardly distinguish between Fernando and Xavier."

"I guess then that we'll just have to reduce your stays up here to a bare minimum. Our other problem is Carlos. He was doing well in kindergarten and is losing that edge here in this backward burg. We have to take him to Santiago. Eduardo Gil-Gomez, the guy I hired to replace me, says that they've opened an American school for the children of the foreigners helping re-establish the Chilean economy. Two of his children go there."

"He loves being here with Elvira, but I can see your point. As for our relationship...I couldn't make it without you and could never love anyone like I love you. I will have to work that much harder to keep Angélica in chains. It would certainly help if you lived in Santiago and I rotated out weekly. Where does that possibility stand?"

"I'm still not a hundred percent sure of my job situation, but everything keeps moving in the direction of Santiago."

"You know that I was happy living in Santiago and for the reasons you just rattled off, I can't live here. Things may seem calm on the surface, but that could change in an instant. I didn't want to burden you, but up until a few days ago a Federal official sat across the street from our consulting chambers monitoring our patients arriving and leaving."

"What made them stop?"

"I don't know...Xavier somehow fixed it. I want us to rent a place for me and the children like the one we had in Santiago before. When your deal comes through, we'll buy a house in Santiago. I can't be away from you as much as this without having serious Angélica problems. I don't know if you'll ever understand that you simply cannot trust Angélica!"

"Perhaps if I could fly you in my own airplane between Santiago and here we'd seem closer to each other."

"You never told me that you had a plane," she said with a tinge of resentment.

"I don't have one yet, but I'd like to buy one. I want a pressurized plane with two engines that can fly easily across the Andes."

"Is this a gadget to please little boy Kevin?"

"Why are you being so disagreeable? I meant it to be helpful. You must admit, being able to leave here at will and be in Santiago within three hours, makes it seem a lot closer. Besides, I'd use it for business purposes as well. Many of my competitors have company planes. That's how I got to San Miguel this trip."

It was Alicia's turn to apologize.

"I'm sorry. I snapped at you. I didn't mean to. I've been losing my temper far too often. I'm still new to the therapy game and some of what I've had to listen to, comes very close to the bone."

"Perhaps being pregnant doesn't help either. You and Elena will have to relieve each other on shorter cycles." insisted Kevin.

"I've been thinking about that ever since I became so edgy with you and Xavier. You didn't deserve it. It's not like me, Kevin. It makes me very unhappy. You mean everything to me!" she said as she buried her face in his chest.

He took her in his arms carried her to the bunkhouse for a long, well-deserved siesta nap.

Rested and relaxed, Kevin cautiously brought up the subject of her dual personality again.

"I sense that much of the reason for the emergence of Angélica has to do with being surrounded by Tucumánis and then instantly having to change into Alicia to conduct your business. When you're alone with Xavier and me, your mind doesn't know which identity to assume. That's what causes you anguish and frustration. What can I do to help alleviate the problem?"

"I've always known that I can't hide my true feelings from you. You're right. I had a Jekyll and Hyde struggle to contend with. Much of it has to do with not knowing what happened to Fernando. Everyone says that he's dead...I don't <u>know</u> that. There's a little person in my conscience who feels guilty about having and enjoying you and intimately sharing his offspring with you. I love seeing you enjoy my children, but I can't help thinking what that would mean to Fernando, were he alive. I suppose my guilt is aggravated by not having loved Fernando with near the passion I feel for you. Far away in Los Angeles or even in Santiago, these thoughts seldom occur. But here, they're constantly with me."

CHAPTER TWENTY

They ended their stay on the ranch on a somewhat happier note and returned to San Miguel to confer with Elena. Alicia wanted her to agree to a consistent protocol for trauma therapy that both would follow.

"Our patients would be less confused when we stood in for each other," she explained.

Kevin was eager to explore a schedule less likely to result in their early burnout which Elena had previously proposed and they agreed to adopt a new two-week rotation cycle. Their coordination and mutual support would be improved while they'd each have a week away every two weeks. Once the practice was going well, they could reduce their overlap to three days.

* * *

Kevin left with a heavy heart. His career was at a critical point and there was much he had to do before there'd be certainty about its course. He missed not having Alicia beside him and now had serious misgivings about her living so much of her life in Tucumán. The pull toward her former life, scared him. On the positive side, he sensed that she had made an excellent choice in Elena for a therapy partner and hoped that her presence in Tucumán would have a stabilizing influence on Alicia.

He and Elena sat together in the small turboprop plane. It was quiet enough for sensible conversation.

"Alicia told me that you also lived in Tucumán in your youth and that you were recently married in Santiago. What's your husband's name and what does he do?"

"I was in my teens when we lived in Tucumán. Alicia was more sophisticated than me—having grown up in Barcelona. Our high school backgrounds were much alike. Our psychology training was almost identical. As for Eduardo, he's a chemical engineer. He has a master's degree from the Colorado School of Mines. He worked for Bechtel in San Francisco on the design of new plants for copper mines in Chile. They sent him to Santiago to supervise their construction."

"Where did you meet him?"

"I went to see a distant relative in Punta Arenas and he was there on vacation. We started dating in Santiago and got married after I graduated."

"Is he a Chileano?"

"No, like me, he's an Argentinean. We both lost family members in the 'Dirty War' and had to get out."

"Will he go back there?"

"No, he's applied for Chilean citizenship. That's where he wants to stay."

"And you?"

"I'm doing the same thing as Alicia. My real feet are planted in Santiago."

"It amazes me how you two can be so dedicated as to live a good part of your lives away from home."

"You know exactly why, so don't give me that line. I know what you did down in Montevideo. She's virtually your creation!"

"Forgive me. I didn't know you were that well informed."

"You bear a great deal of responsibility for what's happening to us. You need to pay closer attention to her needs. You can't just kiss her good-bye and leave her to fight her demons alone. She can't be Alicia without feeling you in her life. Call her...send her notes...little things, every day. She must constantly know that she's the most important thing in your life. Her personality feeds off you. Without you, she'd be Angélica, a sexually irresponsible 'nuera' in the Diaz family. I depend on her vitality, which she gets from you. That makes me dependent on you. You can expect to hear a lot from me."

"What's with the sexual irresponsibility?"

"We lost our virginity to the same man on the same occasion at a college orgy. I know her like the inside of my hand. Until Fernando came along, she was as promiscuous as I was. With Fernando out of the picture, Angélica will revert to her insecure, juvenile behavior. She's been trying to tell you that she can't be trusted when Angélica surfaces."

"With that sort of background, why are you making this sacrifice?"

"I carry the same vengeance you and she have for the same reasons. Let's not make small talk; I can read you like a book. That's why I respect you. It would be helpful if you and I could become intimate friends."

"I didn't know so much depended on me."

* * *

Eduardo Mendoza met them at the airport.

"Eduardo, you and Elena were looking around for living quarters recently. We need a three-bedroom apartment on a month-to-month basis as soon as possible. Please let me know if you hear of anything like that," Kevin asked.

"There are some vacancies in our building," he answered. "We like it there. I'll ask the landlady to call you at your office."

Kevin's replacement, Eduardo Gill-Gomez, was also at the airport and drove him to the office.

"There's a shit-load of messages waiting for you. It sounds like they've arrived at a decision on most points of the merger and wanted your final word on where to locate the southern hemisphere sales office."

"I thought it was up to the merger planning committee to decide that."

"That nice guy from Milwaukee called to talk to you. He said to tell you that they were leaving it up to you to decide. He asked me what I thought your choice would be. I told him Santiago and gave him all the reasons you and I had come up with for doing so."

"Thanks, that saves me a lot of explaining. I'll call him when we get to the office."

"There was a call for you from a guy up in Moses Lake, Washington...he has an Aerostar for sale and said he'd throw in the training and certification in type for free."

"Do you think we'd be able to use a plane like that for our visits to the mines?"

"Where would we get the pilot?"

"I'm a pilot. That plane is pressurized so we could keep the cabin below ten thousand feet while crossing the Andes."

"Aren't small planes too slow?"

"We could make pretty good time at twenty-thousand feet."

"In that case it would save us lots of time and money. Charter flights out of here can get pricy."

"What else have we got?"

"Your wife called to remind you to get a place for Carlos in the school. Since we know everyone there, I took the liberty of getting him accepted."

Kevin talked to his boss, Phil Gordon, who confirmed that he could set up his headquarters in Santiago.

"Thanks a million, Phil. I'll send you our marketing plan for next year in about two weeks."

"That would be good timing. We'll need you here in two weeks to launch the program."

"Where should I meet you?"

"Have dinner with me the night before at the California Club in LA."

"Tell me Phil, is there some way that the company could help me buy a six-place, twin airplane with legs and altitude enough to use in the Andes to get to the mines?"

"I'll look into it. How much do you need?"

"Around two hundred thousand."

"Wow, you could buy a home for that."

"Phil, houses don't fly."

"I'm only kidding."

The phone rang and it was Elena's Eduardo with confirmation that there was a vacancy with three bedrooms in their building. The owner was a professor leaving on a six-month sabbatical in Europe and wanted to rent it furnished.

Kevin called for an appointment and was soon doing a walk-through with the Danish owner. The apartment was nicely furnished with modern Scandinavian wood furniture. It seemed spotlessly clean and was reasonably priced.

This was it and he called Alicia during her siesta break.

"How are you doing?"

"I'm all right today. Things went well this morning and my spirits are up. How's the house hunt going?"

"Elena's husband found us a place in their building. I just took a look at it," and he went on to describe it to her. "What I like most is that it's within walking distance of the school where Gil-Gomez enrolled Carlos. He has to start in two weeks' time. The trouble is I have to be in LA then."

"In LA, what's going on?"

"The merger went through. I get to set up shop here and the company will help me buy the Aerostar. How's that for a home run?"

"Great! I'll be able to see more of you."

"Elena says I don't profess my love to you enough times a day. So, I'm going to mail you a special salutation every day."

"Oh, boy, she got to you too, did she?"

"Just don't forget that you have the reputation of a de la Rosas to live up to."

"Tell her to mind her own business."

"Tell her yourself. I just thought you'd like to know that I love you very much," Kevin said.

CHAPTER TWENTY-ONE

The visit to San Miguel deeply disturbed Kevin. Very much afraid of Alicia losing her balance under Angélica's bombardment, he anxiously searched his mind for a solution. Aside from that, Xavier rang a discordant note. His story about finding the rebel bodies just didn't sound realistic. He said he hadn't done a head count; that the bodies were too bloated, but said nothing about who he reported it to or what arrangements were made to bury the rebel casualties.

In fairness to him, it may have been common practice for each side to take care of its own dead. However, there were other unanswered questions. How did he sustain himself for over a year in the mountains without help from someone? Kevin began wondering if Xavier wasn't a secret scout for the Junta. Perhaps he spotted the fleeing rebels at the campground and set up the ambush. He may have witnessed the battle, seen the rebels drop, without being able to get back there while it was occupied by the soldiers. Surely a posse of commandos would keep careful account of the enemies they killed and would have searched them for papers and other intelligence. They may even have removed the bodies to confuse any surviving rebels.

His vague finger-pointing at Fernando...in a sense, to justify his arrest and probable demise...also seemed fishy to Kevin. Finally, he sensed that there was more between him and Alicia than they could admit to.

He decided to call Alicia's father, Sergio, in San Miguel. His business phone carried heavy traffic, including Telex messages and was less likely to be monitored.

"Hello, Sergio, I'm sorry I couldn't spend more time with you."

"No problem, I was quite busy too. What can I do for you?"

"I've been giving a lot of thought to Alicia's security and have concluded," and he explained the Xavier situation to him.

"He has Alicia believing that he was closer to Fernando than he might actually have been, and I'm concerned that she'll confide in him. I don't dare tell her this on her phone. Could you perhaps ask her over on some pretext and explain what I've just told you. The guy just doesn't ring true to me."

"I'm glad to see you're alert. Your explanation is plausible. I'll get her to come here for lunch, then we'll call to discuss."

"Thanks, Sergio. I'll be in the office all day."

Kevin's next call was to the aircraft broker in Moses Lake from whom he obtained all the information he needed and concluded a tentative deal subject to seeing and flying the airplane in Santa Monica.

The rest of the morning was spent talking to his principal customers and his offices around the world. The good news was that Coldelco had accepted his bid for several new dragline excavators for Chuquicamata.

He had a sandwich brought in and was eating when Sergio and Alicia called back.

"Make a note to tell Elena that I spoke to you twice today," Kevin joked.

"Funny, Ha-Ha. This thing about Xavier upsets me. It never crossed my mind that he might be deceptive. I thought he was my friend—a connection to the past. What you told my father shocked me. But then I have to admit that I also wondered about him leaving the bloated bodies, while taking the time to count the shell casings. So what do I do?"

"Keep on riding with him. Let him feel that he can take you into his confidence, but don't tell him anything about our experiences. Just tell him we fell in love in LA while you were attending Loyola Marymount, that I know zip about Argentina's recent internal politics—I just do business with the air force, the navy and commercial customers as I always have. It won't hurt to let him know that I'm on a first-name basis with the General of their Air Force. Make sure he knows that you have patients on all sides of the conflict. Professionally, you're like Switzerland."

"Kevin! Where have you <u>been</u> these last months! This guy knows *everything*," Alicia exclaimed. "He was Fernando's close friend and mine too—if you count having him as my horse trainer as a friendship. Perhaps I could use him as my conduit to the bad guys. I could bitch about how people in government, who became traumatized, are often neglected when we could be curing them. I could make like I was soliciting their business. If I start getting referrals after talking to him, it could prove your hunch to be correct."

"That's a good idea. Perhaps you should take the initiative by prompting Xavier to arrange a meeting with some of the authorities for you to talk about mental health care for them. Make them feel that you're on their side."

"That's been Elena and my plan for months! Even if you're a bit out of touch, I'm glad you're on our team; it keeps me true to Alicia. I'll let you know what happens. When are you leaving for LA?"

"In ten days. We have to get Carlos in school here before I leave. I'm looking for a governess-nanny for both children. It's not good for Maria to get too attached to Elvira. Perhaps Elvira would like to visit with her here from time to time. She loved to come here before.

"By the way, I always have to ask before you tell me. How's our baby doing?"

"I'm beginning to show; so far, so good. But forgive me, I have to go. I love you"

* * *

Alicia was breathless about the way their conversation had gone. She had felt insecure from the moment Elena and Kevin left. She had lost her temper with Kevin twice in the presence of Xavier. She thought of ascribing it to her dual personality problem and then her father called to repeat what Kevin had just said of his suspicions about *Xavier*.

"Oh no, my God," she thought out load "how on earth will I explain what went on between me and Xavier."

Alicia should never have allowed such unfaithful behavior, but neither could she have mourned the loss of Fernando as passionately. It was becoming a serious dilemma for her to control her split personalities.

That had to change. In Alicia's pro-active way, she immediately began thinking how to reach a government audience to whom she could pitch the value of post-trauma therapy for their stressed-out constituents. She already had several solid examples of officers or their dependents suffering from depression and sleep disorders attributable to trauma.

She contacted the health administrator and made an appointment to see him. She briefly explained what she had in mind and could tell that he had no idea what she was saying...which may have been the reason that he readily agreed to meet with her the next morning.

She found him after a brief search. He apologized for the confusion, commenting that his department had just been staffed.

"So, how may I help you, Señora de la Rosa?"

"Some of the people who came to see us—my partner, Elena Mendoza and me—were from the civil service and from the military. Some suffered so badly from depression and sleeplessness, they couldn't function. They either didn't show up for work, or if they did, they couldn't perform well."

"Yes. We've had a problem with absentees. They don't always seem sick to me."

"What do you do with them?"

"If we can tie it down to something physical, we send them to a physician."

"What about those with mental or emotional disorders?"

"We don't have counselors or psychiatrists here and just send them home to rest."

"Someone with a nervous breakdown won't recover from taking a rest; especially not someone who's been shocked."

"I think I understand, but what can we do about it?"

"You have to get therapeutic help. Some of the ones I've seen will never recover without it. They'll just withdraw and become a burden on society."

"Why are as many as you say, that serious?"

"Tucumán has been through difficult times. Many people lived in fear. There was the Marxist rebellion, then the war to get rid of them, then the search for their sympathizers. Everything was so uncertain for years that it put great strain on many people—especially those who were charged with restoring order. That is why we came here to help. We are specialists in trauma therapy. I trained in Los Angeles and my partner in Santiago."

"How could we work with you?"

"The same way you work with your physicians. Send us your troubled people for evaluation. We'll charge you a modest fee for the evaluation and then, if necessary, we, together, can work out a recovery program."

"I'll have to discuss this with my superior and will call you with an answer."

"That would be fine, here's my card. We are at this address from eight-thirty each week day until siesta and from five until about nine in the evening."

* * *

As if she needed to be reminded of her real purpose for being there, an elderly woman was waiting to see her and began to explain.

"Almost three years ago in November during siesta, a group of hooded men burst into our home and seized five of my relatives. They blindfolded and put bags over the heads of Pedro, Maria, Silvia, and two cousins and took them away. Pedro had been working in the print shop in the front of the house. They told the owner of the printing business that he had twenty-four hours to get the printing equipment out of the house or else they would demolish the building. My husband and I were driven away in a separate car."

"What happened to you?"

"My husband was very old and weak and I pleaded with the driver to take us to the home of a friend. He must have felt sorry for us, because he obeyed me."

"What happened to the ones they took?"

"They 'disappeared' and we never heard from them again. The father of one of the cousin's knew the accountant in General Bussi's office and requested an audience, but he refused. Other friends used their connections to President Videla, but he didn't answer them."

"What happened to your home?"

"They ransacked it and left someone to guard it. It didn't do much good. Men came and drove off with Pedro's car. Others ransacked the house again and again—even with chains locking the front door."

"What happened to your husband?"

"He died of shock and a broken heart."

"How can I help you?"

"I was very sad and angry, but my head stayed clear and I kept functioning. Then, when the worst was over and the Army packed its bags and left, I felt drained of emotion and empty. I loved those children and without them I had nothing to live for. I wanted to know what had happened to them and no one could tell me. I didn't even know if some of them hadn't perhaps survived.

"Then out of the blue earlier this year, a woman who had been a nurse at the Naval School of Mechanics in Buenos Aires came to see me. She was very secretive about everything and obviously didn't want anyone to know that she had come to see me. She said that she had delivered my daughter, Silvia's, <u>baby</u>. I didn't even know that she was pregnant and was about to rejoice that she had been saved, when the nurse told me that they took the baby out of her arms and sent her off to where they executed people! I'm ashamed to say this, but I broke down and went to pieces. The poor woman, after risking her neck to see me, had to comfort me. We wept together and I clung to her as if she was my mother."

"Easy now," Alicia tried to soothe her. "Did she tell you what they did with the child?"

"They gave it to an officer who registered it as his and his wife's child. I asked her if she knew who the real father was. She said that it must have come from being raped in jail, because she had been in custody too long to have been pregnant when they took her from us."

Alicia gasped. "That is the most horrendous thing I've ever heard. How is it affecting you? I <u>really</u> want to help you."

"It's such a waste. She had done nothing to harm anyone. It was all because of that man with his printing machine in our front room— I keep thinking. The trouble is, I just keep thinking—I can't sleep and if I do drop off, I wake up to the most horrible nightmares."

"How are your energy and your spirit holding up?"

"I've never been one to complain or feel sorry for myself, but I've grown weary and sometimes feel I should just end it."

"Do you mean...take your own life?"

"Not in those terms. I don't know how to end it. If one stops wanting to go on, something will happen," she answered.

"Do you live near here?"

"No, but I could come and stay with friends close by."

"I want to see you for two hours each morning for the next week. I want to get to the bottom of your distress as soon as possible!"

"I think you know where I've been; don't you?"

"Yes, and it all comes back so vividly."

"Perhaps it's a blessing that we met. I'll be back tomorrow."

Alicia couldn't hold back her emotions and went to the bathroom to vomit. She could feel the rage well up in her and her need to find vengeance returning stronger than ever. She had to regain control quickly—her next patient was already waiting.

* * *

A few days later, there was a message from the health administrator. He had talked to his superior, the head of public services, who was anxious to meet Alicia. She returned his call.

"I'm glad you called. It seems in my boss' family, they experienced the kind of emotional distress you described to me. He would like to see you soon."

"I could do it tomorrow morning after ten, but I only have an hour open then."

"That will be all right for a first meeting. I'll tell him to expect you here at ten minutes past ten."

Since she had taken the initiative on her own to approach the reigning bureaucracy and since it appeared to be moving ahead, she wanted to discuss it with Kevin. She asked her father to let her make the call from his office.

"Kevin, I called to tell you about a risk I've taken. As result of our conversation about Xavier I decided it would be safest to defuse any rumors he may think of spreading. So I made an appointment and went to see the new man in charge of public health to explain why our therapy would be useful to people in the Provincial civil service. He's a lightweight and needed to talk it over with his boss. He just called back to say that the man in charge of all civil services would like to see me tomorrow morning. He said that he was anxious to meet me, because he had a trauma-related problem with someone in his family."

"That's a smart idea to get them on your side before the gossip starts. Just be careful not to oversell your capability. You don't want them thinking too much about the benefits your services might have for their victims. Keep them thinking that you are beholden to people of means, and their referrals, to make your practice lucrative. Think about it this way...consider that the man you're going to see is already investigating your business and is suspicious. Maybe then you'll be cautious enough."

"The most persuasive way, I think, is to get some of his people saying that we saved someone close to them. We're not hairdressers; if we can pull someone out of a serious situation, word will spread quickly."

"How is your practice going?"

"I had no idea that it would be this tough on me. Someone came to see me and simply blew my mind. I'll tell you when I get there."

"Just take it easy. We don't want you to be the one needing therapy!" Kevin expressed his concern.

"No, Alicia is now in firm command," she lied.

"Glad to hear that. How's Maria doing with Elvira?"

"They're almost too close. You know how strong Elvira's personality is."

"We have to find a way to live as normal human beings."

"I pray every night for it to happen soon."

* * *

Alicia found the Civil Services Administrator waiting the next morning.

"Good morning Señora de la Rosa, it was nice of you to come at such short notice. My colleague explained to me that you had started a practice in psychotherapy here and that you and your partner were specialized in the treatment of trauma-induced dysfunctions."

"Yes, Sir, that's what we do."

"The local government didn't expect to see such advanced specialization here in San Miguel and have been questioning why you set up your practice here."

"I already explained that to your man," and she repeated what she had said before.

"It makes sense to me, but I would have thought that those who suffered trauma the most probably can't afford your treatment?"

"We haven't been able to make that correlation, but some of what you say could turn out to be true. Should that be the case, would it not be reasonable to expect social medicine to make such therapy available to seriously affected residents who could be saved to lead productive lives again? I would have thought that such an approach would actually lower our welfare costs."

"We just don't have the means or authority to pay for therapeutic services of almost any kind."

"That will change in time. For the present, you have a significant number of civil servants and military personnel who need to be taken care of."

"That's why I was interested in meeting you. My eldest daughter, who just turned eighteen, was very nervous when the Army came to take back the province from the Marxist rebels. From her bedroom she could hear shots being fired and people fighting in the streets. Later on, she heard from her friends at school and here in the park that people were being arrested in the middle of the night. She began waking up and crying out because of her bad dreams. At first, we just took her into bed with us to calm her down. But then her laziness started and she began eating too much. She would just stay in her room when all her friends were out playing and going places, so she put on weight, which made her ashamed to go out. And you know how that goes."

"Was she a bright student before?"

"Yes, she was our pride and joy, which is why we're so distressed now."

"We've seen a number of similar cases since we opened our doors. One was the wife of an important official and the other a soldier."

"Who was the official?"

"I can't tell you that. Our services would be useless without absolute assurance of total confidentiality. Your daughter wouldn't confide in me if she thought I would tell someone—even you—about it."

"So, how will we know what you are doing to help her?"

"You'll see the results in her behavior. If there were matters directly concerning you, we would seek her consent to discuss them with you. Suppose her depression was partly your fault, we couldn't solve the problem without talking to you...could we?"

"How did you know that she's depressed?"

"You told me so by describing her condition. Here's what I suggest we do. Make an appointment for your daughter and send her over to my office for a consultation. You can call it a chat, if you like. I won't charge you for her first one-hour visit. Then I'll call you and with her on the phone—or if you prefer, you can join her in my office—I'll describe a program of therapeutic visits that will help her get well again."

"When can she come?"

"Tomorrow morning at eleven."

"I'll make sure that she's there. Thank you for coming. I'm sure that we'll find a way to use your services effectively."

"Thank you for your time and interest."

Alicia walked back to her office alarmed by the knowledge that their practice was under investigation, but pleased that she had probably won him over. She couldn't help but ponder the man's narcissistic attitude, given his responsibility for the welfare of a public so badly in need of help.

* * *

Her next appointment, with the woman who'd had her children and young relatives arrested in her home, stood in stark contrast to the triviality of the meeting she'd just had.

It took all of Alicia's will power to approach the subject of the woman's daughter, Silvia, in a gentle, calm way to help draw the poor woman out of her state of denial and depression. They talked about her life as a young woman, what her hopes and ambitions had been; how she got married, and what pleased her most about her children. Alicia asked about her husband's profession and background and her own beliefs.

"I came from a pious family with deep Christian beliefs, which is why I brought my children up to care for poor and disadvantaged people. I championed Evita for what she did to give them a voice. Perhaps that is why we celebrated when Perón came back out of exile in Spain. Then things went out of control with the Trotskyites rushing in here and taking peoples' property, pretending that it would solve the problem of poverty. But, the poor got poorer and for the first time in our 'Garden of Eden', people were going hungry. We were happy when the Army liberated us, restored order and let the people go back to work. We didn't expect the persecution that happened after the coup.

"I never paid attention to what the man who rented our front room did with his printing machine. He printed stuff that looked like class notes for students at the university. Pedro was studying there and brought the man to our house. He often helped him print the notes. You know the rest of my story."

"If you can, tell me about Silvia."

"She was my youngest. They always get more attention than one's older siblings, so I probably knew her the best. She was very gentle, but smart with a lot of compassion. She was the one who always went down into the poor people's barrio with the food her church group collected or bought with the money they raised."

"What about Pedro?"

"He was our loner and kept to himself most of the time."

"What did he study?"

"He was a sociology student and knew a lot about history; especially contemporary history."

"Did he read a lot of books about Karl Marx or Engels?"

"He read whatever the professors prescribed. I know he had to read Mein Kampf, Hitler's book."

"Did he ever talk about the labor unions?"

"Yes, that was his strong subject. He was concerned that agricultural workers weren't paid enough."

"Was he a union member?"

"No, he was more like an organizer."

"Did he get involved in strikes?"

"Yes, he helped organize them. He made placards and that sort of thing."

"What did the strikers want?"

"Mostly, they wanted more money, but sometimes there were political strikes about voting rights and so on."

"With all of this going on and the Communists in charge of the province, you never thought of seeing what propaganda the man in your house was printing?"

"I guess I didn't want to know, if the truth be told."

"Even if Pedro was in league with the left-wing Perónistas, that still wouldn't justify arresting him and certainly won't lessen the Junta's quilt for taking the others with him," Alicia reassured her. "So don't go feeling guilty about that. You did what you had to do. Someday, when we can get you healthy again, you may have the chance to have your say in court."

"I hope to see that happen and will cooperate with you to get better."

"Very well; here's what I'd like you to do until your next visit on Thursday," Alicia said, handing her a list of things to practice.

CHAPTER TWENTY-TWO

Much to Kevin's delight, Alicia and Carlos arrived in Santiago. He'd missed them much more than he'd anticipated. Carlos was beside himself, talking a blue streak in a mixture of English and Spanish. Alicia heartily approved of his choice of apartment with its nearby playground, and school. The built-in company of Eduardo Gil-Gomez' two children thrilled her. For added convenience, Elena's apartment was within walking distance, as was Kevin's office with its vault and Telex machine.

There had been a series of Telex messages from Carlos Vargas in Spain, containing the descriptions of more misdeeds by the Junta against Spanish citizens as ferreted out by the "Spanish Club" in Montevideo. One of his reports was of a child being taken from its doomed captive mother and given to an official to register as his or her own. This corroborated the report of Alicia's elderly patient in San Miguel, which Alicia described in detail to Kevin.

"Let's talk strategy before we get confused and pursue too many blind alleys," Kevin suggested. "Our objective should be to find rock-solid evidence of serious transgressions by senior officials of the Junta, with which to nail them someday."

"That's right," she agreed. "The challenge is to find a few 'right' ones to pursue. There were so many horrible things done, that we could easily lose our way trying to follow them all. We have to be selective."

"What should our selection criteria be?" Kevin prompted her.

"For one, we now know that they were stealing newborn babies and killing their birthmothers," Alicia suggested. "That is a heinous crime which no one with an ounce of decency can ignore and it can't be justified in the name of national security. I vote that we make those incidents our first priority."

"That's a powerful argument, except it probably can't be pinned on Antonio Bussi in Tucumán, the man you'd most want to get for abducting Fernando."

"No, as far as we know, we can't pin *that* on him. We know it happened at your favorite stomping ground, ESMA, in Buenos Aires and that the man in charge was General Suarez Mason. There were three captains supervising the 'maternity ward' who could also be named in the suit," Alicia continued.

"I'm impressed. You really do good homework for a mere psychologist, except that ESMA wasn't <u>my</u> stomping ground. How do you plan to put the noose around Bussi's neck?"

"Don't get smart with me-you dumb engineer. I have one of his trusted soldiers on record seeing him execute prisoners with his handgun to inspire his firing-squad. I also have at least one credible witness willing to testify that his victims were randomly picked for execution. I'm sure, with a bit of sleuth work, the bodies will be found in unmarked graves."

"What other crimes are you thinking of charging someone with?"

"You, for neglecting your pregnant wife."

"That won't stand up after this evening."

"So, what do you have in mind, Cowboy?"

"Let's get lost in Viña del Mar."

"Can't wait that long, how about a tour of the Scandinavian apartment?"

"What about Carlos?"

"The nanny can take him to the park."

"You sound like Hard-Hearted Hanna, the Vamp of Savannah."

"Try me, Gringo!" she said as she led him by the hand into the apartment building.

She was as tense as a banjo string and craved the gentle affection of the man she adored. He was more than ready for the occasion and made love to her in a gentle, but uninhibited way until they collapsed into each other's arms to lie softly panting with satisfaction.

"Why do we punish ourselves with these long absences?" she asked "We could live a happy family life."

"We had that in LA, and we'll have it again here in Santiago," he assured her.

"Don't hold your breath. We both have heavy obligations. We'll have to learn to manage our time much better," she concluded.

"That reminds me. I made the deal to buy the airplane and will be flying it back here after the company meetings. It should ease our commuting problem. I should be able to take one of you two in and bring the other one out on one round-trip. You guys don't need to overlap any more. On my trips to various mining centers, I may be able to drop into San Miguel to see you as well."

* * *

They had dinner with the Gil-Gomez family who had thoughtfully included Alicia's partner and her husband. Kevin took advantage of the occasion to engage Eduardo Mendoza in conversation about his solvent extraction mining activities. They discovered that they dealt often with the same people and in the design of the extraction plants Eduardo's company used equipment made by Kevin's new group of enterprises.

Elena, having visited Gil-Gomez' office to access the vault, was already familiar with him.

Kevin engaged Elena in conversation.

"What do you think of the progress you and Alicia have made?"

"I'd say we're on firm ground now—that is, professionally speaking. We have a plethora of trauma victims to choose from and many of them are challenging patients to cure," she responded.

"Where are the uncertainties then?"

"There are two. Can they afford our services, given that we have the overhead costs of having to travel so much? More subjectively, how long will they allow us to practice?"

"What do you mean, 'allow'?"

"The Junta still controls everything and if they realize that the majority of our patients are people who they harmed, they may shut us down," she explained.

"Don't you think Alicia's promotion of more business from the administration's side will defuse that?"

"Basically, yes. It all depends on the kind and size of the problems we can solve for them. For instance, if we saved the marriage of one of the top dogs by helping him or his wife to get over a problem, we'd be heroes. On the other hand, if we cured the much more painful problem of a traumatized soldier of low rank, nobody would give a damn. My greatest fear is that they hear of our more spectacular interventions in the miserable lives of their victims and start reading sinister meaning into that."

"I understand, but with each week that goes by, as the Generals become more occupied with the real problems of running the country, that becomes less likely," Kevin suggested.

"I like your optimism. If things do settle down, we may be allowed to go back to doing what we do best.

"I want to start a family and Alicia will have another child soon. As it is, I have to pack tonight for tomorrow's flight back to Tucumán. I'd much rather be staying here."

* * *

Kevin finally took Alicia on the promised outing to Viña del Mar. To relax, they took a long walk on the beach.

Kevin began the conversation.

"I've been thinking. While I'm away in LA, you'll be here for two more weeks. Why don't we invite Elvira to bring Maria to stay with you? You've been too busy in San Miguel to spend much time with Maria. She's extremely bright and impressionable and should have more opportunity to go beyond mimicking her grandmother."

"Are you criticizing me for being a bad mother as well?"

"On the contrary, I'm suggesting a way for you to gain more influence over your little twin. You've no idea how much she's like you."

"I get it, you're afraid she'll become another Angélica. You might be right. I'll call her tomorrow."

"How's your riding buddy?"

"The more I see of him, the more I recognize that he has an agenda. He's good company and a damned good horseman. So I don't dislike him. Now I try to keep our conversation to small-talk."

"What does he talk about?"

"He tries to impress me with the people he knows and how he tried to keep Fernando out of trouble. In spite of his poker face, he's surprisingly compassionate and encourages me to get it out of my system by crying over the loss of Fernando."

"Just be careful. Angélica is naïve compared with you. He could seduce her."

Alicia swallowed hard. I have a confession to make. Until you blew the whistle on him, Angélica had made Xavier her confidante. He was very sympathetic and on more than one occasion they made love. I've been trying to tell you how difficult it is for me to live with this dual personality. So far, that was the furthest she's gone to violate your trust in me. I'm ashamed to tell you this, but you can't have total confidence in me as long as she keeps popping out of her closet."

"I'm glad you told me. I knew that your relationship with Xavier had grown closer than a platonic one. It showed in your demeanor when we were in close quarters with him. I can't hold it against you. I'm largely to blame for convincing you to take the risk of changing your personality. That fact makes me share the guilt with you for Angélica-induced transgression. There's not much I can do about it while you're there in Tucumán. Have there been any more signs of people trying to spy on you?"

"People are curious to know what trauma therapy means, and the provincial sleuths are keeping an eye on us. Why do you ask?"

"I'm just afraid that we may be looking in the wrong direction. You know how hyper-conservative the elite of San Miguel are. After their experience with Communist expropriation, we can expect them to be vigilant about anything new. As conservatives, they view any new technology, especially intangibles, with skepticism or even deprecation."

"So now you think they'll try to spy on us?"

"No, they're more subtle than that. Your practice represents something new which many of them will instinctively oppose until someone explains it to them. Even then, they'll remain doubtful. I can hear them saying that it's just for sissies who take their feelings too seriously."

"That's nothing new. That's how military commanders see things."

"Not quite. Military commanders need fit soldiers, not scared ones. They know what shell-shock is and understand how to lead large organizations. The rich farmers in San Miguel don't."

"I didn't know you knew that much about San Miguel's aristocracy," she added sarcastically.

"I sold them drive gears for their sugar mills when you were still in diapers. My company was one of few suppliers of those gears and they had to deal with me to get decent delivery dates."

"Why are you warning me about them now?" She asked.

"As the influence of the Junta declines in Tucumán, they will increasingly be the ones to watch.

"But let's not talk about that. Right now I want us to remember how lovely it was on the ranch above Puerto Varas. We have to make time to go there to show off Maria," Kevin soothed her. "I'd also like to go back to Montevideo to the Tango Club and the penthouse restaurant of the Sheraton where Alicia de la Rosa made her first appearance. We've been so incredibly lucky and must keep that feeling between us alive.

"I carry so much about those few critical weeks in my heart which I can't explain. I have a sense about you that can never be repeated. Please don't leave me now," Kevin pleaded.

She embraced and clung tightly to him.

"That was the closest you've ever come to declaring your love for me. It makes me happier than you'll ever know. When I'm alone at night, I sometimes wake up in a sweat over the thought that I could lose you. Thank you for loving me," she whispered as she turned to kiss him with extreme tenderness.

They stayed the night in the same inn they had stayed at on their first visit to the seaside town. She was about as pregnant then with Maria. Now as then, they didn't let that interfere in their ultimate expression of love to one another.

CHAPTER TWENTY-THREE

As Kevin arrived in Los Angeles, Alicia waited for Elvira and Maria to arrive in Santiago.

She had debated the wisdom of going with Kevin to help arrange the disposition of their West Los Angeles home and its effects. Emotionally, she *wanted* to keep him company. Professionally, she would have liked to visit her professor for a reality check on what she was attempting to do in Argentina. Instinctively, she knew that she would have been emboldened by his admiration.

In the end, the responsibility she felt toward her baby daughter, who was effectively being mothered by her grandmother, trumped all other considerations and she remained behind.

In deference to Dr. Diaz, Elvira seldom expressed her views on political issues. The shame was that often she was more astute than him. Here on neutral ground, she wasn't constrained and avidly pursued discussion of Alicia's plans and notions.

"You have to look more carefully at the ordinary people around you. We have families in Tucumán who founded and built the community into a prosperous place—so prosperous that it attracted labor we didn't need. In the end, they will have more influence over the community than any outsiders. You and Arnoldo look only at the threats from the military government.

"You have to learn to respect some of those old families for the part they had in founding Argentina as an independent country," Elvira emphasized.

"There must be telepathy between you and Kevin. He just gave me the same lecture in Viña del Mar. We've started courting them," and she went on to explain what she and Elena were doing through the Administrator of Public Services. "If we can find even a few really good cases amongst them to show what relief from post-traumatic stress can do for them, I think, they may be inclined to support us.

"Tell me more about Maria," Alicia changed the subject. "I feel so guilty about leaving her to you so much of the time."

"She's just the sweetest little thing and a well-behaved child. You know how bright she is. I think she understands why you're so busy. She misses Kevin more—she saw so much of him and then it suddenly ended when he brought her to San Miguel. I agree with him. She ought to live here in Santiago. I like visiting you here."

"This living in two places is hard on us. It worries me a lot. I'd die without him. If he wasn't so high-minded, he'd have good reason to leave me."

"He probably feels the same way about you. I hope you'll always be true to each other."

* * *

Once Kevin's family was happily together in Santiago, life began to settle into its own routine and the tension and pressure on Alicia and Elena progressively diminished. Instead of worrying about finding new patients, they became fully absorbed in perfecting their therapy for their growing number of regular patients. Many of them were establishment people, more able to afford their fees. This had the advantage of earning them a favorable reception amongst the community's leaders.

Their greatest challenges lay in curing the effects that trauma had had on their three most valuable witnesses; the firing squad soldier, the young woman who had witnessed some of the executions, and the elderly mother of the ill-fated daughter whose baby was stolen and given to the family of a childless official. They had to bring those people close to normalcy in order to win their cooperation to someday bring suit against the Army's leadership.

Kevin took pleasure in having his airplane, which he used extensively in his business travels as far south as Punta Arenas and as far north as Lima, Peru. Most of his trips were within Chile, where the larger mines were located. Whenever possible, he arranged his trips to the Atacama Desert such that he could drop in to see Alicia and often flew her and Elena to and from San Miguel. This happened so routinely that he enrolled each of them in a "pinch-hitter" flight training program that qualified them to fly and land the airplane if he was in any way incapacitated. He usually flew one of them in and the other out of San Miguel on the same trip.

He had a particularly good intercom system installed to converse easily with his passengers, while at the same time muffling the sound of the engines. It gave the impression of confidentiality—like whispering to each other—and encouraged conversations with less restraint than usual. He liked that aspect when flirting with Alicia, but was a little embarrassed when Elena chose to be personal. She was much more extraverted than Alicia and could come on very flirtatiously.

When the time came, Alicia gave birth to Kevin's son in the same hospital where Maria was born. She instantly named him, "Santiago."

Since it was unlikely that they'd live in Los Angeles again, they sold their home and with the proceeds bought a modest Estancia with a vineyard and space to keep horses just outside Santiago. It had a guesthouse where the seller's parents had lived, which Elena and Eduardo moved into when their first child was born. It was a wonderful environment for the children to grow up in and yet not too far away from the American School which Carlos attended.

There were beautiful riding trials above them in the foothills and enough space on the farm for an arena, a round pen and a pasture. Alicia and Kevin's favorite form of recreation was to ride into the hills where they could talk and fantasize at will.

CHAPTER TWENTY-FOUR

In March 1981, two years into their stay in Santiago, President Jorge Videla lost his grip on the Junta and handed the presidency to his lieutenant, Roberto Viola. Nothing much changed, except that the economy of Argentina, reflecting international financial weakness, was on shaky ground. Later in the same year, Viola was replaced by General Léopold Galtieri, who was more ambitious. The following April he occupied the British Falkland Islands, known in Argentina as the Malvinas. His hope that the British would sue for peace and accommodate him was sadly misplaced. With Maggie Thatcher, the "Iron Lady", in command, the British went to war with him and ignominiously expelled his troops from the islands.

With his credibility and that of the despised Junta, in tatters, Galtieri turned the rule of the country over to the interim government of General Reynaldo Bignone, charged with the task of making the transition back to an elected government. In October 1983, Raúl Alfonsín, of the Radical Civic Union, beat his Perónist opponent to become president.

Alfonsin's campaign speeches made it clear that he found the behavior of the Army repugnant and promised to seek reconciliation. He represented the liberal wing of his UCR party and had many young idealistic supporters, thirsting to avenge the mutilation of their friends by the Junta.

Three days after taking office, Alfonsín issued a decree to the Supreme Council of the Armed Forces to try the Junta leaders under military jurisdiction, for homicide, illegal detention, and torture.

This gave cause for celebration on the Bartholomew ranch and Alicia and Elena were soon huddling with Dr. Diaz to plan the preparation and filing of two suits against key Junta officers. Their principal target was General Bussi, who had been the Junta commander of Tucumán. The charge was illegal execution of prisoners. Their second target was General Suárez Mason who had commanded the ant subversive operations in Buenos Aires where the theft of babies and the execution of their mothers had taken place.

Before the course would be open to bring such actions against military officers, several developments had to take place.

* * *

Through constitutional wrangling and legal arguments, the trials initiated against the Junta leaders didn't close until two years later, in September 1985.

In the meantime, almost two thousand denunciations involving 300 officers of the military and security forces had piled up. This is not what Alfonsin had in mind with his decree, which didn't require that indictments be drawn up for trials before the Military Supreme Council. This left a huge loophole through which the National Commission on the Disappearance of Persons, was able to present evidence it said supported the contention that the military had carried out a vast program of repression on ideological grounds against innocents. This non-specific charge energized all manner of human rights organizations to accuse hundreds of officers of violations, which could theoretically now be brought before the military bar.

This was precisely what Alicia, Kevin and Carlos Vargas in Montevideo had aimed to avoid by carefully structuring clear, specific suits in support of innocent victims based on strong, verifiable evidence to convict particular perpetrators.

The distraction from their cause by over-zealous activists, made Alicia more determined than ever to attain her objective and she proceeded systematically to build their two cases. Her subjective priority was to nail Bussi's hide, since he presided over the disappearance of Fernando.

* * *

Most important to their case against Bussi, was the evidence of the handsome soldier who had witnessed him executing prisoners with his side arm to motivate his firing squad. He had been one of her first trauma patients. Curing him had taken a long time through many hours of therapy, during the course of which, he had grown exceedingly fond of her.

In tracking him down, she found that he had reenlisted in the Army and had been deployed to the Falkland Islands where the British captured him. Upon repatriation, he elected to resign his commission in the Army.

He was extremely pleased to hear from her and agreed to meet her in Santiago del Estero, a town some distance towards Córdoba, where he now worked and lived. They met in a small café where he had been waiting and rose to greet her by kissing her hand.

"You have no idea what a pleasure it is to see you again. When I was a POW—with not much else to do but sit and think—I often tried to imagine what you were doing. I've had no bad dreams and haven't felt depressed since you pronounced me cured."

"Well, that's wonderful. It's always nice for a professional to hear someone praise their work. I would never have guessed that you'd reenlist. What made you do that?"

"They trained me in advanced communications which is what I liked doing, the ant subversive activity was over and they wanted me to come back because of my expertise."

"Why didn't you stay in?"

"When the Junta crashed, I could see senior officers retiring in droves. That could expose their junior officers to the brunt of responsibility for all the awful things they had done. I'd been in the front line of ant subversive operations, engaging the guerrillas and carrying out the orders of guys like Bussi, who has retired. I had every reason to be distrustful of the military hierarchy.

He went on, "That wouldn't have been so bad if people still respected the military, but there was no way for me to be considered praiseworthy for being in the military."

"Are those the only reasons?"

"No, these charges being filed against us by the human rights people are nothing but their way of winning votes for their radical left supporters by condemning us for actions we did under orders and to punish hundreds of officers for doing their duty."

"What else is there?"

"This Alfonsin government is running a publicity campaign through government-controlled media to sully the honor and ethics of our military institution."

"How would you like to get even with Bussi? He's one of principal officers who brought the military to this."

"He's a big man with a lot of political influence up here in the north. There's nothing I could do that would touch him."

"Would you at least help me nail his hide to the wall?"

"For you I would kill a bull."

"But, it's not for me. It's for the future of Argentina."

"Bussi did some very bad things, but he also did many good things."

"A man who shoots a defenseless person in cold blood— especially one who may be completely innocent—to impress his troops, can never do enough good to make up for it."

"You feel strongly about that."

"It was under his command that they took away my husband, who had done nothing against anyone and they probably murdered him. They would have killed me too if they knew where I was."

"If it means that much to you, what do you want me to do?"

"Testify in court to what you saw him do. That's all."

"Jesus! They'll skin me alive."

"No, they won't. You'll help people to see that the military also has officers as good and as honorable as they were supposed to be."

"How much does it mean to you?"

"It means everything to me."

"Like my love for you means everything to me?"

"I didn't know you felt that way."

"I was a broken person with no self-esteem. You nursed me back to being whole again. I never knew a person as lovely as you. If I do this for you, can we always be close friends?"

"Yes, of course."

"I don't mean as a patient. It has to be a personal relationship."

"I'm a happily married woman with three lovely children, but I have many men friends also."

"I'll take my chances. Just remember, I'm in love with you."

"I take it then that you'll cooperate?"

"Yes, where and when do you want to start working on the case?"

"How about next week in San Miguel?"

"That's fine as long as it's on a Saturday. I work days during the week."

"I usually go home on the weekends, but next Saturday will do. Come to my office at, shall we say, eight?"

"Hold on, I have to drive all the way from Córdoba!"

"Why don't you come up the previous evening?"

"Where will I stay? The town's booked up because of the independence day celebrations."

"Oh, all right, you can stay at my house," and she gave him her address and stood up to leave.

He ushered her to her car and opened the door for her. As she past in front of him, he embraced her and held her for a moment before kissing her.

"Drive carefully, will you please," he waved her off with a broad smile.

She couldn't believe what had just happened and thought about it almost all the way to San Miguel. He certainly was handsome and seductive. Angélica would have loved to date him. However, that was hypothetical nonsense. She owed her life to Kevin, was the mother of three children and a well-respected professional. She had to stop this nonsense of Angélica.

The question was how. She absolutely needed his cooperation for her prime case. She wanted Elena's opinion, since she'd treated the soldier much of the time. However, her progressive flirtation with Kevin bothered her...even if Kevin ignored it.

* * *

Her mind moved to the other half of the case against Bussi...the young woman detainee who also witnessed Bussi shooting prisoners while in captivity. She recovered well from her post-traumatic condition and seemed beholden to Alicia for her recovery. They went over what she remembered in great detail to be certain that her memory of what she saw hadn't changed. Her description corresponded exactly with the contemporaneous notes Alicia had made about her first consultation with the woman. More importantly, she was anxious to testify.

She stopped by her in-laws to discuss the case with "Arnold" as she had come to call him.

"I think we have the makings of a good case against Bussi. I just fear that the judges in our division of the Appellate circuit may be too partial to the military," she said.

"Since Bussi resides in Buenos Aires we'll sue him in the central division where we know which crony judges appointed by the Junta were removed by Alfonsin," he offered.

"When can we start putting together a petition for an indictment?" Alicia wanted to know.

"The sooner, the better. There's quite a queue of motions in line ahead of us. I've heard that there may be as many as two hundred cases wending their way to the Supreme Council."

"Why the Supreme Council? That's the military court! I thought this would be a criminal case?" Alicia said in amazement.

"Alfonsin's declaration stipulates that one has to go to the Supreme Council of the Military first. If they don't take action within six months, it automatically rolls forward to the Federal Appellate Court. So far, the Supreme Council has declined hearing complaints of this nature let alone hand down indictments."

"Only in Argentina! No wonder you have to look where the sun comes up when Argentineans say 'good morning.'"

"When can we sit down with your two witnesses to get started?" asked Dr. Diaz.

"The ex-soldier will be here on Saturday morning and the young woman lives here in town. I can invite her to come at the same time if you like."

"No, let's do them separately in series for now," Arnold suggested. "That way they'll meet between sessions without being distracted."

"You know what concerns me most," Alicia added. "These ideologues from CONADEP have filled the Supreme Council's schedule with complaints that amount to little more than political propaganda, dressed up to look like requests for indictments. All they do is strengthen the military's contention that the evidence gathered by the human rights organizations is self-serving and void of substance to arrive at the truth."

"Yes, that's why democracies are so much messier than dictatorships," Arnold pointed out. "However, there is an important provision in Article ten which places crimes that aren't of a military nature, directly in the hands of the civilian courts. There can be no pardons in the way of those cases.

"Your second case, about the prisoner's baby they stole is a crime and will go directly to the civil court."

"If this goes on much longer, I'll be talking like a lawyer," Alicia concluded. "See you on Saturday morning."

* * *

Alicia talked to her elderly witness about the Army nurse who had informed her about delivering her daughter, Sylvia's, baby in prison. "Do you ever hear from her?"

"Yes, we've stayed in touch. As a matter of fact, after what you did for me, she showed interest in consulting you about her own nervous problems."

"Where is she living and what is she doing?"

"She moved next door to Catamarca, after Alfonsin cut the defense budget and the Army gave her early retirement. She works in a clinic."

"Do you think she'd be willing to testify about the babies who the childless officials stole?"

"I don't know. She's certainly no fan of the Junta, but she may be afraid that they'll take her pension away."

"Could you ask her if I may come to see her?"

"I'm sure she'd be delighted to see you."

"Is she married?"

Johan Wassenaar

"No, her husband left her several years ago. There were no children. If you know of a man looking for a wife, she's rather attractive and doesn't like living alone."

"I'll see what I can do. Let me know when I can see her."

"Sure, I'll let you know at our meeting with Dr. Diaz on Saturday."

CHAPTER TWENTY-FIVE

Alicia caught Angélica several times during the Friday, thinking about the handsome soldier with an avowed crush on her. It was flattering to be told that he was in love with her.

By nine o'clock when she heard his car pull up to her house, she was on pins and needles. She put on a nonchalant face to answer the door. He was dressed to show off his attractive black curly hair, trimmed moustache, lean, muscular body and aristocratic Seville features.

Under his arm he had a large portfolio, tied with ribbons, which he put down against the wall to extend his hand to her. She came forward to shake it; instead he took her fingers, bowed formally and kissed her hand, saying, "It's a great pleasure to be invited to stay here. To thank you, I wish to take you out to dinner."

"That would be very nice. What do you have in mind?"

"When I was stationed here, there was a fine flamenco place I liked. They served excellent paella."

"I love flamenco, and paella sounds good to me. But, what's in that important-looking folder?"

"That's for later. It's some art I did when I was a POW. The British treated us well and gave me access to art materials and instruction. I spent much of my time drawing."

"Will you show it to me?"

"Yes, after dinner. For atmosphere at dinner, would you wear something like Carmen wore?"

"You mean boots, black embroidered skirt, white embroidered blouse and a flat-brimmed leather hat?"

"That would be perfect. I'll add the red rose for your hair when we get there."

"Get your things from the car, while I dress."

She could see his car from her bedroom window and was curious about the large suit bag he brought into the house.

He must have phoned ahead, because at the restaurant they were expected and were seated at the best table in the house. Almost immediately, a waiter placed a single red rose on a silver platter before her. Her soldier resembled a Spanish nobleman in his Seville outfit, much like flamenco performers wear, and behaved like one too, as he ceremoniously arranged the red rose under her hat brim in her auburn hair, which she had pulled back tightly into a knot, held in place by a silver comb.

"There now, you look precisely as I imagined you in my dreams—astonishingly beautiful," he said smiling affectionately.

They poured from a bottle of their best red wine and he toasted her with his first sip, "To our success!"

"To our success," she echoed and asked "Where are you from?"

"When I was born, my parents lived in Brazil. I grew up in Santa Catarina until I was eight. Then we moved to Argentina. My father was from Seville. That's where I was educated."

"No wonder you like flamenco!"

"Yes, I was my school's champion flamenco singer."

"Will you perform for me?"

"If they'll let me."

He called the waiter over to their table and whispered something to him. A few minutes later, the leader of the flamenco group came over. Her soldier politely stood up to converse softly to one side with him. He thanked the man and with an apology to her, sat down.

"He said he'd be happy to let me chant one of the numbers," he told her as he reached for her hand. "I can't thank you enough for having me. This is something I've dreamt about for a long time."

They ordered paella and as they were enjoying the wine, he asked her about her youth in Barcelona.

"Who told you I was from Barcelona?"

"It's obvious from your accent; I know many things about you."

"I never once mentioned my private life to you."

"That's right, but as you helped me more and more to regain my confidence, I felt a growing need to know more about you. By the time I realized how important you were to me, I had found out a great deal."

"Like what?"

"Your marriage to Fernando, your escape to Montevideo, then to Chile and on to Los Angeles."

"Who gave you that information? Nobody knows it," she gasped.

"When I reenlisted, they gave me my old job in communications. Because of the importance of my expertise to them during the Malvinas occupation, I had access to all sorts of information and got into the intelligence files for Tucumán Province. When I saw your name 'Alicia de la Rosa, nee, Angelica Diaz', I lifted the file and when I saw what it contained, I removed it from their computers."

"Why did you do that?"

"It incriminated you and I didn't want to see you hurt any more. I was madly in love with you and while I almost worshipped your American mentor for what he did for you, it makes me jealous to think of him."

"My God, you really scare me. I feel naked standing before you. What else do you know?"

"Don't worry. As long as we're together, your information is totally safe with me. There's nothing in writing for anyone to discover."

The guitar players came on stage and were soon joined by a male and a female dancer. They were top performers from Spain and the patrons showed their appreciation with effusive applause.

The leader signaled her soldier. He stood up and with a polite bow to her, said: "This number is expressly for you."

He took up position between the two guitarists, who began playing and at their signal, he stepped forward and began chanting. He had a great stage personality and at the urging of the patrons he began to dance as well as sing. The rhythm was fantastic and his chanting rose to such passion that the audience began calling out "Bravo!" repeatedly. He then moved off stage to stand in front of Alicia and gave a private performance. The audience went wild when she presented him with the red rose out of her hair. He took the stem between his teeth and danced back into position on stage.

They drove home and to break the silence, she said, "That was a fantastic performance you gave. I had no idea that you were that talented."

"Did you mean to give me the rose, or was it just to be polite?"

"It wasn't a gesture."

When they arrived home, he presented her with a colorful silk robe. "I want you to exchange your clothes for this robe. It has a purpose in showing you my art."

Curious to see his art, she came back into the living room looking about as seductive as she could be. The garment was superbly cut to fit her. It presented her cleavage tastefully and her legs showed suggestively through strategically placed slits in the skirt. He had set up a portable easel to the left of her full-length mirror covering a section of the wall. He too was wearing a handsome silk gown.

"I want us to stand here where we can see both, our images in the mirror, and my drawings. I want to know how accurate my recollections of you were out there in isolation."

The first of the charcoal drawings was of a man and a woman in close embrace with her head tilted up to look into his face. Her likeness was unmistakable. The detail was exquisite and the presentation artful in composition. She was dumbfounded and almost didn't notice him embrace her and prompt her to mimic the drawing. He looked down into her sparkling dark eyes with feeling and brought his hand up to softly trace the outline of her lips with his fingers while smiling with satisfaction.

The next pose was of the same two people, now naked, embracing behind a backlit, translucent screen. The outline of her bosom was so precise that she didn't know how to respond.

Casually he peeled his gown off his shoulders to show his naked chest while helping her to do the same. She was shy about being so exposed and tried hide her bosoms.

"Don't be shy. I worked hard to be precise and would like the assurance of success. Try to mimic the drawing exactly."

She straightened up her shoulders and embraced him as boldly as in the drawing.

"Not bad for a lovelorn POW who had never seen his lover naked," he commented.

"No, it's incredible!"

Next came a drawing of her standing naked in front of him slightly to one side, with her hand holding his penis while looking up into his face—his hand fondling her breast.

He dropped his robe to the ground and placed her hand on his penis as he reached over her shoulder to fondle her breast.

She hesitated when she saw how well-endowed he was and held him tentatively.

"No, you must hold me firmly. Don't be afraid, you won't hurt me."

With that she held him so tightly, she could feel the blood coursing to increase his erection. It felt deliciously erotic. She had never seen, let alone touched, one that size with such elegant symmetry.

"Now look up at my face as in the drawing."

She felt her resistance fading as she obeyed his command. His gentle fondling of her bosom excited her and she couldn't resist the passionate kiss that was obviously coming. If she refused him his information about her would not be safe.

He brought their lips together tenderly and gently opened them until they were fully engaged in a French kiss. She experienced a floating feeling as she gave in to him. He knelt down and delicately holding her bosoms, softly kissed them while exciting her bloated nipples with his tongue. She was intensely aroused as he sat her down on the footstool of the loveseat and politely urged her to open her legs. With fingers lubricated from a small vial, he began lightly tracing the folds between her inner and outer lips moving haltingly toward her clitoris. She had never been touched this way and the effect was electrifying, causing her to sharply draw in her breath. By the time he'd moved to fondle her clitoris, her breathing was audible. He lifted her flesh to expose more of it. The effect of moving it up and down stimulated her more than she expected and she involuntarily encouraged it by rhythmically moving counter to his hands. She was beside herself when he lifted it even higher to insert his tongue onto the upper surface of her small protrusion. She heard herself panting softly, "Yes...Yes," to urge him on. She was rapidly coming to a climax and he paused to freshly lubricate his forefingers and ever so gently began inserting one of them into her swollen passage. His lubricant magnified her sensation and as he went deeper and began rubbing against the front lining of her passage where she was most sensitive, her breathing turned to soft moans of intense pleasure. He slowly withdrew his finger as her passage was dilating and inserted two fingers to invade her even deeper. She was finding it difficult to stay still and started to lift her pelvis toward him to increase his motion.

Johan Wassenaar

Then he sucked her clitoris into his mouth, teasing her un-hooded protrusion with his tongue, while stimulating her with his fingers. She went wild, couldn't hold back and began having an orgasm. He controlled its intensity until he had her climaxing continuously. She had never felt so aroused and was unashamed to cry out aloud.

Thoughtfully he withdrew and after her breathing had subsided, he said, "I have something else that you've never experienced," as he brought out a small mirror and a little pouch of cocaine. He carefully laid out two lines on the glass and showed her how to inhale it through her nostril. "I'm not a junky and neither will you be, as long as it is only used in this way."

They both sniffed and as it worked its way into their bloodstreams he resumed stimulating her orally. The sensation was exaggerated but it didn't cause her to orgasm. She was all over the stool as he pleased her. When she could take no more, she began stimulating his large organ. He moved her into positions that pleased him most and showed her how to open her throat to take in more of him. He bent forward and fondled her bosoms that were swollen until her nipples were smooth and stood out straight.

Finally he had her embrace her knees to hug her thighs up against her body. Then he carefully entered her, in small increments until he could go no deeper. He withdrew to rub repeatedly against her clitoris before entering her again and dwelling around her hot spot before going deeper. This time, she moved her body so that he would slide in under her cervix and thus gain several more inches of penetration. He then began reciprocating slowly, increasing the pace until she was screaming with delight. And still, neither of them climaxed.

They stopped for a drink of water and another snort of cocaine before proceeding with different positions of intercourse until they were physically spent and drifted off to sleep.

* * *

She awoke tucked in her own bed. My God, she thought, how will I explain <u>this</u> to Kevin? If I don't go along with the soldier he could blow our whole case and in the process expose me. Besides, what he did to her just blew her mind. She had no idea that sex could be that satisfying without a serious component of affection. As the full import of what had happened, began to sink in, her feelings alternated between swells of anguish and a desire for more — especially after ending without an orgasm.

When he surfaced and confidently breezed in to resume their intimacy she felt compelled to set limits.

"There's a woman not far from here, who, like you, witnessed things her conscience wouldn't allow her to hide. She was a nurse at ESMA and delivered babies from female prisoners who were then murdered and their children awarded to childless families of officials, to register as their own. I have other eyewitnesses to these atrocities, but our case would be much stronger if an insider would also testify. She's an attractive single woman with a feeling about the military much like yours. I want you to convince her to testify for me."

"What do I get for bringing home the bacon?"

"First, you'll have the chance of romancing a very responsive woman and if I have to, I'll sleep with you one more time before the case goes to trial."

"Only once, given all I know about you? What happens after that?"

"I told you up front that I was happily married with three children and a respected professional practice and could offer you nothing permanent. You agreed and said that you would take your chances. Those are your chances."

"I don't think so. I love you too much to give up that easily. Where is your heart, woman? I know you have one. You cured my screwed-up emotions. Don't you have any more room for me?"

"Not in that way. You have incredible charm and sexual prowess. You proved it so strongly last night, I can hardly wait for more, but then it must end after two more times?"

"OK, I guess I'll take my chances," he said as he crept into bed with her and began kissing her. She held him firmly to feel his tension rise until he was as hard as bone before giving him access to her. They went at each other with the desperation befitting a last opportunity. Without the help of the drug, they exploded in ecstasy. He drew her to him and they kissed long and fervently.

"Oh, no. Look at the time! We had better get cleaned up fast. We have an eight o'clock meeting. Whatever you do, play it straight. No personal affection, please; do this professionally. And, by the way, if you ever spill the beans about my identity, I'll have you killed."

"Like the agent you brought down in Montevideo?"

"Damn you, is there anything you don't know about me?"

"A bit more, but after this morning I won't need it. My love for you is at least as strong as your commitment to your Gringo."

"After what I've just done to him, that doesn't amount to much."

* * *

The meeting with Dr. Diaz was hard on Alicia. She tried to keep the discussion strictly on the merits of their case against General Bussi, while he was in command of Tucumán Province between 1976 and the beginning of 1978. Under his command many atrocities were committed. Amongst the five thousand people he made "disappear", more than half may have been innocent of any form of subversion. That is where their focus had to be.

"The most conspicuous atrocity we've been able to document, is the General's propensity to shoot prisoners, made to kneel down in front of a communal grave, with hoods over their heads waiting to be executed by a firing squad. He did so with his hand gun, to cow his troops into subverting their consciences and shoot defenseless prisoners in cold blood," Alicia started the discussion.

"How many eyewitnesses, willing to testify to these atrocities, do we have?" Dr. Diaz asked.

"We have a young woman who inadvertently saw two such incidents while being held in a secret detention center near San Miguel. Rodolfo, here, was one of the troops assigned to the firing squad. He saw more than one such event."

"I can understand why a person wronged by the military would want to turn State's witness, but why a soldier?" Diaz asked, looking at Rodolfo.

"Sir, I was horrified by what I'd seen and experienced what my therapists, Alicia and Elena, called a 'post-traumatic stress disorder'— I couldn't sleep, had repetitive nightmares and was so depressed that I thought of taking my own life."

"Is that your only reason? There are many people who would see the act of a soldier giving evidence against his commanding General as treason."

"I would not have thought of turning State's witness, had I not been helped so generously by the two women to regain my emotional balance. When Alicia asked me to cooperate with her, I felt an obligation to do so."

"I find that hard to believe. Surely, you understand that the hierarchy still running the military would try to punish you?"

"Sir, after I regained my mental health, I reenlisted and served honorably in the Malvinas where my communications technology was of vital importance and for which I was awarded the Army's highest medal. I think, they'll think twice before punishing me, given that the new Generals think well of me."

"If that's so, why did you quit the Army?"

"My reason was selfish. The defense budget cuts by the civilian government made it punitive for me to stay in and the public image of the military had sunk so low that many of us were embarrassed to be part of it. I had far better opportunities on the outside, Sir."

"How will we know that we can trust you to testify as you promised? You could say one thing now and do something else in court!"

"I'm a man of honor, Sir, and swear that I will do exactly what I promised."

"How does that square with your oath to loyally serve the military?"

"I wouldn't do it if I was still in the military, Sir."

"What happens if—after you appear in court and are on record, under oath—the case is appealed or for other reasons held in abeyance? Won't someone from the old school have you harmed or killed?"

"That's the risk I have to take if I'm to be honorable to Alicia."

"What's this got to do with Alicia? We're talking about a horrific atrocity by a senior General! She was just your psychotherapist."

"Yes and no. What she did for me was such a kindness that I feel a serious obligation to help her."

"What obligation? You paid her for her professional help...didn't you? Next you'll be telling me that you fell in love with her!"

"Let's just say that I came to regard her with great affection."

"Come on, son, that's no guarantee that you won't change your mind. We have to deal in specifics."

"Sir, I'd hate to be cross-examined by you. I'll tell you the truth. When my communications detail was getting ready to go to the Malvinas, I had free access to all the Government's computer databases. I looked up 'Alicia de la Rosa' and found a file with incriminating details about her escape from Argentina and killing a

Junta agent in Montevideo...I had no choice but to destroy the file. If I stepped out of line, you could hold that against me."

"Not a chance, young man. It would destroy you, but in the process it would expose us to unacceptable danger. Besides, how can we be sure that you really destroyed those files?"

"Arnold," Alicia interjected in English, "I made a deal with him to not only testify on our behalf, but also to help us persuade the nurse from ESMA to do the same. Her testimony about the baby business would be dynamite."

"What makes you think that she'd be influenced by him?"

"They share the same disillusionment with the military establishment. I really think it will work."

"What do you have to produce at your end of the deal?"

"Look, I swore an oath with you to avenge the loss of Fernando, come what may. This guy's in love with me and insisted on receiving sexual favors in return."

"Dear God, say it isn't so. Don't you realize how dangerous that could be? The more you give, the more he'll want."

"That's why I threw in the chore of convincing the nurse—to give it a point of finality."

"Does Kevin know about this prostitution lark of yours?"

"Arnold, don't be so judgmental, I have yet to tell Kevin. I wish it wasn't so. It breaks my heart, but how else can I secure his cooperation and safeguard what he knows about me?"

Dr. Diaz turned his attention back to the soldier. "She told me what your deal was. I find it despicable that you would sink that low. If you don't abide strictly by the rules you agreed to and try to blackmail her, you will most assuredly die. What are those rules?"

"She agreed that I could sleep with her two more times before we file for an indictment; then it's over."

"I want you to sit down here and write down exactly what you saw General Bussi do—when, where, how and why—which I will use in preparing the petition to indict Bussi. You will have to swear to the authenticity of your statement before a notary public. I hope you understand that this memorandum will be addressed to the Supreme Council of the Military. They proclaimed beforehand that they will not act on any requests for indictments, which, after six months, automatically grants us an appeal to the civil Appellate Court in Buenos Aires. There is no guarantee that the contents of our memo won't be read or leaked by the military staff."

"I hope you understand that I truly love Alicia and am willing to testify only because of her."

"If you truly loved her you wouldn't hold the secret file on her over her head to obtain sexual favors. Don't expect any respect from me, young man."

Alicia was pale with fright from the consequences her involvement with the soldier had wrought. If only she could honestly say that she had done so totally against her will. Clearly he had conned and seduced her, but she had not found it offensive. On the other hand, there now was no other way for her to ensure his cooperation than to give in to his passion.

"Alicia," Arnold addressed her in English. "I want you to sit down at that end of the table and write down precisely what you've agreed to do to secure Rodolfo's cooperation for the entire case from beginning to end. I also want you to indicate what part of the deal you've already satisfied—and I didn't mean to use that phrase indelicately."

"Oh, Suegro," she said, lapsing into Spanish, "I find this so difficult. I can't stand losing your and Kevin's respect, but I don't know how to live up to my oath any other way."

"Just write what I asked you, child."

He reviewed what they'd written. With minor changes and the addition of several caveats, he added spaces for them to initial and sign.

"I will go through this once more to be sure that you both fully understand what this requires of you and what limitations it places on you."

"You, Rodolfo, will testify, as you have described, in any and all hearings pertinent to the case, however long it takes to reach a verdict as well as a sentence. Furthermore, you will use any and all talents you possess to persuade the nurse, formerly from EMSA, to testify for the State in a different case dealing with the theft of newborn babies from prisoners."

"Yes, Sir, I understand all of that."

"Now for the most painful part of my entire career—do you, Alicia, understand that you are prepared to have sexual intercourse up to two more times with Rodolfo before the case in which he has agreed to testify for the State goes to trial? After that you will have no further obligations whatsoever to him."

"Yes, Suegro, regrettable as they are, I understand those terms."

"And, Rodolfo, do you understand that you have no further right to sexual favors from Alicia after that and that you will not be allowed to make any future overtures to her of a personal nature?"

"I wish that it didn't have to be, but I agree and accept those terms and constraints."

"All right, then, I expect you both here at ten o'clock tomorrow morning to sign these agreements in the presence of a notary."

"Rodolfo, I'm done with you for today and you may leave. Alicia, we have another interview here in thirty minutes. Please, be here on time?"

They sheepishly left his study and she walked Rodolfo to his car. "Please don't make light of these agreements, whatever you do. You can't stay in my house tonight. My partner will be returning any time now. Tomorrow morning after we sign the papers, we immediately have to leave for our visit to the nurse. She is expecting us at two in Catamarca, which is quite a long drive."

"When will I see you after that? I can't wait to make love to you again."

"Jesus, is that all you ever think of? Perhaps if we get back here early enough, there may be time tomorrow evening."

He stepped forward to kiss her, but she waved him off and went back inside.

She needed time to herself to figure out how to handle her situation with Kevin. In spite of her infidelity, her devotion to him was unchanged. She hated the thought of how deeply he'd be hurt. She knew that he wouldn't raise his voice in anger, but his icy silence and cryptic conclusions would be devastating. She had to find a way to make amends. She couldn't live without his approval and intellectual support. At that moment she despised Angélica for what she'd done.

* * *

The presence of the elderly woman in the next case was startlingly different from that of the sex-crazed soldier. She was calm and collected and wasted no time making Dr. Diaz cognizant of the circumstances surrounding the disappearance of her youngest daughter, Silvia. Her daughter had subsequently surfaced in the Naval facility's child birthing ward in Buenos Aires where the nurse delivered her baby and witnessed it being taken from her and given up for illegal adoption.

"The nurse couldn't live with her conscience and after several years, voluntarily came all the way here to tell me about it. Her news caused serious psychological problems for me, which, thanks to Señora de la Rosa and Señora Mendoza, I was able to overcome. I believe that the nurse is brave enough to testify about it in court."

Dr. Diaz explained to her why this would be a civil trail in Buenos Aires against the top commander who was responsible.

"We are in touch with the nurse and Senora de la Rosa will go there tomorrow to seek her cooperation. Then we will file a petition to indict the guilty party or parties. We hope to get a guilty verdict, but even then, we expect them to appeal. For today, I just need you to fill out the details on this form and bring it back as soon as you can."

"May I just fill it out here and save another trip? Transportation is a bit difficult for me right now."

"Of course you can, and when you're done, perhaps one of us— Señora de la Rosa—can drive you home."

That was not what Alicia wanted to hear, she had hoped to get up enough courage to call Kevin. Somewhere in the back of her mind Angélica had images of seeing her soldier again.

CHAPTER TWENTY-SIX

The news from Elena, that Alicia would be staying an extra week in San Miguel, bothered Kevin. It meant that he'd either have to fly Elena there on Saturday and return home empty, or persuade her to take the airline.

He opted for the latter and since her husband was away, he drove her to the airport. In the car she began telling him of the difficulty she and her spouse were having.

"Eduardo was getting tired of me being away so much and started complaining more and more. I altered my schedule—much to Alicia's discomfort—but he started staying over in Valparaiso longer and more often until we weren't seeing more of each other, any way. So I went back to my original schedule."

"Is there anything we can do to help you? I don't suppose it would do much good if I spoke to him?"

"Don't, he's jealous of you. He accuses me of showing you more affection than him."

"How can that be?"

"You're too blind to notice how much I care for you. Perhaps you ignore it not to upset Alicia."

"That's absurd. You're naturally flirtatious and you're fun to flirt with. But that's nothing for Eduardo to be jealous about," Kevin objected.

"That's what I mean about you not noticing."

She embarrassed Kevin and he was relieved when they entered the passenger terminal. He pulled up to the curb at her departure point and opened the trunk to get her bag. She stood on the curb and reached out to take her bag, then pulled him toward her. He gave her a friendly hug and let her go, but her arms were still around his neck and she lightly kissed him as she handed him a hand—written note.

He blushed as he waved good-bye and drove off, thinking that it may have been a mistake to invite her and Eduardo to live in their guesthouse on the ranch.

He sat down at the ranch kitchen table to read her note. She began by expressing her thanks for everything Alicia had done for her professionally and hoped that her observations would not be construed as criticism.

She wrote: "*Since the election of Alfonsin, Alicia has become obsessed with her desire to avenge Fernando's murder. It was as if she had suddenly changed back to being Angélica.*

"*We started the practice on the premise of gaining incriminating evidence. It was always our intention to do this together. We jointly selected the information we had acquired that would make the most compelling cases, and began talking to Dr. Diaz about drafting petitions to indict the guilty ones.*

"*Then suddenly, she went ahead with two prospective cases without my involvement. The Tucumán case is based on credible evidence from an eyewitness who was incarcerated where the shooting took place. Alicia and I agree that we need stronger evidence and needed to enlist the help of a soldier who, as a member of a firing squad, saw his general shoot condemned prisoners with his handgun.*

"*I don't trust this soldier, since I conducted much of the therapy to cure him of his distress from the trauma caused by that incident. I think he formed an unhealthy emotional attachment to both Alicia and me during his treatment and that he may resort to any method— even blackmail—to endear her to him in compensation for turning State's witness. I voiced this concern to her, but she blind-sided me, as Angélica of old would have done, and proceeded without me.*

"*I don't want to jeopardize my professional relationship with her. But since she suspects me of desiring you I can't influence her. Someone has to prevent her from making a serious mistake. It is quite possible that, if he doesn't get the attention he craves from Angélica, this soldier would expose what we are doing to his former military peers. I also don't trust Angélica to resist his overtures."*

Kevin thought long and hard and then picked up the phone to call Xavier at the stables.

"How are you Xavier? Can we ride with you again?"

"Since you took Alicia's horse to Chile, I haven't heard from either of you, but we have good horses for you to ride. When would you like to come?"

"I'm not sure, but there's something I'd like you to check out for me—just between the two of us. Would you be kind enough to see if any of your friends saw Alicia out with a tall, handsome, man at one of the better restaurants last night? If you hear anything, feel free to call me collect as soon as you can?"

"Sure, that will be easy," Xavier replied. "I have several of my chaps scouting for other clients."

"I didn't know that you were a private investigator!"

"Not quite yet," Xavier explained, "but we are beginning to build up such a business."

"That's good to know. I sometimes need services such as yours, but I'm in a bit of a hurry with this one."

"I'll move it along, I hope she's OK."

"So do I. Thanks Xavier."

Late Sunday morning, Kevin received a detailed account of the soldier's flamenco show in front of Alicia, complete with a description of the red rose ritual. Xavier's comment was that Kevin certainly appeared to have serious romantic competition.

Kevin called Alicia, but there was no answer. He called the Diaz residence.

"Arnold, I'm glad I caught you. I fear that something terrible has gone wrong with Alicia. On Friday night she was seen in..." and he described what he had heard from Xavier. "This guy was seriously coming on to her and by the way she gave him the red rose, she wasn't showing much restraint. Elena gave me a note at the airport on her way to Tucumán in which she described him as emotionally untrustworthy. I know that he's after Alicia with all the sexual drive in the world and will use it as his price for cooperation. What do you know about this?"

"I hate to tell you, but he's well ahead of us. I tried to nip it in the bud with a contract which they both signed this morning. He will not be allowed more than two more sexual encounters with her before the case goes to court and an indictment is granted. They left here for Catamarca to persuade the midwife nurse to also turn State's witness in the other trial. As part of their deal, the soldier has to do his utmost to convince the woman. After all, they are both disillusioned military officers."

"What can I do to save my marriage?"

"There, I can't advise you. In your shoes, I'd go to her as quickly as possible. If you took off now, you could be here in time to confront them."

"Thanks, Arnold, that's good advice."

He grabbed a few essentials and called Elena at her office to ask her to meet him at the airport in three hours.

* * *

Alicia and her soldier drove most of the way to Catamarca in silence. She was very much aware of her father-in-law's disapproval of her conduct with the soldier and petrified at the thought of how Kevin would react to it. She hoped that he was still unaware of what had happened, because she couldn't get up enough courage after the wrenching experience of facing the hidden wrath of her Suegro, to explain it again to Kevin. Besides, there wasn't much to explain. He would immediately know that largely she had acted out of lust. How was she going to survive without his respect and encouragement?

Without that she'd be reduced to "Angélica". Only this time she'd be the slave of a man with a huge sexual appetite, but a miniature soul—a level of morality she could not expose her children to. She absolutely had to find a way back into Kevin's comfort zone.

At each stop for refreshments or fuel when they switched seats, Rodolfo tried to lift her somber mood by reflecting on the exuberant moments in their brief relationship, pointing out how beautiful she looked at the flamenco restaurant, the marvelous feelings of comparing his art to reality, leading up to her exhilaration when he induced her first extended orgasm. He did it with style to evoke in her the fringes of an inextricable desire for more. At one point, when she was at the wheel, he began stroking her neck and shoulders to help relieve her stress and it felt good enough that she didn't discourage him. She leaned forward on the wheel as he messaged her back. It felt wonderful as he moved down along her backbone, working on the knots in her tense muscles. She didn't notice when he unhooked her bra, until she felt his delicate touch of her breast nearest him. It was so natural that it seemed right to her. He gradually grew bolder until he was fondling her nipple, which had become swollen, soft and full.

By the time he placed his hand on her thigh and began moving up under her short skirt, she had drenched her panties and almost welcomed his titillating fingers moving into her bloating passage. It wasn't until he unzipped his pants and exposed his large, elegant protrusion, that she caught herself and removed his hand from her genitals.

"This is not the time. We have to focus on how to persuade the nurse"

"That's what I was practicing," he joked.

"You are incorrigible."

"I know, but you love it."

She felt better, but was cross that she had again succumbed to his treachery and instinctively knew that sooner or later he'd use up one of his "privileges" that day. She was angered by her body's refusal to reject the idea and remained damp between her legs most of the day.

The nurse turned out to be more attractive than the elderly patient had described. She was taller than Alicia, had soft, curly, black hair, very pale skin and vibrant blue eyes. Her build was athletic with beautiful long legs and shapely bosoms. Alicia noticed the overt look of approval in her soldier's eyes and felt a pang of envy.

They introduced themselves and Rodolfo explained his experience in the military and what had become so offensive to him that he resigned. Alicia talked about her own experience and what she had seen through the eyes of her trauma patients. They all agreed that it was an unacceptable state of affairs that needed to be addressed aggressively before it got swept under the rug.

"Rodolfo has decided to testify for the State against certain officers for particularly heinous conduct he bore witness to. Our patient told my partner and me about your experience in like circumstances and thought that you may be persuaded to testify against the military commander in Buenos Aires in civil court for the theft of newborn infants. As a direct-witness, much as in Rodolfo's situation, you would strengthen our case several fold," Alicia emphasized.

"If I may add," Adolfo elaborated "when Alicia asked me the same question, I immediately saw the contribution I could make towards restoring some sense of decency in our country to add to my undying gratitude to her for helping me out of my depression."

"While I'm partial to the idea, it would be a far-reaching decision for me. I have to study the risks and liabilities of turning State's evidence," the nurse said, dodging a quick answer.

"I understand your caution. Would it be helpful if I went through my own justifications for taking the risk," Rodolfo offered. "After I was cured of my emotional dysfunction, I reenlisted as a Captain to serve in the Malvinas, where the British captured me and my squad. The Army subsequently decorated me and I resigned my commission at the rank of Major. Looking back at my Army career, I decided I owed it to my country to help set the record straight. I felt that people like us with solid credentials have an obligation to stand up and be counted, in view of the utter brutality we saw."

"In general I agree, but I need you to walk me through your rationale step-by-step."

With a warm smile, the soldier answered, "I'll be happy to show you. I'm available on weekends."

"Where do you live?"

"Down in Córdoba."

"Do you have room for us to work and for me to stay?"

"I have a house in Córdoba."

"Do you live there with your family?"

"No, I'm a bachelor. I live alone."

"You, live alone?" the nurse questioned.

"Why, are you surprised?"

"You seem very eligible to me!" she added.

"Is that a come-on?" Rodolfo asked.

"Perhaps, I'm getting tired of living alone out here in the sticks. I was used to being pursued by eligible men in Buenos Aires. You're not gay are you?"

"No, you'll be perfectly safe working with me. Can we do it next Saturday?" he said with a knowing wink and gave her driving instructions to his residence.

Alicia interjected, "What particularly concerns you about testifying?"

"I don't want to jeopardize my pension income from the Army."

"I know how to minimize that risk," Rodolfo added.

On the way home, the soldier expressed optimism that the nurse would cooperate and his manner suggested enthusiasm for something other than the purpose at hand.

Alicia found herself beset by pangs of jealousy. He was at the wheel, and as she thought about sharing his unusual prowess with an overtly available, luscious woman, she began craving his assurance that she would remain his preferred partner. She gradually succumbed to the urge of drawing his attention away from the nurse by moving closer to him and placing one hand on his thigh while stroking his forearm with the other. He pretended not to notice and then gave her hand a squeezed to reassure her. She took his hand by the fingers and just barely touched the back of his hand with her lips. He responded by opening her lips with two fingers to nibble on. The symbolism was inescapable and strangely aroused her as Angélica took the stage. For emphasis he moved her hand toward his fly and unbuckled his belt. She responded by unzipping him. He'd been getting hard and fascinated by its size; she held and encouraged him with gentle strokes under its mushroom head. He loved the sensation and put his free hand on the top of her head, to gently nudge her face toward his erection. She complied eagerly, seductively moving up and down his shaft until he was lodged deep in her open throat. His driving was getting erratic and it wasn't long before she was swallowing repeatedly and kissing him passionately on the mouth. They were laughing when he pulled over to give her the wheel.

She moved around the front of the car, stepping out of her panties, handing them to him while unzipping her skirt. She had hardly steered back onto the highway before he was feeling under her skirt.

"Halloo," he said. "When did you shave? You must be expecting me to claim another of my precious 'rights' tonight. It's much better that way," he said and gently moved his hand between her legs. She moved her right knee to his side of the gearshift and urged him with her free had to touch her. He did so delicately with care to excite her in small incremental steps until he went down on her. Once again he extended her ecstasy until she was climaxing in small repeated bursts. They had gone no more that ten miles before she had to turn the driving back over to him.

Between rest-periods they repeated the cycle several times before reached San Miguel where they stayed in the car on her doorstep to finish their last round of foreplay. They were virtually naked and highly aroused as they stumbled into her living room. He could hardly hold still long enough to lay out the lines of coke which they snorted in haste to start their full ritual.

* * *

Kevin landed in San Miguel after dark where Elena was waiting to drive him home. "If you don't mind, I'll be staying with the Diaz family tonight," Elena began. "I think you need to be alone with Alicia."

"Thanks. That's thoughtful of you," he answered and told her what he'd heard from Xavier.

"I can vouch for Xavier's veracity. There's talk all over town about their flamenco show. You know what a small gossipy place this is."

"But, there's more serious stuff happening," and he explained to Elena what Dr. Diaz had told him. "For Christ sake, can you believe it? She paid for his silence and willingness to testify by promising him sexual favors! The ass-hole is entitled to sleep with her three times before the case goes to trial. Ostensibly, he also has to enlist the support of the nurse to testify. The two of them are off talking to the nurse as we speak and probably also to screw their heads off."

"Take it easy, Kevin. That soldier has to be handled carefully to secure his testimony. I know, because I treated him. You have to stay cool or you'll blow everything...your marriage and both our cases."

She went on to explain.

"Last Friday he seduced her, or perhaps more precisely, he seduced Angélica. Having served time in a POW camp, you can be sure that his perversions are well developed. She must have found his technique exhilarating, going far beyond her own sexual experiences. As a sexually active woman, as she and I both were in our late teens, I'm sure that the expectation of additional encounters with the soldier would have mesmerized Angélica. I her position I too would have wanted more. He clearly is a superlative lover. This may be reflected in the fact that she let her father-in-law write the contract in such a way as not to impose constraints on her to seek sexual 'favors' from <u>him</u>.

"Her huge dilemma is that she couldn't stand letting you know about her planned infidelity and now has to convince you that it was the only way she could get him to testify," Elena completed her analysis.

"What satisfaction does the bastard offer that she can't get from me?"

"This is pure speculation, but I've seen credible data that the studs in the Malvinas POW camps prided themselves in artificially enlarging their Johns. There's a myth that an outsize penis offers a woman better sex, which is anatomically incorrect. Artificially lengthened tools are usually too long to fit into most women. Without care these bozos can punch the devil out of a woman's cervix and cause serious damage."

"How do they enlarge them?"

"With exercises and dietary supplements."

"You've got to be kidding, what exercises?"

"There are many routines of dubious quality and some bizarre ones; like hanging weights from or putting splints on them."

"That sounds depraved to me."

They arrived at Alicia's house, there was nobody home, and Kevin rushed in. After three hours of flight he urgently needed to use the toilet. He had taken off his jacket and shoulder holster and was about to put his pistol down, when he heard the commotion coming from the front parlor. He doused the lights and cautiously moved to the front room, his handgun at the ready, only to find two naked bodies frantically entangled sexually pleasing each other on the carpet of the living room. His inclination was to destroy the soldier, but mindful of Elena's warning, he forcefully controlled his emotions and just quietly stood watching.

They moved with precision, almost seamlessly from one routine to the next. He stood anchored in amazement. It surprised him the way she relished oral sex. With him, she'd always had inhibitions about oral sex. Now she even encouraged it by shaving her pubic hair. He envied the man for being able to draw such phenomenal responses from her.

Then he saw the drug paraphernalia on the floor and it dawned on him why she was able to conduct herself in such explicit ways. She flung her legs wide open and guided his huge erection into her. There was much groaning of satisfaction to accompany the slow gradual invasion of her, which increased and then paused to visit around her most sensitive areas before continuing inward. It was done so elegantly that he felt inferior. The soldier became increasingly aggressive and was soon pounding her until she screamed in agony, pleading with him not to be so rough. He paid no attention and increased the severity of his movements until Kevin's natural instinct to protect his wife overwhelmed him.

He leapt over the bodies, grabbed the man's legs and savagely jerked him off her.

With drug-crazed eyes the soldier came at Kevin who sidestepped, sending the man flying across the room, giving him time to raise and aim his pistol. The bullet parted the man's thick mop of curly black hair and stopped him dead in his tracks.

Johan Wassenaar

"You crazy son of a bitch! Don't you know what damage you can do with that artificially large thing of yours?" Kevin yelled at him.

With tremendous effort he swallowed his temper and his angry blue eyes turned to ice.

"I've been standing here totally animated by the precise and practiced manner in which you've perfect the art of fornication. You were so good it made me feel inadequate. I was never permitted the luxury of such marvelous oral sex with Alicia. It amuses me that she went so far as to shave her pubic hair. You're a privileged man, soldier!

"But, on to realities. I saw nothing in any of your routines that I have not used or would use if called upon. I just lack three things:

"I don't have an unnaturally enlarged penis;

"Sex with me lacks the nefarious excitement of doing it with a stranger;

"On principle I regard it immoral to use addictive narcotics to enhance sexual gratification.

"You are ill-advised, soldier, to have used sex as a bribe. It's a form of extortion which you will ultimately pay for."

He waited to let his words sink in before continuing in a calm, reasoned voice:

"So where do we go from here? If Rodolfo has one ounce of decency left in his bones, he would relieve Alicia of any further sexual obligation to him and agree never to have personal contact with her again, so that she can come home to rebuild her and our lives.

"Even then, the problem remains that Alicia is free to seek more sex from you. She will have to swear never to have personal contact with you again.

"The only alternative is for Alicia to break off her relationship with me and with her family, which I hope she will find unacceptable."

"You have two days in which to decide which it will be," Kevin stipulated. "Until then, it will not be acceptable for Alicia to visit her children. They are too young and vulnerable to be exposed to any of this."

"Please Kevin! Don't think so badly of me. I am what you made me. Without your approval I can't go on. I needed Rodolfo's help to nail those bastards and fell for his seduction."

"So soldier, is she relieved of any further sexual obligations to you?"

"I need time to think. You're too fast for me."

"I should warn you, soldier. If you dare double cross Dr. Diaz and blow your commitments to testify, you're a dead man. If I can part your hair with a bullet, you can be sure that I'll remove both your gonads with a single shot."

Kevin grimaced, the color returned to his eyes and he addressed his wife in a gentle voice, "Darling, I'll get you a clean towel to put between your legs. Your clean-shaven lips look like you tried to put lipstick on them. Your soldier must have punched a leak in your cervix. We'll have to get you to a hospital real fast."

"Oh damn, look what you've done, you stupid idiot," she said to the soldier.

Kevin called Elena to fetch them. The obstetrician at the hospital wanted to know how it happened. Kevin lied that they had been careless with a dildo. She had a tear where her cervix joins her uterus. The doctor told Alicia to wear sterile absorbents—as if she had her period—until the bleeding stopped. She injected her with a heavy dose of antibiotics, gave Kevin antibiotic pills to give Alicia twice daily and forbade any form of intercourse for the next four weeks, after which she'd examine Alicia again.

They drove her home in silence. The soldier's car was still there.

"Please Kevin, come in with me? I'm scared of what he'll do to me."

"No, after the damaged I did to his ego tonight, you have to make sure that he will testify. If he stays on the team, which I'm sure he will, you can hand him his walking papers. Call me, I'll come and get you."

"Oh God, do I have to?"

"Yes, only you can do this."

"Does it really have to end this way?"

"You must come home to me and your family. It's your only hope. It will take hard work to heal the wounds you've opened, but we will go on loving you."

* * *

In the car on the way to the Diaz residence, Kevin described to Elena what he'd witnessed.

"It was the worst experience of my life. What really scares me is the guy's use of cocaine to enhance their sexual senses. Clearly, he's got her hooked on supercharged sex. It won't take much to get her addicted to that stuff. I'm not even sure that she'll decide to come home!"

"My God, if it's that bad," Elena ventured, "we can't leave her to handle the nurse. If anything, the nurse's testimony is the most valuable of all. Alicia has the nurse meeting the soldier at his home next Saturday!"

"You've got a point," Kevin agreed. "Let's discuss it with Arnold."

"Who's Arnold?"

"I'm sorry, that's what we call Doctor Diaz when we converse in English."

"Kevin, I am desperately sorry for you. I'll do anything I can to help you," Elena said as she squeezed his arm.

With the torn copy of the soldier's sex deal in his hand, Dr. Diaz greeted them at the door.

"He came here looking unusually contrite and said the he would relieve her of any further obligations."

Dr. Diaz agreed to let Elena assume responsibility for handling the nurse and the rest of the details of their second case.

Kevin tried phoning Alicia, but received no answer. Her fear of Rodolfo's response bothered him to the point where he borrowed Elena's car to drive home. The place was in total darkness and both her car and the soldier's were gone. He went inside to find the place neatly picked up, except for Alicia's room, which showed the chaotic signs of a hasty exit.

He reported what he'd found to Elena and asked her to be ready to leave with him at dawn.

"Please call the nurse now and ask her to meet you at the airfield at six thirty. I've been there. It's a good airport. We need to stop her from meeting with the soldier. If anyone found out that they'd been colluding, it could cast doubt on her testimony. Ask her for the soldier's address and phone number. I'll be flying on to Córdoba to check on Alicia and will pick you up on the way back. I'm sure she took off after him when he left. They must have argued over him tearing up their sex deal and blaming her for proposing it."

"I think Alicia felt threatened by Rodolfo's seductive response to the nurse. She's probably attractive and tired of living in the sticks on her own," Elena concluded.

CHAPTER TWENTY-SEVEN

To see the nurse in time, Kevin and Elena left for Catamarca at daybreak. Elena used the cozy privacy of the intercom to remind him of her feelings, which were strengthened by her sympathy for both Alicia and him.

"I can understand your anguish at seeing them having sex so outrageously in front of you, but try not to be angry with Alicia over her bizarre behavior. Right now, she's a very sick person, with almost no control over her emotions. She's possessed by a devilish drive to be Angélica and to avenge the loss of Fernando in her own way. Like a child, rebelling against authority, she seized upon the conquest of her own sexual inhibitions as tangible evidence of her drive. I remember her telling me about proving that she had left her Catholic aversions behind by having oral sex with you."

"Yes, it held the promise of her also challenging other hang-ups," Kevin mused. "Are your problems with Eduardo perhaps associated with similar elements in your makeup?"

"With us, it's the other way around. I love sex in almost any form."

"I didn't know you were that relaxed about your sexuality. Was Eduardo that way too?"

"Heavens, no! Eduardo is the world's quintessential prude. I had to resort to a form of psychotherapy to make him tolerable in bed. Even then, it had to be in total darkness."

"Doesn't that frustrate you?"

"Off the record, I have a secret drawer, which I keep locked, in which I maintain a supply of sex toys. Without them, I doubt that our love affair would have lasted this long."

"Well, I'll be damned, I never thought of you that way. How often do you unlock that little drawer?"

"It's not so little. I gave you my thoughts about Rodolfo's artificially enlarged one. Well, Eduardo needs that kind of therapy. So I have to offset his shortcomings...no pun intended."

"Perhaps I should ask the soldier for his formula. I wonder if that could be part of my problem with Alicia."

"That's possible. I've never seen you naked"

"I really would like to know whether I come up short enough for it to have mattered to her."

"I don't think you'd be wise to mimic the soldier and I don't ascribe his sexual attractiveness to his bloated Wiener."

* * *

The nurse was waiting and seemed pleased to see them.

"Alicia explained to me what you were trying to accomplish, and almost had me sold...until she turned that smooth-talking soldier onto me. He came on too strong...I could smell his ulterior motives. So, I let him think that I was open to a heterosexual relationship. He got so eager about having me spend next Saturday with him in Córdoba that I could see what his real intentions were. I felt sorry for Alicia. It was clear that he had her in his clutches already and that his flirtations with me were designed to make her jealous.

"After years in the service, I know his type and can tell that he's making up for his failures in life by winning sexual control over as many frustrated women as he can lay his hands on."

"Can we start over fresh with regard to you testifying?" Elena asked.

"Yes, I have my own personal reasons to be interested, but there are many questions I need answered."

"Good. I can stay here as long as you need me to answer them. Kevin has to leave for Córdoba to talk to the soldier. You wouldn't have his address and phone number handy? We left so early, I forgot to bring my notebook."

* * *

Kevin took off for Córdoba with deeply anguished. What the nurse said, about Alicia being jealous of the soldier's attention to her, almost made him panic. He had seen the whole horrible spectacle as one of lust and hadn't even considered the possibility that his wife could be enamored with the man. If she was truly smitten under the spell of Angélica, there was no telling how far she'd go. He was a damned fool not to have gone in with her, as she begged him to do. She was crying out for help, not out of fear of what <u>he</u> would do, but rather what <u>she</u> would do.

He took a taxi to the soldier's address and found both the soldier's and Alicia's cars parked out front. Braced for a torrent of anger from the soldier, he politely knocked on the door, which a dressed Rodolfo, ready to leave for the office, answered.

"I owe you an apology. Perhaps I was too judgmental last night. Doctor Diaz told me that you relieved Alicia of any further obligations to you. I'm grateful for your consideration."

"It really wasn't my intention to insist on favors from her. Her therapy helped me regain my sanity and the further away from her I got, the more convinced I became that I loved her, especially during my months in POW camp in the Malvinas. I dreamed of her constantly and even took art classes to draw pictures of us together.

"If you were that smitten, why did you wait till now to approach her?" Kevin said, throwing him a curve ball."

"She tracked me down to ask me to testify and suddenly, I was on cloud nine with opportunities to see her and be with her. I didn't think for a minute that she would be receptive to my romantic approach. She was too advanced intellectually to fall for that. She told me to my face that she was happily married, a mother of three and held a respectable professional position in the community."

"What happened to change that?"

"I took her to dinner and entertained her by chanting and dancing flamenco, then I showed her my drawings and before I realized how receptive she had become, we were making passionate love on the living room floor."

"Didn't you also tell her how much you knew about her and how culpable you thought that made her?"

"I told her what I had found out, but assured her that I had destroyed her file in the computer database and that as her intimate friend I'd keep it a secret."

"Perhaps you should have substituted the word 'lover' for 'friend' to be honest. I believe that you meant to imply that if she didn't cooperate, your information about her could become insecure."

"I didn't force her into anything. I certainly didn't rape her. She came willingly."

"Yes, 'willingly' as in the seduction of someone."

"I did no more than romance her."

"Even if that were true, you didn't have to go through with it. A man of honor would have stopped."

"You are right about that and I will go to my grave regretting what I did. But worse, I foolishly introduced her to cocaine to heighten her sexual perceptions and we got carried away. She had never felt like that and wanted more. That's when she negotiated the details of our 'deal.'"

"Are you telling me that you weren't reluctant to testify?"

"I had some reservations, but as I told you, I felt passionately about her and would have testified even if she hadn't had sex with me."

"After that first evening, why didn't you stop?"

"We were both charged up and when she began coming on to me on the way home from seeing the nurse, nothing could stop me."

"Why then, did you make a date with the nurse that reflected ulterior motives on your part?"

"I wanted to see if Alicia would get jealous, but I didn't expect it to make her obsessive about our sexual relationship. You saw the rest and I hang my head in shame. I don't know how to make amends for it. I will go to court with testimony that will bury that bastard Bussi, but what can I do to earn your forgiveness?"

"You can begin by telling me where she is."

"Last night when you took her to the hospital, I went to see Doctor Diaz and tore up that bloody piece of paper with the handwriting of the devil. I swore to God that I would never use drugs again and went to fetch my things to come home. I was about to leave when you dropped her off at the house. She came in sobbing and pleading with me to forgive her for being such a sissy about me banging her too hard. She insisted that she wanted to show me that it didn't matter to her if I needed to be rough."

"Good Lord, didn't she tell you what they did at the hospital? The doctor forbade her to have intercourse for at least a month!"

"No. She said it was only a small bruise and that she had stopped bleeding. I told her that I had to leave...it's a long drive to Córdoba and I that I had to work today. My real reason was that I couldn't bring myself to make love to her after seeing what I'd done to you. I was afraid of what you would do to me, but my sorrow over what I had done was even greater."

"So you left her?"

"Yes, she clung to me and cried aloud to have me stay, but I shook her off and left. Early this morning there was a knock on my door and she stumbled in. She was loaded and offered me a large stash of cocaine, if I'd make love to her one more time. She said she couldn't live without the sexual highs I had taught her and that she would commit suicide if I didn't take care of her."

"Why didn't you just tie her up or call the cops to hold her until she was sober again?"

"God knows, I wanted to stop her, but I still love her and she was very persuasive. She kept urging me to bang her hard so that I could see that she didn't mind. I couldn't do it and as I pulled out I saw the bleeding. It was a dark moment in my life. I almost wished that you would have come to her rescue and shot me. I couldn't take her to a hospital—she was too high on the stuff for them to admit her. They would have tossed her in jail to detoxify on her own."

"Where is she now?"

"She's in the back room on the bed. Take a deep breath. It will shock you to see her."

Kevin rushed in and stopped. He could hardly recognize the ugly heap of drugged protoplasm lying in a fetal position on the bed, softly groaning between sobs. He picked her up whispering, "Oh, my darling, what have you done to yourself? You can stop crying now. You're safe with me. I've come to take you home."

"Kevin, is that you?" Why didn't you come in with me? I needed you."

"Just relax. I'm here to take care of you. You'll be home safely soon."

"Kevin, please forgive me. I have to have your love, else I'll die," she moaned helplessly.

"Rodolfo, will you please drive us to the airport? Next time you have to see Doctor Diaz, please drive Alicia's car back up to Tucumán."

The two men bundled her up in a sheet and soft blankets, put her in the back seat of the soldier's car and proceeded to the airport.

"Rodolfo, we've decided that it's too risky for you to be seen talking to that nurse; it could be construed as collusion. We are taking care of it another way. Please call her as soon as you drop us off at my airplane and ask her to tell Elena to meet me at the airport in an hour and a half."

"I know Elena, she's a sweet lady. I'll be glad to call. Believe me, someday I'll find a way to make amends for the pain I've brought on your house. Adios, you're an honorable gentleman!"

* * *

Elena and the nurse were at the small airfield to meet him. While they refueled the airplane, Kevin went in to file a cross-border flight plan to Santiago and to pay a visit to the toilet. The nurse climbed onboard to examine Alicia who had fallen asleep and was breathing deeply. She lifted an eyelid to see into her eye. The pupil was dilated. She was still stoned. Besides that, she smelled of vomit and booze. She examined Alicia's genitalia. She was still bleeding and when Kevin came out, she sent him to the drug store in the terminal to buy sterile napkins, over-the-counter antiseptic and anti-inflammatory pills. With the help of Elena they did as much as they could to prevent vaginal or intra-uterine infection.

"What a crying shame, she seemed like such a bright person," the nurse was saying. "I find it disturbing to see her in a condition almost as bad as any I saw in the secret detention center. Whatever his excuse, the soldier should be made to pay for this. I'm glad I don't have to deal with him."

"What could possibly have driven her to this?" Kevin asked again.

"There has to be something deep-seated in her psyche to make an educated, decent woman sink so low. Did someone wrong her in a barbaric way, perhaps?" the nurse questioned.

"The Junta's men abducted, tortured and murdered her innocent husband and tried to kill her for knowing too much," Kevin answered.

"I suppose that alone is enough reason for me to testify," she concluded.

* * *

The flight to Santiago over the mountains was rough. Kevin had to give up the idea of handing the controls to Elena so he could go back to sit with Alicia and perhaps even take a short nap. She often piloted the airplane from the left seat, but not in weather like this.

"How are you going to handle the nurse and that case?" Kevin asked Elena.

"The testimony of the nurse will be devastating and I'm certain that she'll turn State's evidence. I will know tomorrow what she is willing to do. The elderly lady's evidence will give the court and the public a dramatic description of just how heartless and brutal the Junta's officers and men were allowed to become."

"When does Arnold expect to have the petitions for indictments ready to file?" Kevin asked.

"Before the end of this week."

"Then, you'll have to go back to San Miguel, won't you?"

"Yes, but not until Thursday."

"Will I be needed?" Kevin enquired.

"Yes, probably on Friday and Saturday for Diaz's final interviews with the nurse and the soldier, respectively."

"Please remind me to call Xavier tomorrow morning?" Kevin requested.

"I thought you didn't trust him."

"I'll pay him for information which I've reason to think he has access to."

"Like what?"

"Whether the soldier told the truth about destroying Alicia's government file. What do you think her chances of recovery are?"

"If the nurse is correct about it stemming from her bitter loss of Fernando, it may take years of therapy. If it's an addiction, as you say the soldier thinks, her treatment will be more intense, but yield quicker results. At this moment, I don't believe either. I get the sense that she can't bear to look you in the eye, because of her abhorrent behavior, which she knows you think involved lust. If I'm right, many years may pass before she feels sufficiently comfortable with you to make love again. No matter what, she's going to be frigid for a while."

"What about her obsession with the soldier?"

"She'll get over him. With you around, he won't come near her."

"What options do I have? I've got a major professional responsibility plus the children, including yours."

"What makes you say that?"

"You and Eduardo split the sheets."

"How did you know that? I never told anyone. I can't go on leaning on you!"

"Why not, you said you loved Alicia and me."

"What if Alicia is seriously impaired? You can't leave her."

"I know that, we love each other."

"Will you love me too?"

"How do you think I survived these terrible days?"

"Does that mean I can make love to you?"

"Someday...perhaps."

"You're a complex person and I don't know how to handle you."

"Elena nobody 'handles' another person. You just saw what happened between two deeply devoted people."

As they approached Santiago, Kevin asked the air traffic controller to call an ambulance to meet them at the executive terminal.

He asked Elena to follow the ambulance and sat in the back with Alicia to the emergency ward.

"Can you understand me, Alicia?"

"Yes, I can hear you."

"We are first going to the hospital to have your reproductive system examined. Then you're going to the detoxification center to get rid of all the narcotics in you. You will never again be able to use narcotic drugs. Is that clear?"

"Yes, I understand. What's to come of me?"

"First, you're going to be my wife and the mother of our children again. Second, you will gradually go back to practicing psychotherapy. Third, in time you'll be my lover again and if all goes well, you'll be given a chance to help Arnold and the others with the court cases again."

"What will happen with the nurse?"

"Elena has the matter under control. She'll agree to testify."

"What about Rodolfo?"

"He's working with Arnold. You're never to have personal contact with him again."

"Will you forgive me?"

"How could I not? All you have to do is love me—merely love me."

"I will always love you, Kevin. Please try to forgive me?"

"I'm trying."

The prognosis at the hospital wasn't good. In spite of what the soldier had said about his caution, he had seriously damaged her organs and it was far from certain that they could be cured. The alternative would be to remove them surgically.

She had lost a lot of blood and was given a transfusion. They also put her on a drip to keep adding antibiotics to her system and transferred her on a gurney to take her to the detoxification center.

By then the analyses of her blood samples taken at admission had become available. She'd essentially overdosed on cocaine, they said. Detoxification would take several days. By Chilean law, that would have to be followed by extensive anti-addiction therapy.

"When may I visit my wife?" Kevin asked.

"You can talk to her briefly now, but then she goes into the drying oven and you won't have contact with her for about ten days. Before you go in to see her, we need to ask you some questions, so please take a seat."

"I had no knowledge of her sexual encounter or her involvement with drugs, if that's what you want to know."

"Where did it happen?"

"It started as an argument in San Miguel de Tucumán and ended in a disastrous emotional engagement in Córdoba."

"Who abused her?"

"A retired Argentinean soldier."

"Will he be apprehended to avoid further savage incidents of this kind?"

"I doubt it...not in the present political climate of Northern Argentina."

"How do you plan to safeguard your wife against repeat incidents?"

"By keeping her on our Estancia and treating her with love and respect. She's the mother of three adoring children."

"What provisions will you make for continuing psychotherapy?"

"She is one herself and her partner is a post-graduate in trauma therapy from the Catholic University."

"Do you know what caused this to happen?"

"I think I know, but it's too early to tell for certain."

"Thank you, Mister Bartholomew you may go in to see your wife now. We have no jurisdiction where this happened and will have to let it rest there."

They led him in to the post-examination holding area where Alicia lay in a strait jacket, strapped to a gurney.

"My darling, whatever happens remember that I will never stop loving you. The children and I will do everything we can to bring you back to good health and sanity."

"Kevin, I'm scared, they have me tied down and are putting me away somewhere. I may never see you again. Please stop them! I want to go home with you. I promise I'll never go near Rodolfo again."

"You overdosed on cocaine and you have to stay here until it's all out of your system."

"Kevin, my tummy hurts so badly, it feels like someone stabbed me with a knife. Please, can I have something to take the pain away?"

"You can't have pain killers until you're detoxified," Kevin replied.

"Kevin, hold my hand. I want you to know how sorry I am. It breaks my heart that I did this to you, please forgive me, please!"

He held her hand through the material of the straight jacket.

"In time we'll get over all of this, but you mustn't languish in remorse, you weren't consciously hurting anyone. Try to understand, your problem was like a sickness. Together we will cure it."

"Excuse me, Sir," the nurse interrupted "You have to go now."

They kissed and she was wheeled off trough the swinging doors into the ward.

* * *

On the way to the ranch, he and Elena reviewed the situation.

"I could never have imagined that Alicia would fall prey to such bizarre circumstances," Elena said and went on to explain.

"We were drawn together in our late teens by neither of us having a mother to turn to. Both our fathers were respected businessmen, but they were too busy to give us the kind of guidance mothers give their daughters during puberty. That caused us to be more experimental than our classmates, which tended to bind us together even more. As we became sexually aware, I'm afraid, we were too exuberant. Some in our crowd viewed us as nymphomaniacs, which we certainly were not, but selectively we were borderline promiscuous. We avidly compared notes about our exploits and if one of us found a particularly live partner we'd share his affections—without his knowledge, of course. In retrospect, I think it helped us grow up and mature ahead of our class and awoke us to the marvels of psychology. Fortunately for us, venereal disease in those days in rural middle class Argentinean society was virtually non-existent and we escaped physically unscathed.

"I moved away with my father before Angélica entered the university, but I heard from others that she pulled herself together when she met Fernando. However, she could never have grown as strong as the Alicia I've come to know, respect and love. Alicia always knows how to handle the most difficult situations. That's what made her such a good trauma therapist."

"The Angélica I encountered on the ferryboat," Kevin added "was a somewhat subservient, uncertain personality. She could not have survived in Montevideo had she remained that way. We had to change her. She chose the name of Alicia de la Rosa."

"That opens a whole different constellation to me. Alicia was <u>your</u> creation!"

"Yes, now you know why it leaves me with a heavy burden of guilt for this tragedy. I seized on her passionate commitment to Doctor Diaz to avenge the murder of Fernando, to mold Alicia."

"Why did you feel compelled to do it? She meant nothing to you then."

"Our emotional involvement came later. She began as my potential vehicle to grind my own axe with the Junta."

"You lost someone too?"

"Yes, but I don't want to talk about it."

"Why didn't you have the same sympathy for me?"

"I didn't know enough about your grief and you're so mind-driven that sympathy seemed inappropriate."

"Why then do you love me also?" Elena asked.

"I found out by accident how much you need the comfort of being loved." Kevin replied.

"How far does it go?"

"That's in the hand of the gods. I'm vulnerable too and after this last week, my emotions are at their breaking point. Have you any idea what it's like to have to stand and watch someone you absolutely love, engaging in hard core sex with a stranger? It's a nightmare I don't know how to live with!" Kevin confessed as he strained vainly to stem his emotions.

"Kevin, pull over and let me drive," Elena commanded.

He complied and as he stretched to get out of the car, she came around the front and embraced him. "Please don't cry alone, Kevin. Let me help you, please. Can you hold out until we get home?"

"Thank you, I'll try," he said holding his breath.

CHAPTER TWENTY-EIGHT

In the morning they called Arnold to review their situation. On Saturday he and Kevin would put the finishing touches on the two memoranda petitioning the courts to indict the Generals concerned with their two cases.

Then they would just have to wait until the cases wended their respective ways through the judicial system.

Thankful for the respite, Kevin turned his focus on the challenging tasks of his business and on Alicia's recovery.

To give the children the greatest possible feeling of security, Elvira Diaz, agreed to fly home with him at the end of the week.

* * *

Elena reminded him to call Xavier.

"Xavier, since you're in the PI business now, I have my first paid assignment for you."

"That's great! We're short on business. What do you need?" he replied.

"Before I tell you, I need your solemn oath that the information will remain strictly between us."

"That's a guarantee, so shoot!"

"Get into the intelligence database and see if you can find anything about Alicia de la Rosa, Angélica Diaz or me, Kevin Bartholomew. Call me back by Friday with the results."

"Consider it done."

"What will I owe you?"

"One hundred American bucks."

"OK, make it happen!"

He stayed in close contact with the hospital. It was beginning to look more likely that they would have to remove her cervix surgically, but the detoxification people remained tight-lipped.

Elena worked hard to get the children organized and to deal with her own marital problems. Eduardo was shacked up with a young woman in Valparaiso and since there was no such thing as legal divorce in Chile, she had to pretend to still be his wife. There was such a thing as a separation agreement, which dealt with child custody and estate distribution. Eduardo had not developed meaningful ties to his little son, who looked up to Kevin as a father figure and since Eduardo and Elena each had their own professional careers and incomes, the agreement was rather simple. She would have full custody of the child.

The few evenings she was there, she did all she could, to comfort Kevin. On the surface he looked tough as nails, but emotionally he was a mess. Her empathy tended to make her appear more amorous toward him than she already was. Fortunately, she wasn't the type to wear her heart on her sleeve and tolerated loving him without sexual involvement—at least for the time being.

"As a psychologist, tell me," he asked, "what's the chance of Alicia turning frigid as result of this horrendous experience?"

"I planned to avoid discussing that...any prognosis I'd offer you'd be skeptical about...I thought. Normally, women who were treated roughly during rape lose their sexual appetites. Their husbands wind up with the challenging task, through love, affection and consideration, to bring them back without too many inhibitions. For example, they may not want their partners to see them in the nude, or they may have an aversion to having their genitalia fondled, others pretend to enjoy sex, but never climax."

"What effect, would you say, is it going to have on Alicia?" Kevin asked again.

"Since she was shy about oral sex with you and after the excessive concentration of the soldier on oral foreplay, she will probably eschew oral sex. If I were you, I'd be more concerned that his macho hotdog because the agony it caused her may make her resist any invasion. That could make your marriage a sexless one."

"You mean like yours?"

"Yes, like mine. The difference is that Alicia is your creation...she can't survive without you, so, unlike Eduardo, she can't move out. I crave making love to you and if you weren't so honorable, you'd reciprocate my feelings. So what's it to be? You've suggested a living arrangement of three, why not a Ménage au Trios?"

"You make a compelling argument," Kevin said, dodging the bullet."

* * *

Kevin woke up more relaxed. He was extremely comfortable in Elena's company and had accepted her as his family member. He also enjoyed the comradery she shared with Alicia. He could truthfully say that he loved them both.

He called the hospital and talked to the matron of the detox center to convince her of his need to see Alicia.

"Matron, I have to travel a lot in my business. Can't you bend your rules just a little to allow me to see her on Friday, before I leave? By now, you must have discovered that she only used drugs that once and that she has no history of drug addiction."

"I'd gladly oblige, Señor Bartholomew, but it isn't up to me. She's under psychiatric care now and you'll have to talk to Doctor Snow, our chief psychiatrist. I'll see if he's available to talk to you. Please hold..."

"Hello, Snow speaking."

"Yes, Doctor Snow, Bartholomew here."

"What can I do for you?"

"My wife, Alicia, is in your care and I'd like a chance to visit her before I leave on business Saturday."

"I have to talk to you first. Her problem stems largely from her relationship with you."

"Good God, in what way?"

"You're her mentor and she looks up to you with almost religious verve. She'll do supernatural things to live up to your expectations. You may have set the bar too high for her and she crumbled when she came up short."

"Doctor, what does that have to do with getting high on cocaine in order to behave like a slut?"

"The man had her feeling in control of her own destiny without judgmental constraints. She felt free to fly on her own."

"I've never constrained her, doctor. Her goals were her own inventions. I did no more than facilitate their accomplishment."

"You obviously don't know how powerful your influence over her is. She feels that she's a personality entirely of your making; one which contrasts sharply with her natural one. The way she puts it, she's Angélica whereas you made her into Alicia, a stronger, more confident creature, which she has difficulty measuring up to."

"If I hadn't changed her identity she would have been tortured to death. So what was I supposed to do?"

"I think you need to come in for a consultation with me. If we're able to agree on certain ground rules, I'll let you see her. Whatever you do, don't show any anger over her scandalous transgression."

"When can we meet?"

"How does Friday morning at eight in my office sound?"

"Thanks, I'll be there."

Kevin was baffled. It seemed that Alicia had succeeded in deflecting the blame for her ghastly behavior in large part onto him.

He felt a flash of anger. Shit, what was he to do? Elena would know, but it would force her take sides.

He needed to clear his head and went out to the barn to see if there was someone to keep him company. Carlos and Maria were in the stable. For a ten-year old, Carlos had become a good horseman, and at age eight, Maria was <u>seriously</u> in love with horses. He seldom had the opportunity to ride with them alone and they jumped at the chance to ride in the foothills. They eagerly helped load the horses into the trailer with the necessary tack and they set out for the foothills of the Andes to an area where there they had a wide choice of trails.

The views from the high terrain were incredible and to ride in that country was exhilarating. What he liked most about the experience was the opportunity to talk one-on-one with them. He loved them more than life itself, even though they were his adopted children. He spent more time with them than their mother could and they accepted him as their mentor.

They wanted to know when Alicia would be home. They were used to her being gone only a week at a time.

"Papa," Maria asked "Mama has never been gone this long. We think things happened which you won't tell us. Is she all right?"

"Maria, you're so smart, I will never hide important things from you. That's why I invited you to ride with Carlos and me. Mama was involved in a serious accident in Argentina and <u>tía</u> Elena and I brought her back to the hospital in Santiago on Monday night. We must thank God for saving her life and that she's getting better every day."

"Will she be home soon? We miss her," Maria whimpered. "She promised to take us to the beach at Viña".

"You have to be patient. We hope she can come home next week, but she will still be sick and it may take a long time before she'll be able to take you to the beach. If you'd like, I'll be happy to take you there."

Johan Wassenaar

"But, that's still not the same as going with Mama. We love you, but I miss Mama."

Kevin found the child's anguish hard to take and made an excuse to ride ahead to get hold of his emotions, praying silently to his maker to deliver them from this terrible impasse. He couldn't consider even the possibility of going on without Alicia, regardless of how she currently felt about him. He'd just have to learn how to slow his pace and bolster her self-confidence. He'd had no inkling that he was putting too much pressure on her.

He dismounted to open a gate and sat down on a rock to gather his emotions. They were beyond containment and sorrow just poured out of him.

Suddenly, he felt Maria's arms around him, pulling his face against her little chest. "Papa, please don't cry, we'd love to go with you to the beach," she said.

The irony of her innocent remark struck his funny bone and he laughed out loud, clumsily blowing his nose and wiping his eyes.

"Thank you, my little one. You made me feel <u>so</u> good," he said as he hugged and kissed her.

He couldn't face more of the same with Carlos and challenged him to a race to the far end of the sloping meadow. They raced and Kevin had to exert himself to beat Carlos.

"That's not fair, you beat me!" he complained.

It broke the ice and by the time they returned to the horse trailer they were all smiles and laughter. As he was putting away the tack and washing down the horses, Carlos joined him.

"Papa, I know that things are not good between you and Mama, but I believe in you to make it good. Tell me what we can do to help."

"The best thing you, Maria and Santiago, can do, is to love her. I mean, really let her know how much you love her. I'm hoping to see her tomorrow. Why don't the three of you make up your own get-well cards tonight for me to take to her?"

* * *

On the way to the airport for Elena's flight to San Miguel, without mentioning his conversation with the psychiatrist to her, Kevin asked whether he may have put too much pressure on Alicia.

"You made the observation that Alicia lost her grip largely because I masterminded her change in personality. Where did you get that idea?"

"We talked about it a lot during our early days in San Miguel, when we were deathly afraid of being arrested. I don't recall either of us mentioning it for the past four years. To me she seemed comfortable in her 'Alicia' skin. She reminisced about having to be flamboyant in the beginning…dancing the tango…dressing a bit like a vamp to throw the Junta's dogs off your tracks. Perhaps she craved another fling like that."

"Anyway, I'll see you on Saturday. <u>Vaya bien</u>," he said as her let her off at the terminal.

"She came close to his window to caution him, "Don't make too much out of catching her in the act with another man. It happens a lot these days and has little social stigma. Where she went wrong, was to become obsessed with him."

"Are you saying that adultery is fashionable in Latin America?"

"South America has always been adulterous. Only now, the *women* also enjoy that liberty."

"Was Alicia particularly promiscuous?"

"She and I were pretty wild as I told you. Since you'll be talking to Xavier, why not ask him? He dated her too."

"Thanks for the tip. Bye."

He called Xavier from the company office in the city to see what he'd discovered.

"The file on Kevin Bartholomew says that you are dangerous by virtue of your American connections...probably a CIA agent...and to steer clear of you.

"Alicia de la Rosa is to be viewed with suspicion, but is to be left untouched because of her connection to you. However, there is evidence that she really is Angélica Diaz, whose husband was arrested and 'disappeared' in nineteen seventy-six. It suggests that Alicia shot and killed a Junta agent in Montevideo and then fled to Chile where two soldiers who were sent to apprehend her, also died."

"No shit, are you sure that you're not making this up?"

"No, Kevin, I truly like you guys and wouldn't lie to you."

"While I have you in the mood, what do you know about Angélica's sex life?"

"I dated her once, and she was virtually out of control, screwing fellows left, right and center—at times more than one guy on the same day. After she hooked up with Fernando all that ended. The story about her and the flamenco dancer, points to something different. I don't know if she told you, but we had a few rolls of our own in the hay when you guys were out of touch with each other."

"She told me that she seduced you."

"Yes, it should not have happened."

"Thanks, Xavier, I'll bring you your hundred bucks on Saturday."

Kevin was astounded. How could he have been so naïve? If what Elena said is the social norm, he'd have to rethink his heartfelt, but pious, response to Alicia's trysts with the soldier, who was now turning out to be a liar.

He drove to the hospital for his appointment with Dr. Snow and stopped at a flower shop to buy a dozen beautiful red roses. He truly loved Alicia and would now have to adjust his response to what she had done to him. There could be no outrage about the sexual aspect as such. He had to focus on the whole nature of her association with Rodolfo and the danger it posed to her health and their entire family.

The consultation didn't start well. Dr. Snow was unreasonably aggressive about Kevin's alleged penchant to dominate and control his wife, to which he ascribed nearly all her harmful behavior.

"She was crying out to you to stop steering her and to cut her some slack," he insisted.

"Doctor, there may be some truth in what you say, but in all honesty, I'm not domineering and never cracked the whip over her head. All our decisions were made jointly. We come from different cultures with different social mores. There may be things where, either she or I may have a fetish that we don't share. It could be a generational thing too. For instance, my generation is less tolerant of promiscuity and infidelity than hers. However, we love each other passionately and are capable of forgiving almost any transgression. She has three dear children who fill both our hearts. Please, let's concentrate on a way for her to regain her sanity and health," Kevin almost begged.

"That is our common interest," Dr. Snow replied "but I can't leave important stones unturned. Alicia is deeply depressed by the fact that she disappointed you so badly that your relationship with her may be permanently impaired. She can't conceive of you forgiving her for stubbornly going back to the soldier even after you had offered her a graceful exit. I hate to say this, but if you'd been less honorable...had more of your own skeletons in the closet...she may not have been as terrified."

"What about addiction? I have nightmares about her possible addiction to cocaine from this episode."

"I don't see that as a problem yet. Her withdrawal went smoothly, her mind cleared very quickly and she hasn't mentioned any continuing desire for the substance. I think it was used as a form of date rape to lower her inhibitions and expose her to a heightened sexual sensation that she would crave. Obviously she did. In your position I'd be strongly motivated to castrate the son-of-a-bitch."

"Doctor, I think we can work this thing out between us. Please let me in to see her? I brought roses to give her and cards that the children made. I'm sure it will help her surmount her depression."

"OK, you can see her for an hour, if you promise not to get into anything heavy."

* * *

He found Alicia appearing vastly improved and in possession of all her senses. Her eyes were clear and her parched, cracked lips had returned to normal. More significant, she was no longer in a straightjacket.

He smiled broadly as he entered the room which she shared with two other patients.

"Darling, I'm so pleased to see you looking so much better. The kids and I've been counting the days when you can come home. Maria can't wait for you to take them to 'Viña.' They each made their own card to wish you well. Please look at them carefully. They put so much effort into making them. It took all day for Maria. Oh, I *am* glad to see you!" he said with tears pouring down his cheeks "Please get well so you can come home?"

Her eyes lit up at the sight of him actually weeping with joy just to see her. "Thank you God, he's forgiven me, thank you, thank you," she whispered.

"The only thing that matters is that you get well. What does the obstetrician have to say about your insides?"

"If I wasn't still bleeding, I wouldn't be in bed," she said. "They think they may have to do a complete hysterectomy to remove my damaged cervix. I wouldn't give them the go-ahead without you. It means I won't be able to have any more children."

"How do you feel about that?" he asked.

"I'd like to have another daughter, but even if I heal fast enough to avoid serious uterine infection, they're not sure that I could risk being pregnant again. But, you didn't answer me."

"I've only Santiago to call my own, even though Carlos and Maria may just as well be part of my flesh. If it's not too much to risk, I'd opt for the chance of having my own daughter."

"I'll see what they say after my next examination. If my equipment has to go, you can always have Elena bear us that child."

"Are you crazy? Even if she was willing to do something as selfless as that, me having sex with her would make all sorts of waves and could wreck your professional relationship with her."

"You Anglo-Saxons can sometimes be so literal and proud of your DNA. What difference does it make, as long as she and her offspring remain integral part of our family?"

"Who said we could be like that?"

"Kevin, it's so obvious. She and I are linked in lockstep professionally. We're as close as any two straight women could ever be. We totally depend upon each other. On top of that, she worships you as much as I do."

"I guess I'm just too old fashioned to have thought of it that way. But, we're getting off the subject of your cervix. I think you ought to listen carefully to the alternatives they give you and make your decision. I'll live with whatever you decide."

"Aren't you going to give me those fabulous red roses?"

"Sorry, I forgot. But don't let that detract from their meaning. I love you as passionately as I did that evening by the river on the ranch near Puerto Varas."

"Do you really mean that?"

"I do with my whole heart."

"You won't hold my awful betrayal of you against me?"

"Just don't do it again, please?"

"After that ghastly night when you stumbled on me with that soldier, I had an epiphany which almost made me self-destruct. I would have died with gratitude, had you not rescued me. You have a noble soul, Kevin, and you can't believe how happy I am that you forgave me. Please kiss me before they chase you out of here?"

They kissed. As he got up to leave, he added,

"I've also forgiven you for rolling in the hay with Xavier. He did some sleuthing for me and discovered that your soldier lied about destroying our files in the intelligence database. I'm still there...as a probable CIA agent, not to be touched...and you're an escapee with one notch on your pistol for bringing down one of their agents in Montevideo. Fortunately, they link you to me, which also places you in their untouchable category."

"Why is it that you always know everything before I could tell you? That's been one of my greatest fears. Now I know better. Adios, my wonderful man."

"I'm bringing Elvira back with me on Sunday. That will keep them happy until you get out of this catacomb. Bye, sweetheart, don't forget to smell the roses."

CHAPTER TWENTY-NINE

Kevin was wheels-up at dawn and arrived in San Miguel in time for Elena to pick him up at the airport for Arnold's ten o'clock meeting with the soldier. He was obviously uncomfortable in Kevin's presence.

"Rodolfo, the fact that you've told at least two lies, leaves me in serious doubt about your reliability as a witness."

"What lies?"

"You said that you exercised particular care when Alicia followed you to Córdoba and begged you to have more intercourse with her. Your care was so great, that she will probably now have to undergo a total hysterectomy. Great care, my ass!

"You also bragged about destroying the files you found on her in the government's intelligence database, to make her feel beholden to you and subtly to imply that, with that information, you had leverage over her.

"Those files are still there and what you didn't tell her was that they include instructions not to touch her, since she is closely linked to me, a suspected CIA agent."

"I didn't want to hurt her," Rodolfo protested. "She stuffed me full of coke and without knowing, I may not have been gentle enough."

Kevin raged on.

"With excuses like that, how in hell can we trust you to give clear and consistent evidence in a case which will go through many hearings and appeals? You may have to appear in court four or five separate times with enough time between hearings to be threatened or bribed into changing your testimony."

"I told you several times that I will keep my word," Rodolfo protested again "if for no other reason, than that I deeply regret what I did to you and your family. Another reason is that I still love Alicia."

"That and a peseta will buy you a cup of coffee. You don't almost kill someone you love! Your propensity for lying makes me doubt that you know what 'regret' is. I want something more concrete to bind you to your commitment."

"You told me that you'd shoot my balls off if I double crossed Doctor Diaz. Isn't that concrete enough?"

"That gives me an idea. Arnold, how would it be if this man gave us irrevocable instructions to have him surgically castrated along with a side letter in which we agree to destroy his instructions once he's delivered all his eyewitness accounts in court?"

"How would I know that you've destroyed it?" Rodolfo asked.

"We could appoint an impartial referee to hold both documents," Dr. Diaz explained.

"You guys will be holding my most unique capability hostage," he protested.

"OK, Don Juan, what'll be? We expose to the military what you promised to do and go without you, or you sign up with us for the full course?"

"Damn, I knew you'd get me. Now I'm left with no option."

"Arnold, how soon can we have the directive and side letter done and ready to sign?"

"When you come back here this afternoon to go over the final account of what you saw General Bussi do, we'll have the documents ready to sign. I'll also have the name of a referee for you by then."

Elena sat dumb-founded throughout the whole discourse, and waited until Rodolfo had left, before venturing her opinion.

"I hope I never have reason to cross swords with you. You really gave it to him. Poor bastard, I almost felt sorry for him. As we discovered when he was our patient he's indecisive by nature. There's nothing worse for someone like that to be placed between a rock and a hard place."

* * *

In contrast to the soldier, the nurse was self-motivated and eager to right the wrongs of the vile establishment she was made part of seven years earlier. Her descriptions of the circumstance under which the poor pregnant girls were kept to term to have their babies jerked out of their arms on their way to a certain grave, were worthy of a Pulitzer Prize.

The testimony of the elderly mother of one of the victims was truly heartbreaking, in the selfless way she expressed herself.

They broke for lunch and a siesta.

* * *

Kevin and Elena went to Alicia's house where Kevin brought her up to date with his discussions with Alicia and Xavier.

"I discussed the possibility of Alicia ending up being infertile with her. You know what? She invited me to have a child with you! She even articulated the reasons for the three of us living as a single family. I hadn't understood how close the two of you had become."

"I'd better learn to phrase my sentences more precisely" Elena responded: "that's exactly what I told you."

"I also had no idea that your generation was so liberated" Kevin added; "like infidelity wasn't a sin...as long as it's not done in secret or to hurt someone."

"That's what an age of revolution and insurrection brings. Speaking of which, isn't it about time for you to start showing me some affection?"

"I don't think this is a good time for shenanigans."

"Why not? We have two hours before we meet again and I'm frustrated. As my male partner you've been singularly unforthcoming."

"Now, wait a minute if you were in Alicia's position in a hospital ward, wouldn't you expect me to give you all my attention?" Kevin asked.

"When she suggested that we make a baby for the family, she didn't expect it to be immaculately conceived, you know! I've known her much longer than you have. For a while she and I were the hellions of this town. She expects us to be intimate with each other."

"You may be right, but let's just say that I'm still too old fashioned to cross that line. I know what hell Alicia is going through in that hospital and it would be obscene for me to make love to you, her best friend."

"We could try to duplicate the soldier's routine," she suggested temptingly. "You could discover the secret behind his way with women. That could assuage your feeling of inferiority after watching him outdo you with Alicia."

"Elena! That was nothing short of gratuitous cruelty."

"Except you know it's true," she continued "and neither Alicia nor I want a lover with broken wings. With a bit of practice I could have you besting the soldier at his game. You'll need that skill to lure Alicia back, you know. She could go cold on you, still craving his excitement. Don't make light of it. It's the strongest urge a woman can have and usually transcends logic or reason."

"There's some sense in what you say, but I'm just not ready to start that now. Perhaps we could try it when we know what Alicia is going to turn out like."

"That would not be fair to me. It keeps me playing second fiddle to Alicia. In business we're co-equal."

"Call me old fashioned, or if you prefer, an Anglo-Saxon prude, but I just can't accept adultery as an everyday thing. As you like to say, I virtually created Alicia. I have to be loyal to her, because I know how devastated she'd be if I made love to her closest friend."

"I'm not just her closest friend. We share practically everything in life. We live together like a commune. Our children are everyone's responsibility. My son thinks you are his father. You're the only man I've truly loved. Our thoughts are co-mingled and I adore Alicia as much as you do. Doesn't that give me the privilege of being intimate with you? I know Alicia thinks it does."

"Look I don't want you to think I'm not attracted to you. You are more sensuous that Alicia and far less inhibited. Making love to you would be awesome, although I don't think I'm virile enough for you. Your reference to my size in relation to the soldier's makes me doubtful that I could live up to your expectations."

"You just made a perfect case for making love to me. How would we know without trying?"

"Speaking of trying, how did you know that the soldier was so hot?"

"He made love to me about five years ago, when he was my patient. That was before he enlarged himself and learned about coke."

"Good God! Did Alicia know that?"

"Yes, I had to tell her. I was in breach of professional ethics. She quizzed be about it and seemed satisfied when I swooned about how hot he was."

"Jesus! Why didn't you warn me when she started sucking up to him?"

"I didn't know *what* she was doing. I told you how unhappy I was about her going off on her own without me. When you told me what had happened on Sunday, it was too late. I didn't know about his bloated whopper or cocaine use. If I'd known, I'd have blown the whistle."

"Why did you make love to him when you were just married?"

"Rodolfo is loaded with sex appeal; the quintessential Don Juan of smooth seduction. He became my primary therapeutic responsibility and he caught me off guard when his condition improved in leaps and bounds towards the end. There I was, still bolstering his ego, when I should have been putting on the brakes. He got me all excited before I understood what was happening and then nothing could stop him...nor did I want him to stop. I was already frustrated by my inability to break through Eduardo's excessive reserve."

"Could it be that Alicia, in her Angélica mode, overplayed her hand because she was jealous of your relationship with Rodolfo?"

"I don't think so. He was just a one-night stand for me and then he was gone, out of sight, out of mind."

"If you love me, will you still play around?"

"I don't want to, but I have to be sure about our physical compatibility. As long as you can take care of me, I'm all yours."

"What does it take to keep you on a leash?"

"I don't know, but we'll find out...soon, I hope.

* * *

The afternoon session with Dr. Diaz went smoothly and out of it emerged the final drafts of two memoranda with motions to indict in each of the two cases. They were to be filed the following Monday. Once their petitions had been accepted, there would be little more they could do, except wait.

The newborn baby theft charge against General Suárez Mason and Admiral Emilio Massera went straight to the Federal Court in Buenos Aires.

They were early enough in a growing queue of complaints to make a list of approximately three hundred cases with serious potential of being tried.

CHAPTER THIRTY

Elena stayed behind to carry on the therapy business and to stand in for Alicia. Kevin returned to Santiago with Elvira, the children's grandmother. He brought her up to date with Alicia's condition and the fact that Elena's son, Ricardo, would essentially now also be her grandson.

She was a good woman and brought calm and an aura of peace with her. The children were delighted to see her.

Kevin had stayed in touch with the hospital and was anxious to go there since the diagnosis of the obstetrician was marginal. They would have to decide whether to let him perform a total hysterectomy or take a chance on her cervix healing.

He was uncomfortable with the prospective idea of being intimate with Elena. What was he to do since Alicia was promoting it?

He stopped to buy more red roses and was quickly admitted to her ward.

"Doctor Snow said that you can now see her whenever you wish," the duty nurse announced. "She's in room four-twenty, straight down the hall."

There was a man visiting her and she introduced him.

"This is Francisco Salazar, one of the trauma experts here at the Catholic University and a good friend of mine. Francisco, this is the Kevin you've been hearing so much about."

"I'm pleased to meet you, Professor. What exactly is your expertise?" Kevin asked.

"I'm regarded as an oracle on rape-induced trauma. With all the political upheavals and chaos of the seventies, social mores relaxed. It encourages promiscuity amongst our young people, which often leads to over exuberance and rape. There has been an increase in psychological dysfunction resulting from women, and men too, being sexually violated."

"Interesting! What are the typical signs of that kind of dysfunction?"

"They're all over the map, but most frequently it leads to fear of sex in almost any form."

"Like what?"

"Reluctance to engage in it. Inhibitions about being seen naked. Inability to be aroused and frigidity in general."

"How does one cure this phobia?"

"With patience, love, tolerance and respect for their dilemma. We've seen many spouses who greet their wives' dysfunctions with anger and push, or even force, them into having intercourse with them. Of course, to the woman that seems like more rape and her condition gets worse."

"You obviously know and respect Alicia. How do we avoid going down that long, dark tunnel?"

"Do you love her?"

"Yes, beyond words."

"Then I will help guide you through it. Come to think of it, Elena Mendoza was my star pupil in this area. She'll know what to do."

"Thank you, Professor."

"Please call me Francisco, or Frank, if you like. Those are truly beautiful roses. I had better get out of your way," he said as he kissed Alicia's hand and left.

"I couldn't wait to see you; and with more roses!" Alicia greeted him.

"After all, you are Alicia de la Rosa," he said as they embraced and kissed. "Tell me that you're not going to go frigid on me, please.

If you still crave what the soldier gave you, I'll soon be at least as good as him, I promise."

"Kevin, I couldn't love another person more than I love you. I will try with all my might not to disappoint you."

"That's the wrong answer. You must only do things you really want to do. Your fear of disappointing me is at the root of our problem. I'm not God. I make mistakes. I can be disingenuous. I'm not above infidelity or lying."

"You have something bothering you. Is it Elena?"

"How did you know?"

"Woman's instinct. You could never love her like you love me, so it doesn't matter. I've never been jealous of her. We grew up wild together in San Miguel and got wise by sharing our experiences. She never found a Fernando to tame her. It may interest you to know that the soldier also seduced her."

"Yes she told me. Why couldn't she find a suitable man to marry? She certainly is eligible."

"She probably is too self-centered. That's why you have to adopt Ricardo."

"Let's talk about you and your cervical damage. Your condition is either the result of rough sex or rape. Obviously, you weren't raped, so it has to be the influence of cocaine. As Doctor Snow will tell you, cocaine causes a sense of euphoria, empathy, self-acceptance, and emotional closeness, none of which I would have thought you lacked. He will also tell you that the idea that it provides for prolonged sex without orgasm is nonsense. That only happens when cocaine dulls the senses. You have to take a lot of it to get there and it's counter-productive; that is, if the object is to achieve a heightened sense of euphoria. Your soldier had taken too much cocaine when I came upon you. He didn't know what he was doing. He was oblivious to the fact that he was hurting you, and drugged so much, that he tried to attack me with a gun in my hand. A trained soldier just doesn't do that."

"Why are you telling me this? It hurts to hear it."

"It may influence your choice. If you have a hysterectomy, the surgeon will sew up the end of your vaginal canal where the uterus and cervix used to be. That means that you'll have less depth to accommodate a large penis. The stitched wall is weaker than the surrounding tissue and will rupture if pushed too hard. Without the uterus in the way, the rupture would directly expose your abdominal cavity and that's very bad news. The other aspect of a total hysterectomy is that it reduces the demand for blood flow, since there aren't ovaries to feed. In the process, your sexual appetite will diminish."

"What alternative is there?" She asked.

"Try to mend the damage to the cervix. You'll have to lie on your back much longer to prevent hemorrhaging until it's healed and, obviously, rough sex will be off limits."

"Which would you prefer?" She asked

"Healing the cervix."

"Good, but what's so attractive about rough sex?" She asked.

"I don't know. *You* have to explain that, since that's what brought us here in the first place."

"My Lord, you don't think that I could go back to that?"

"I don't *know*, Alicia. *You* have to tell *me*. You went back *twice*."

"I couldn't stand facing you. I was so desperately ashamed after you stood there calmly, mouthing words which I knew would break your heart. I just ran away senselessly. You have to forgive me! I'll never be like that again, *please*!"

"Thank you. That's what I had hoped to hear," he said as he cradled her face in his arms and held her. "Let's tell the doctor to try healing it. We can serve you in bed on the ranch for just as long as it takes."

She smiled brightly, "You can't imagine what a load that is off my shoulders. Now tell me about the trials?"

He quickly ran through what Arnold had done and what they expected from the filings.

"Our hope is to get on the Federal Appeals Court's docket before Alfonsin decides he's had enough and pardons the rest."

"What do you mean by 'pardons'? Surely he has to follow his own decree when he took office?"

"He spoke too soon and found that all the human rights people in the world were filing complaints and overwhelming the courts. So he added a measure called the 'Punta Final,' which put a time limit on having these alleged cases filed. With the deadline approaching, the claims are pouring into the system in torrents, most of them vague or vacuous.

"So now he has another gimmick called 'Due Obedience,' which absolves nearly all junior officers of responsibility for bad deeds they committed under orders from their superiors."

"What will it mean to us?"

"Both our claims are well substantiated and involve only top officers. So we should stay in contention."

"Gosh, after all these years of doing therapy to get the dirt on them, I'll go nuts if they just slap everyone on the wrist and send them home. We could have stayed in Los Angeles and had a lovely life."

"Our way out is that the theft of those new-born babies is clearly a criminal offense and that's not covered by the 'Punta Final' declaration."

"When do you think we'll know?"

"Probably next year, or it could drag on till eight seven."

"Why that long?"

"There's a lot of unrest in the Army and different groups are rebelling against the government. The economy is in a mess and if Alfonsin can't fix it, he could lose his job."

"Shit. That means we'll go back to the Perónistas and they'll probably pardon everyone that's been convicted!"

"That's life."

"I wish I hadn't sworn that oath to seek vengeance. I'd just like to crawl in under your skin and languish in your love."

"Please call me after the obstetrician's been. Elvira is dying to see you. I'll bring her here tomorrow. Perhaps they'll let you go home with us."

Kevin looked into her eyes.

"Thank you for allaying the worst fear I've ever had to face. Don't ever stop loving me."

"Go well, my beautiful Bartholomew."

* * *

The doctors agreed to release Alicia the next day with a ton of prescriptions for her cervical injury and strict instructions to remain prone in bed until the bleeding had stopped permanently.

The whole establishment on the ranch turned out to greet her. Most touching was the reunion of mother and daughter. Maria's little face lit up like a candle.

"Mama, will they let you stay this time? Please say you'll stay long enough to take us to 'Viña'?"

It took several months for Alicia to heal well enough to move about out of bed and another month before she could go back to work. The doctor continued to oppose intercourse, which Alicia had no appetite for anyway. She loved being embraced and kissed by

Kevin and they slept intertwined with each other as lovers do, but that was as far as she could bring herself to go. The doctor strongly opposed any idea of her bearing another child and suggested tying off her tubes against that eventuality.

Elena had found a graduate from the National University of Tucumán as an understudy to help carry the therapy load. It was hard on her, but she never complained, although it took much encouragement from Kevin on his travels through San Miguel to keep her going. She had become highly dependent on him emotionally and craved his attention when they were together. Gradually, as the traumatic effects of almost losing Alicia wore off, he became more receptive to her overtures.

When Alicia began working again, Elena was visibly relieved to spend more leisure time on the ranch. She had agreed to let Kevin adopt Ricardo, which made her more comfortable about being part of his ménage. On her second layover she broke through Kevin's reserve and they made love in the most fantastic way.

* * *

The complaint against the General and the Admiral who commanded the Buenos Aires "ant subversive" zone, moved forward and an indictment hearing was scheduled.

Dr. Diaz put the mother of Silvia...the one who was executed after her child was born...on the stand first. Her testimony, delivered in an unassuming way, was heart-wrenching and starkly revealed the unconscionable brutality with which prisoners had been treated. The judges questioned her on how she knew about the theft of her grandchild. She pointed at the nurse.

"That brave angle from heaven couldn't stand having it on her conscience and came all the way to San Miguel at great peril, to tell me. Pray to God that there should be more such angles in our midst."

When Dr. Diaz called the nurse to the witness stand, there was little doubt left that the court would indict the officers. Her testimony was devastating with specific times, dates and places of the babies she delivered and how they were wrenched out of their mother's arms and taken away. She concluded with equally lucid descriptions of how the mothers were killed by lethal injection, naming the physicians who had administered the lethal doses along with the identities of officers in control.

"How did they dispose of the bodies?" the presiding judge asked.

"I can't be specific, Your Honor, but I understand they were taken in transport aircraft and ejected into the Rio Plata estuary. Some of the bodies washed ashore in Uruguay."

The panel of judges deliberated for less than twenty minutes before handing down the indictments and setting a trial date two months hence.

* * *

Unbeknown to Kevin, Alicia was sliding into depression over her inability to fully satisfy her aspirations. This came piled on top of her continuing guilt about the incident with the soldier. She was grateful to Elena for satisfying his physical needs, but knew that it still struck him as infidelity and that he craved regaining her sexual attention. The fact that she couldn't give him the daughter he wanted, weighed on her conscience too.

She finally confided in Elena.

She couldn't find answers to why she'd been so vulnerable to seduction by the soldier. Kevin filled her life and gave her everything she'd ever dreamed of. The soldier had nothing but a very smooth line, good artistic ability, the information to subtly threaten her and an extraordinary, large organ. What, in God's name was she thinking to let him seduce her? There was no question about him being a superb lover and she understood why she lusted for more, but if she wanted it so badly, why didn't she help Kevin give it to her, as she could see Elena was doing. His spontaneous promise to her in the hospital that he would at least equal the sexual prowess of her soldier, gave it away.

Elena was always more pragmatic than her and looked for direct solutions to her problems.

Oh God, if only she'd known how deeply she really loved Kevin, none of this would have happened. Why then, is she not anxious to lavish her ultimate expressions of love on him now? In the cloud of her emotional confusion she felt tarnished, as if her physical offerings to him had become cheap and tawdry. When she closed her eyes she could still feel the ice-cold derision as he mentioned her shaved pubic hair.

Oh God, how awful! If only he'd screamed in anger instead of gently taking her to the hospital. If only, in a mad rage, he'd beaten the soldier and taken her home. Instead, he enumerated the alternatives and left the decision to her.

For him to forgive her so magnanimously and beg her to come back into his loving arms was so much more than she deserved. She truly felt unworthy.

Elena skillfully comforted her before addressing her responses.

"Darling, don't be so harsh on yourself. We both gave Kevin fair warning of the deceptive nature of the Angélica within you. He knew what the risks were for you to assume a vastly different personality. If I know how much better you are, Kevin knows it ten times over. He loves you so far beyond reason that I'm genuinely jealous of you. He doesn't see you as the slut you paint yourself to be. He adores every inch of you, warts and all. He wants Alicia and needs her. He's a damned good lover and will elevate your spirits, if you'd just let him. You don't even have to make the first move; just snuggle up to him and let him take it from there. He'd like nothing more than to seduce you. Give him a chance. His style is better than you've ever experienced...I'll guarantee that. I wouldn't be saying this if I didn't love both of you so very much."

* * *

The news of the outcome of their first case buoyed Alicia's spirits and improved her outlook on life dramatically. Her greeting of Kevin when he arrived home was exuberant and very personal.

"I think this calls for a celebration," she said. "Let's call Roberto and Analise to see if they have room in the bunkhouse on their ranch in Patagonia for just you and me this weekend. They are cornerstones in our lives. I want to start over fresh."

"Will you let me show you?" he asked with mock childish pride.

"Nothing would please me more."

"Great, bring your shaver along."

"You're just an animal!"

"Aren't we all?"

CHAPTER THIRTY-ONE

Kevin had been under the gun to keep his company's factories busy in the lean times they were having. He was elated to land a large excavator contract from one of the world's largest coal and iron-ore mining companies in Brazil.

Large dragline excavators are as tall as three-story buildings and are fabricated from huge amounts of steel. Kevin was having the heavy steel sub-assemblies made by a steel fabricator in Santos, the port city of São Paulo.

It required frequent visits by him. From Santiago, his flight path went directly over San Miguel and Asuncion, Paraguay, to São Paulo.

It became convenient to fly either Elena or Alicia up to Tucumán on Sunday and bring them back home the following Saturday.

On his second Brazilian trip, it was Elena's turn and she asked if they could leave on Saturday for something she had to do. They left in the afternoon. He planned to fly the rest of the way on Sunday after conferring with Dr. Diaz.

They had their usual flirtatious bantering on the intercom along the way, but it wasn't until they arrived at Alicia's home, that he realized Elena had something special up her sleeve.

"How was your visit to Patagonia with Alicia?" she asked.

"It was great. We relived committing ourselves to each other. For the first time, since she came home from the hospital, she was completely open to me. It was like magic and she loved what your training had done for my skills as a lover."

"You're having me on. She wouldn't be that transparent."

"Why not? She wants me to sire a daughter of your making to add to our communal family."

"Damn her for blabbing! I've been treating her for her depression, and she asked me if I would consider letting you sire a baby with me. That was going to be my surprise for you this evening."

"Have I spoiled it?"

"No. I've been looking forward to this for weeks," she said. "I normally don't believe in negative thoughts, but your reconciliation with Alicia won't be complete for some time—depression doesn't just evaporate—and pragmatic as I am, I regularly need your full attention. As the pregnant mother of your child, my chances are improved. So, let's hope it's a girl."

"You've probably figured out to the hour, when you'd be most susceptible to conceive?"

"*Si, Señor*, it happens to be tonight. There's a special procedure we have to follow to make sure I get pregnant."

"Don't tell me I have to stand on my head!"

"No, but I practically have to."

"Sounds crazy, but lead on..."

* * *

Elena's prediction, that Alicia's depression would recur, was correct and they found themselves periodically looking for euphoric reasons to cheer her up.

One such joyful reason came about when the trial against General Masson and Admiral Massera for the theft of the newborn babies went Dr. Diaz' way. With the guilty verdict, a sentencing date was set for several weeks later.

Alicia's response was amazingly strong, revealing a surprising passion in her to have the truth about the brutality of the Junta's men laid bare in public. It lifted her spirits and caused her to turn her attention with great energy to the forthcoming trial of General Bussi.

The Buenos Aires Federal Appeals Court had responded positively to their petition to indict him for gratuitously executing unproven "ant subversive" prisoners in 1977. A trial date was set three months hence.

To their relief, the soldier acquitted himself honorably by providing conclusive evidence to implicate the General. The young female prisoner, who had witnessed similar executions by the General with his handgun, added her horrifying description of the torture of her inmates to great effect, including the incident of the burial alive of a man, which had traumatized her.

Dr. Diaz expected the trial to face strong opposition from the General's enthusiastic political supporters amongst the conservative elite in Tucumán.

This moved Alicia to focus her attention locally in San Miguel. She simply had to know everything there was to know about this enigmatic man who was brutal in uniform, but supposedly thoughtful and compassionate in civilian life.

She had developed many acquaintances through her psychotherapy practice. Some of them knew Bussi well or had worked on his staff. From them she learned that since he retired from the military, he had aspirations to run for office in Tucumán and that he had already begun putting a support organization together. That prompted her to enlist the help of her old friend, Xavier, now in the intelligence business, to help identify Bussi's political supporters.

"Why do you want to stick your nose into that hornets' nest? Some of those maniacs could sting you pretty badly."

"I want to know who is standing in my way of getting him indicted."

"Have you gone off your head? That's one of the ways left around here for folks to get killed. These guys just bombed the offices of Alfonsin's radical party in town last week! The cops are on the take and the Army's gone. On your own, you'll have no protection.

"Look, Alicia, you know how paranoid the wealthy people here are. They literally live behind walls and only pass through the proletariat swiftly when they have protection. That's why they like Bussi. 'He must be good, because the city was never as "clean" before he came,' they say."

"I can't just walk away. We at least have to get him indicted before this Government falls apart," Alicia pleaded.

"The only guy I know who has the smarts to do that is Fernando's father. Why don't you explain your fears to him? He'll give you good answers. The only thing I have to offer you, is physical protection, should they turn on you."

"What will that cost me?"

"For you, nothing."

"Oh, no, I don't do favors in return."

"After what happened to you, I don't blame you."

"What do you know about that?"

"In my business I have to read between the lines. I knew the minute Kevin called to get the dirt on Don Juan. I would have killed the bastard. You just don't know how lucky you are."

"Oh God, do I ever! That's why you have to help me vindicate myself in his eyes."

"You'll have to keep what I tell you to yourself. I'm not ready to be assassinated. Give me two days. Come up to the stables wearing jodhpurs and boots. We can ride and talk where no one can hear or see us."

What Xavier disclosed really scared her. In effect the Bussi organization contained a militia element along the lines of the Nazi Brown-Shirts, used principally to intimidate those unwilling to accommodate the wishes of his supporters.

She started spending more time with Arnoldo, wrestling with the legal challenge of finessing the plaintiff's lawyers who were trying everything possible to block Diaz's claim against Bussi by using the "Punta Final" provisions. They tried every way to drag the indictment proceedings out beyond its time limit. In the end it looked like a contest of who could influence the presiding judge most. To complicate matters, the court had combined their complaint with several others of a like nature to shorten the overall process, hopefully to sentence him while the momentum was still in the court's favor.

While the trial was in the limelight, she and Dr. Diaz felt reasonably safe from physical attack.

Alicia prayed constantly for the opportunity to prove her worth to her father-in-law and to Kevin. She was so charged up that there was no room left for depression. By the end of the week when Kevin picked her up on his way back from São Paulo, she was ebullient.

They got home just in time to take Elena, already in labor, to the hospital. She gave birth to a healthy little girl, whom she named Elvira in honor of Grandmother Diaz. Alicia was so exuberant that Elena and Kevin could plainly see it as her way of assuaging her guilt.

Now her family was complete, and every one could concentrate on being happy...or so they hoped.

* * *

As the calendar flipped from 1986 to 1987, the decline in the Argentinean economy reached critical proportions. The same extremist factions on the left and on the right, that had driven the country into anarchy before, were coming back out of their rat-holes. Bombs were going off in the offices of opposing political parties and danger signs of civil unrest were everywhere. President Alfonsin's regime was rapidly unraveling.

Dr. Diaz, working regularly with Alicia, filed motion after motion to respond to the stream of nuisance motions filed by Bussi's attorneys.

Fortunately, the court found the time to sentence General Masson and Admiral Massera, each to long periods of confinement. They appealed and were released on bail. General Masson fled into exile in the United States. At least Alicia and Dr. Diaz had succeeded in drawing a line on the wall for the whole country and the world to see.

* * *

The Bussi case dragged on until Alfonsin resigned in July, 1989, a year short of his six-year term. Perónist, Carlos Menem, succeeded him. Barely three months after his inauguration, Menem began pardoning convicted military officers and by December, 1990 he had pardoned them all.

Their frustrations were palpable and the impact on Alicia's demeanor was dreadful. She reacted as if she was beset by autism, seldom spoke and often seemed dislocated, unaware of the people around her; not recognizing even her own children. Then early one morning she tried to slit her wrists and they had to commit her to a neurological institution. As fate would have it, she was placed in the care of Dr. Snow.

"We meet again, doctor. Where do we go from here?"

"Suppose you could sit down and walk me through everything important about her behavior you know of."

"You were right about her having recurring bouts of depression, but we were always able to cheer her up," Kevin began and told him everything that had happened.

"Was she animated by the news that the General and the Admiral were found guilty?"

"Yes, that was what really made her crawl out of her shell and made her participate so actively in the pursuit of General Bussi."

"I think you're missing the cardinal point. She disappointed you and her father-in-law and never got over it. Regardless of how much you forgave her and how kind and loving you were to her. She was desperately seeking a tangible contribution she could make that would vindicate her. The pardon robbed her of that chance."

"So how do we help her get healthy again?"

"With drugs and therapy we'll get her over this, but we can't grant her happiness. There's the probability that she will become a loner; keep things to herself, do things on her own. Don't be surprised if she even shuns you and the rest of her family."

"When and how often may I see her?"

"Give me a week to get her over the worst of this. Is there a close friend out of her past who knows nothing about her life with you, who we could have her talk to?"

"I don't know of anyone, except her partner, Elena."

"Ask her and let me know, please."

* * *

Kevin was heartbroken and leaned heavily on Elena in his sorrow. What had overcome Alicia was well beyond his comprehension.

"How could she, surrounded by doting people, want to commit suicide?" he asked.

"She disappointed herself. In <u>her</u> mind she was a failure. On her own, she couldn't even satisfy the man she worshiped. She had nothing to give for what she'd received from him. Her only hope was to make a difference by forcing the perpetrators to acknowledge their sins. In her mind, she would then be vindicated; while all the time she really only wanted your uncompromised admiration."

"But I gave her that; didn't I?"

"No, you never approved of what she had done. She knew that it remained repugnant to you. That's why she was so magnanimous about me being your paramour. She wanted you to share in her guilt."

"How can we win her back?"

"I don't have to. She never left me. It's you she's crying out to."

"Is there <u>any</u> way for me to turn back the clock?"

"No the clock of life only goes one way. But, you may be able to establish a different relationship with her that satisfies a modified you and her."

"Here, together under this one roof?"

"That would be wishful thinking. She can't stand lying in the bed she made for herself. She wants to be on her own, I surmise."

"That's what the psychiatrist said."

"It looks like we're stranded together while she flees the coup."

"Could we stand to see that much of each other?"

"I'd love it. It's up to you."

CHAPTER THIRTY-TWO

Dr. Snow worked wonders on Alicia and sent her home after four weeks of intensive therapy and treatment with anti-depressants. Her eyes were clear, her skin tone healthy and, on the surface, her demeanor appeared normal.

"Her condition remains tenuous," Dr. Snow advised "and you'll have to be very careful not to do anything to make her feel inadequate. She never got over the derision you felt when you found her with that soldier. She believes you will always hold it against her. To redeem herself she feels compelled to do something remarkable. When all her efforts against the Junta were swept away by the Menem pardon, she lost hope and simply collapsed."

"I understand. Can we not find new objectives for her to pursue—objectives important enough to restore her self-esteem?"

"That's the correct remedy. Just don't set the bar too high. Start with something easy and build up to more challenging objectives as her condition improves."

"You're a great guy. I'm sorry we started off on the wrong foot."

"Those were trying times. You're forgiven."

He drove her home and was delighted to hear her prattle about the staff and routines at the hospital. He'd organized the children to give her the most welcoming reception possible and they came through like Trojans.

As she entered, they began singing a "welcome" song composed by Maria, set to a Chilean folk tune. The words spoke of how they had missed her and how happy they were to see her. It brought tears to Alicia's eyes as she hugged them each in turn, and gracefully accepted their homemade gifts.

"I'm so glad to see you all so happy together. Where I just came from, there was no pleasure. I want to stay here from now on. Thank you for your wonderful presents. I will always treasure them."

It was a good start to a long journey. Alicia clung desperately to Kevin becoming distressed whenever he was out of her reach for long. He began asking her special favors such as teaching little Ellie to read and to draw the letters of the alphabet.

He took her riding often. Riding into the mountains brought smiles to her face and she began responding humorously to his flirtatious banter. He tried to emulate the atmosphere they enjoyed, deeply in love, while riding on Roberto's ranch.

She embraced Elena fondly for always being there for her.

In a team effort, Elena, Kevin and Carlos promoted projects for her to embrace...from helping Maria with her homework, to playing parlor games with the younger ones and providing her with multiple choices to keep "little El" out of mischief.

As she gradually gained confidence and could again drive a vehicle, she began car-pooling children to various places for sports practices and events and wound up helping in the classrooms as a teacher's aide.

By the middle of 1991, Dr. Snow pronounced her fit to return to work. On her first visit to San Miguel, Elena introduced her to the new staff she'd hired and to some of their new patients. Alicia seemed fearless and at ease as she began conducting therapy sessions and the partnership was back on track.

Then election posters of Antonio Bussi's campaign for Governor of Tucumán Province began appearing. It angered Alicia to a point that Elena had to ask Kevin to take her home.

"In all conscience," she argued "how can anyone in his right mind allow that asshole to run for public office? He's not fit to be dogcatcher," she objected. "That's our problem. People are so stuck on their petty routines that they can't see beyond their noses! That butcher killed at least five hundred Tucumánis...most of them innocent. Is it now fashionable to reward murderers?"

"Take it easy," Kevin calmed her. "Bussi's supporters don't <u>want</u> to know that he did bad things. They <u>believe</u> what his posters and newspaper ads say. There are no courts to find him guilty, so the myth prevails. People believe what they <u>want</u> to believe. They say he did a good job as military administrator and would do more good for the province than his corrupt, weak competitors. Even Arnold acknowledges that Bussi did a good job. The place was clean, the local economy improved, more people had jobs...."

"You're always so reasonable. Why can't I be like you?"

"You can and shortly will be, so relax and enjoy this beautiful place we live in."

It took several more tries before Alicia was up to full productivity as a therapist. Fortunately, under Elena's management the practice was thriving.

Bussi was ignominiously defeated by a pop-star, singer called, "Palito" Ortega, who ran as a Perónist. Determined to win the next election in 1994, Bussi formed a uniquely Tucumánian, right-wing, political party, which he ominously called the "Republican Force".

Family life in Santiago almost returned to normal, except that Alicia was still not satisfied with her and Kevin's relationship. She often was short-tempered, but didn't take it out on the children. Little Ellie filled her heart and she lavished love and attention on Maria.

As the children grew older their demands grew increasingly cerebral. Carlos graduated from high school in 1994 and at age nineteen, gained acceptance as an engineering student to Kevin's alma mater, UCLA.

Maria was a late-teen in high school and, fortunately, still in love with horses rather than boys. She too wanted to attend an American university and tentatively showed interest following in Alicia's psychology footsteps.

Elena's Ricardo was somewhat of a problem, complaining that he was treated differently from the other children. He seldom saw his biological father and hadn't become completely at ease with Kevin. He was fascinated by mining machines so Kevin began taking him along on his visits to the mines. Even so, Elena couldn't be available enough to fill the gap and they suggested that Alicia try taking him under her wing. She jumped at the chance and soon had him even feeling superior to his siblings.

* * *

The 1994 elections came, and this time Antonio Bussi narrowly won the election for Governor of Tucumán. Once again, it had a devastating effect on Alicia.

She just lost interest in everything except her need to seek vengeance. The whole family pulled together to bring her back to sanity, but to no avail. She confined herself to the guest house, ostensibly to "plan her comeback".

Finally, Kevin convinced her to go with him to Spain to see their old friend, Carlos Vargas, in Segovia. Her spark began to return as they sat together comparing notes. Vargas had done his homework superbly by documenting precisely the most egregious criminality against Spanish citizens and had found surprisingly strong interest in his material from a judge by the name of Balthazar Garzón in the Spanish National Court.

They began working together to construct a series of legal charges against Junta members for crimes committed against Spanish citizens. Much of the gruesome and repugnant details which the judge selected had come from Alicia and Vargas' documents.

Kevin suggested a meeting for Alicia with the judge. They had to wait several weeks for an appointment, which gave Alicia time to add her own details of atrocities committed against Argentineans.

They found Dr. Garzón receptive and Alicia was invited to join his team. Kevin had to leave on an urgent business matter in South Africa and promised to return. To his surprise Alicia begged him not to.

"Bartholomew, you mean everything to me," she explained "but this is something I have to do on my own. I can't stand not being able to give you my full measure of love. I must have the opportunity to prove myself. Please, I beg you. I must do this alone if I'm ever to redeem myself in your eyes. I crave your unconditional approval...*please*!"

"Are you sure you'll manage without a relapse?"

"Of that I can never be sure, but I'm certain that I will if I don't do this."

"How long will you be gone?"

"My darling, it could be years, but I promise you, it will be worth waiting for."

"What about the children and me?"

"They will thrive under your care and you have Elena. Give her all your love. You two are all I've got."

Kevin refrained from helping her and during his visits to Spain he strictly limited their activities to recreation. They went on vacations to Majorca, the Andalusian Mountains, the Greek and Turkish Islands, Egypt and other exciting places. In spite of all their travails, they were still very much in love.

* * *

Two years later, in 1997, Judge Garzón launched a formal investigation into the kidnapping, torture and murder of 266 Spaniards by the Junta and asked the Argentine government to summon 97 Argentinean officers to give evidence in his court. Argentina denied his request and a year later, in 1998 he issued a dozen international arrest warrants...one of them for Antonio Bussi. 60 more warrants followed for officers who were complicit in the horrendous crimes committed in the Navy's Mechanical School, ESAM.

Judge Garzón's pressure on Argentina was amplified when the Italians, Germans and French began filing similar suits for crimes against their citizens.

Cracks were appearing in the stone walls of former Junta members. More confessions by officers, who'd been complicit in the campaign of terror, were coming forth. A former Navy Captain voluntarily confessed to flying aircraft and casting sedated prisoners into the sea and had his face slashed in reprisal.

In 1999, when his term as Governor of Tucumán expired, Antonio Bussi successfully ran for a seat in the Argentinean Congress. By then, his reputation for brutality was so sullied that, for reasons of "moral inability", his peers in Congress voted to deny him taking office. His supporters in the Republican Force were furious, once again placing Dr. Diaz, Alicia and Kevin seriously in harm's way.

The intensified press coverage, internationally and in Argentina, resulting from the work Alicia and her colleagues had done in Spain, led Argentina's Prosecutor, Adolfo Bagnasco, to declare:

"I hope Argentina can send the message to the world that despite its flaws, my country has a serious and effective justice system."

All of this animated Alicia and her partner Vargas as they labored to keep Judge Garzón focused on Argentina, even as his notoriety for pursuing Chile's General Pinochet distracted him.

In October, 2003, the judge completed his examination of crimes committed by the Junta and officially closed his investigation, referring cases for trial before a panel of judges in Spain's special court for serious international crimes.

* * *

By then, Antonio Bussi was back in Tucumánian politics, now running for the job of Mayor of San Miguel. A new case was brought against him for allegedly embezzling money when he was military governor and sheltering it in offshore financial centers. This energized the Republican Force militants who Xavier had previously identified to Alicia.

The charges against Junta members by Dr. Diaz, Alicia, Elena and Kevin had become public knowledge as was Alicia's cooperation with the Spanish judge. Their actions acutely embarrassed Bussi, who was still smarting from his rejection by the Argentinean Congress. Xavier alerted Kevin to Bussi's growing frustration, which he saw as an increasingly serious threat of assassination against each of them by the militants.

They began taking precautions whenever they entered Tucumán. When Kevin flew in to fetch Elena, he kept a close watch and went to extraordinary lengths when performing his fight checks prior to takeoff from San Miguel. In addition Elena engaged Xavier's company to guard her.

Dr. Diaz believed that his reputation gave him enough insulation from attack and took no unusual precautions. One morning, in his car on his way to the Courthouse, someone took a shot at him, shattering his windshield and lightly wounding him. The incident so undermined his confidence that he essentially became housebound. Naturally hypertensive, his health had been deteriorating for some time and being attacked didn't help. This was of great concern to Kevin and he began visiting him more often.

Brushing aside his promise not to meddle in Alicia's activities in Spain, Kevin engaged a security agency to protect her in Barcelona and in Madrid.

After visiting Dr. Diaz on one occasion, Kevin detected a partially sawed-through hydraulic line on the landing gear of his plane. This clearly was a deliberate attempt at sabotage which he reported to the airport authorities. They agreed to post guards by his airplane from then on. He commissioned Xavier to investigate and to identify the saboteur.

Some weeks later on takeoff, once he had retracted his landing gear, the hydraulic pressure dropped to zero. Instead of flying to Santiago, he and Elena circled for an hour to burn off fuel, before making an emergency landing. With flight maneuvers, Kevin got the left-hand gear to drop by gravity, but the right-hand gear wouldn't budge.

His approach was precise and as he put a small amount of pressure on the unlocked, extended gear, it collapsed, sending the aircraft into a slithering ground spiral. Elena's head was thrown against side of the fuselage, knocking her unconscious. The plane continued to slide in a cloud of sparks, causing the right hand engine to catch fire. Kevin couldn't open the jammed door and before the rescue crew got to them, the fire had spread. They managed to extricate Kevin, but couldn't reach Elena.

Kevin suffered severe burns on his legs and was met at the hospital by Xavier, who had immediately started an investigation into the causes of the crash.

"Do you have any idea who could have done it?"

"Yes, since Bussi started running for office again, we've been receiving threatening messages and as you know they tried to assassinate Dr. Diaz.

"Who do you think sent them?" Kevin asked.

"The militia of the Republican Force did it. Their threats are mostly directed at Alicia to drop the cases she has filed against Bussi in the Spanish courts. As you know, it caused him to be placed under house arrest in Buenos Aires. What more can I do to nail the bastards?"

"Call the New York Times and the Miami Herald. Tell them what's happening and give them my phone number here. I'll give them a lot to talk about!"

"How are you taking the loss of Elena?"

"Bloody awful...Alicia and I loved and depended on her. She is the mother of two of my children. I can't stand the thought of her not being here for me. What gave *you* the courage to finally stand up and be counted?"

"I've always known that you suspected me of being Bussi's mountain scout. I know that you figured out that I was responsible for Fernando's arrest. When we met on that long ride, the consequences of my actions really hit home. I never thought they'd go beyond scaring Fernando into shutting his big mouth. But, I couldn't stop them. It has weighed heavily on my conscience. I could never tell Angélica the truth and could never understand why you didn't tell her."

"I wasn't sure at first and I needed her to get information out of you."

"What did she learn from me?"

"The identities of Bussi's key militia guys."

"OK, now you know why it's payback time."

"Make those phone calls to New York and Miami while you're still alive."

"OK, I'm on my way. The coroner's office wants to know where you want Elena's body sent."

"Have her cremated and bring me her ashes. Thanks for coming, Xavier. It's nice to really have you on our side. The most important thing you can do is find out who sabotaged my plane, who commissioned that person and who shot at Doctor Diaz. This time I'm going to blow these extreme bastards all the way to hell!"

Two hours later the New York Times editor called. Kevin gave him the broad picture and described what had happened. The fact that he was an American, weighed heavily in his favor and the editor asked where their correspondent could interview him.

"I'm in a burn ward in the hospital of a small city in northern Argentina, waiting to be evacuated to Santiago de Chile."

"Our most knowledgeable Argentinean correspondent is in Buenos Aires. Are there direct flights to where you are?"

"Yes," and Kevin described how to get to him.

"Her name is Susanne White. Expect to hear from her soon."

The nurse came in to prepare Kevin for his treatment. He had second-degree burns over 20 percent of his body, which made him a borderline case for hydrotherapy to remove the dead skin. All of it was painful, but not nearly as painful as the loss of Elena. That would haunt him for the rest of his life.

The correspondent arrived from Buenos Aires in the early evening and, after some negotiation with the hospital staff, was permitted to see him. She was fully conversant with all the important aspects of the "Dirty War" on both sides of the Atlantic and knew a lot about Alicia's activity in Spain.

"We've been following the career of Antonio Domingo Bussi closely; from Army General to Provincial Governor, to member of the Congress and now his run for Mayor of San Miguel. We know his military record in detail and are aware of the charges brought against him by your wife and her father-in-law. But so far we've not had indications of foul play in this election."

"It has little to do with the election for Mayor. It involves the fervor with which they are trying to whitewash his tawdry military record, which my wife has struggled for the past three decades to expose. His zealous supporters in the Republican Force, which he founded some twenty years ago, will go to the extreme of murder to silence his antagonists. They just proved it by attempting to assassinate me, murdering my wife's psychotherapy partner and wounding Dr. Diaz.

"I want you to write a news flash about the attempt on my life...me, an American citizen...by sabotaging my aircraft. In return, my wife and I will furnish you a comprehensive revelation of the misdeeds of this man who sent over five hundred people to their demise in Tucumán. In fact, we have enough verifiable data on him to fill a series."

"OK, let's start with what happened today and what led up to it. I hope you won't mind me using a recorder."

"No, go ahead."

In the next half hour she questioned Kevin until she had a full grasp of the situation and left to question Xavier further about evidence pointing to sabotage by Bussi's people.

* * *

Xavier had tracked down the mechanic who damaged Kevin's hydraulic system and coerced him into disclosing who had hired him. He fingered the son of a leading member of the Republican Force. Xavier was well on his way to making him confess. His next step would be to incriminate the father.

In spite of the excruciating pain in his legs, Kevin was anxious to get back to Santiago where he'd be safe and could obtain a higher level of medical care.

He fretted about funeral arrangements for Elena whom he deeply mourned. She had been his stalwart supporter through all his difficult times with Alicia and during her long absence in Spain. Why did she have to be the one to pay the ultimate price? He knew in advance that he would miss her too much to go on living on the Estancia. Since several of the children were already studying or living in California, he began contemplating going home too.

* * *

The outcome of the Spanish cases had almost become superfluous to Alicia's objective. She and Vargas' Spanish activities had helped force the Argentinean Congress and its new President, Néstor Kirchner, to annul all the pardons and to abolish the mid-eighties "Punta Final" and "Due Obedience" laws of President Alfonsin.

The die-hards appealed on the grounds that Congress didn't have the legal right to do so. Alicia felt confident that with the house-cleaning Kirchner had done amongst Supreme Court justices, that the resolution would stand and clear the way for prosecution in the Argentinean courts.

As the realization dawned on her that she had essentially accomplished her goal, her thoughts turned inward to find that a spiritual sense had grown in her, which dulled her previous need for revenge.

The gravity of what had happened to Argentina now lay indelibly exposed before its citizens.

She was in full possession of her emotions; her transformation to Alicia de la Rosa was complete. The time had come for her to repay her debts. She longed to see Kevin's face when she showed him her new strength.

Then Xavier phoned.

"Alicia, I'm calling on behalf of Kevin. Please sit down and steel yourself. He's in serious condition with burn wounds in the Tucumán Hospital and can't face telling you about the accident and Elena's death."

She could feel her angst going through the roof and struggled to maintain her composure.

"Xavier, what happened?"

"Bussi's people tried to assassinate him by tampering with his airplane. There was a fire. He got out...Elena didn't make it."

"Oh, my God, will he survive?"

"He'll make it all right. I've never seen a man so outraged. He has already interviewed the New York papers and won't quit until Bussi is totally discredited. He urgently needs you! The loss of Elena broke his heart. He blames himself for her death. Please come soon!"

"I will, I promise. How is my Suegro taking this?"

"Not well, Alicia. They think he suffered a stroke when Elvira told him."

"Will he survive?"

"They don't think he'll be able to hang on much longer."

"All this, just as I was thinking how well things were going," Alicia mused.

"You must hold yourself together," Xavier encouraged her. "You're the only pillar left standing. Call me with your flight numbers, I'll come and get you. It's too dangerous here now for you to move around on your own."

"Thank you, Xavier."

CHAPTER THIRTY-THREE

Dr. Diaz passed away peacefully in his sleep. His funeral was a private affair. His abundant friends, colleagues and clients arranged a grand memorial service for him. Through the intervention of Xavier, Alicia was invited to make the address to celebrate his life.

As she was flying from Madrid, her Spanish Judge reissued his extradition orders, including one for Antonio Bussi.

The great hall fell silent as she walked to the podium and calmly put down her notes to take a sip of water before beginning:

"Arnoldo Diaz was a high achiever from modest beginnings. He excelled to win a scholarship to Harvard's Law School, where they instilled in him a higher purpose. He came home not just to practice law, but to begin his life-long struggle to help make Argentinean justice independent, fair and free of corruption.

"He bit off more than he could chew. In the course of the last half century, our country's rule has been chaotic under self-serving demagogue after demagogue, each corrupting the bench by appointing his own cronies as judges.

"In spite of this, Doctor Diaz never gave up his diligent efforts to work within each successive regime, bringing a stronger sense of justice to the judiciary. He even got the Marxist rebels to respect the legal institution when they invaded Tucumán. When the men of the Junta, without the slightest reason, arrested his son, Fernando, my husband, and tortured, mutilated and obviously murdered him, Doctor Diaz' determination to reform the justice system soared. His path to that dream was blocked by the lawlessness of the Junta and he and I swore an oath to avenge their atrocities.

"In the course of trying to find my husband, I became too knowledgeable about their gratuitous brutality, to be left alive, and I had to flee the country. I found myself at the crossroad with many Spaniards who told of horrors they experienced in Argentina and

began accumulating a catalog of ghastly incidents, perpetrated by men of the Junta. The place was crawling with secret agents, which so imperiling my existence, I had to adopt a new personality and move on. But for the generosity and compassion of an expatriate American stranger, I would have perished. He gave me the protection, courage and enterprise to continue my drive to bring the perpetrators to justice. No innocent, pregnant, Argentinean mother should ever have to suffer as I did, simply to survive.

"After several years on my own in Spain, my transformation to Alicia de la Rosa is complete. My deepest regret is that Doctor Diaz can't be here to see me finally make amends to my family for the pain I caused them.

"When I returned to Tucumán, I rode extensively on horseback in these beautiful mountains, where I discovered what savagery the Marxist rebels had indulged in. It strengthened my resolve to fight gratuitous barbarism of any sort.

"Doctor Diaz and I persevered and finally found a way to indict top members of the leadership with incontrovertible evidence of newborn baby theft from incarcerated mothers in Buenos Aires and the criminal execution of untried prisoners here in San Miguel. Two of the three senior officers indicted were found guilty and sentenced, before President Menem pardoned them.

"Neither, Doctor Diaz, nor I, could give up the fight and with the encouragement of my American mentor and husband, I returned to my birthplace of Barcelona to work with Balthazar Garzón, the Spanish judge, seeking the extradition of those pardoned by President Menem for trial in Spain. President Duhalde outlawed any response to the Spanish courts. The result was an international outcry so loud that it reduced this wonderful country's standing to that of a pariah. President Kirchner finally reversed the decision and arrested those wanted by the Spanish courts, including your mayor-elect.

"The only honorable way out for Argentina is to prosecute those who stepped over the line of human decency. As a proud nation, that obligation cannot be delegated to a foreign jurisdiction. When Argentina prosecutes them, this nation will understand the vicious cruelty that dictatorial governance, in the absence of an independent judiciary, is bound to lead to...not only the brutality of government, but also the savagery of its enemies.

"I no longer despise people such as San Miguel's mayor-elect for the horrors committed under their stewardship. But they have no right to impose their will through assassination or to hide the truth from their constituents. Antonio Bussi must face trial as surely as any common criminal must.

"If you share my craving for the freedom of a just society in Argentina, you must learn to die for me and for the tens of thousands like me. Only then will we achieve the goal to which Arnoldo Diaz dedicated his life.

"I honor him with the deepest sense of loss.

"For all these years, I craved seeing the look of redemption in the eyes of the man to whom I owe everything. Thank you for your unyielding love, my beautiful Bartholomew.

"I ask you to join me in prayer that justice will be done in the brutal death of my colleague, Elena Mendoza."

She ended with a soft, tender voice, choking back her tears "Vaya con Dios...my faithful friend."

As she stepped down, a young man with a gun in his hand yelled "Traitor!" Xavier pushed Alicia to the ground as a shot shattered the edge of the podium and a second shot followed immediately. The assassin fell to the ground. Propped up in his stretcher, Kevin was astonished to see Rodolfo, the soldier, with gun in hand salute him in a gesture to signify that they were now even as he promised that fateful morning in Córdoba.

* * *

For their personal safety, Alicia immediately left with Kevin on a charter flight for Santiago. Having lived through so much violence, she was enthusiastic about returning to California.

After a series of skin grafts Kevin was again able to walk and sit comfortably. Alicia took him on a voyage to rekindle their deep, abiding love for each other. It started in Montevideo where they stayed at the Sheraton Hotel, hosted the Spanish Ambassador to dinner in the posh penthouse restaurant and danced the night away in the Tango Club. Their journey ended on the ranch near Puerto Varas.

They interred Elena's ashes on the Estancia in Santiago where her first-born, Ricardo, assumed the role of manager. Kevin's daughter with Elena, Elvira, left with them, thrilled with the specter of reuniting with her siblings already in California.

Kevin endowed the de la Rosa Chair for Argentinean Studies at Loyola Marymount University to serve as a cross-discipline, study center and a depository of documents relating to contemporary Argentinean history. They also created the Argentinean Heritage Foundation to manage and build a large collection of authentic information about the "Dirty War" to dramatize the tragic episode in digital format on site and on-line.

Alicia was in great demand to give lectures and address gatherings interested in learning more about her traumatic, thirty-year experience. Kevin engaged a top talent agency to manage her public appearances.

They went looking for a modest-sized ranch in a valley where they could keep horses near high mountains and established a new Bartholomew family home.

For the most part, they spent their time authoring and publishing exposé's under the collective title, "Lest They Forget", emphasizing the cruelty imposed by Argentinean governments on its citizens.

On June 14, 2005, Argentina's Supreme Court, in a 7-1 decision, struck down the country's two amnesty laws that had granted impunity for gross human rights violations committed under the country's military dictatorship.

The crimes of Argentina against its citizens were too serious to be forgotten. No matter how many years it took to come to this realization, the way should now be open for Argentina to redeem itself in the eyes of the just and to begin its journey towards becoming a truly civilized society.

The Moving Finger writes; and, having writ,
Moves on: nor all your Piety nor Wit
Shall lure it back to cancel half a Line,
Nor all your Tears wash out a Word of it
-Omar Khayyam//